DEMOCRACY AND THE "KINGDOM OF GOD"

STUDIES IN PHILOSOPHY AND RELIGION

Volume 17

The titles published in this series are listed at the end of this volume.

DEMOCRACY AND THE "KINGDOM OF GOD"

by

HOWARD P. KAINZ

Marquette University,
Department of Philosophy,
Milwaukee, U.S.A.

KLUWER ACADEMIC PUBLISHERS

DORDRECHT / BOSTON / LONDON

Library of Congress Cataloging-in-Publication Data

Kainz, Howard P.
    Democracy and the Kingdom of God / by Howard P. Kainz.
        p.   cm. -- (Studies in philosophy and religion ; v. 17)
    Includes bibliographical references and index.
    ISBN 0-7923-2106-5 (hard : alk. paper)
    1. Kingdom of God--History of doctrines. 2. Kingdom of God-
-Political aspects. 3. Christianity and poilitics--History.
4. Democracy--Religious aspects--Christianity.   I. Title.
II. Series: Studies in philosophy and religion (Martinus Nijhoff
Publishers) ; v. 17.
    BT94.K3 1993
    231.7'2'09--dc20   92-40289

ISBN 0-7923-2106-5

Published by Kluwer Academic Publishers,
P.O. Box 17, 3300 AA Dordrecht, The Netherlands.

Kluwer Academic Publishers incorporates
the publishing programmes of
D. Reidel, Martinus Nijhoff, Dr W. Junk and MTP Press.

Sold and distributed in the U.S.A. and Canada
by Kluwer Academic Publishers,
101 Philip Drive, Norwell, MA 02061, U.S.A.

In all other countries, sold and distributed
by Kluwer Academic Publishers Group,
P.O. Box 322, 3300 AH Dordrecht, The Netherlands.

Printed on acid-free paper

Printed in the Netherlands

"The kingdom of the world has become
the kingdom of our Lord and his Christ." —*Revelation* 11:15

PREFACE

The idea for this book has come to me gradually over the last decade. In my *Democracy East and West* (1984), I devoted a chapter to the speculative question about whether there is any discernible "necessary relationship" between religion and democracy. Later I began to search for a way to pinpoint the question more precisely. Teaching an interdisciplinary colloquium on War and Peace in 1986 and surveying the literature on the ethics of nuclear warfare, I came across an article by James Rhodes, entitled "The Kingdom, Morality and Prudence—The American Bishops and Nuclear Weapons"[1], which brings out some fundamental ambiguities in the concept of the "kingdom of God." The Catholic Bishops had focused on this concept as a paradigm for world peace, in the survey of Scripture which constituted the first section of their joint letter concerning disarmament and deterrence. Some of the ambiguities—e.g. the incongruous and possibly compromising intermingling of Old Testament and New Testament versions of the Kingdom—were eliminated in the Third Draft, at the instigation of Rome; but Rhodes argued that ambiguities still remained. He proposed to clarify these ambiguities by distinguishing a number of differing interpretations of the "kingdom of God" within Christianity, especially a) the Augustinian tradition, b) the Lutheran tradition, c) the millenarian and d) the liberationist tradition (associated with liberation theology in Latin America and elsewhere). Rhodes was especially dubious about the Bishop's idea of a "progressively realized Kingdom," which seemed to incorporate liberationist elements without supplying the necessary theological clarifications.

Soon afterwards I came across an article in *The Lutheran Forum*[2] by Paul Kuenning concerning the present split in Lutheranism

---

[1] *The Center Journal*, 3:1, Winter, 1983, pp. 31-79.

[2] "The Two Kingdoms: Weighed and Found Wanting," *Lutheran Forum* 20:21, Lent, 1986.

between the German (pietistic) interpretation of the "kingdom of God", and a current attempt to restore the original "Two Kingdoms" doctrine of Luther—a doctrine which Kuenning and others refer to as "the weakest link" in Lutheranism.

It occurred to me that the split in Lutheranism seems to parallel the ambivalence among American Catholic bishops concerning the "kingdom of God"; and I became interested in exploring the extent and the political implications of the diversity of interpretations. I decided to proceed in my investigation as follows: First examine the scriptural bases for the idea of a "kingdom of God," the history of its interpretation, and the main contemporary tendencies in interpretation; then trace out the influence of the idea in history and in the history of political theories; and finally explore the implications for both religion and democracy in the contemporary world. This will explain the overall succession of topics in the present book.

My investigation has necessarily brought me into contact with the classical political theologies of Augustine, Hegel and others, but also with masterful twentieth century works in theology and scripture studies, political philosophy and democratic theory, and history—including John Bright's *The Kingdom of God*, Benedict Viviano's *The Kingdom of God in History*, Paul Tillich's "History and the Kingdom of God" (in Vol. 3 of his *Systematic Theology*), Eric Voegelin's *Israel and Revelation* (Vol. 3 of his *Order and History*), Karl Löwith's *The Meaning of History*, William Everett's *God's Federal Republic*, and H. Richard Niebuhr's *The Kingdom of God in America*—to name a few. The present book will not compete with such works, but hopefully will complement them. My own contribution, as I see it, will be to collate the considerable research already done on the various facets of this topic and to bring theology into rapprochement with philosophy, as far as possible, in drawing implications for contemporary politics and political philosophy.

In the course of my investigation, I have discovered: 1) that there is a consensus among both Protestant and Catholic theologians as to the central importance of the doctrine of the Kingdom, although there remain sharp differences as to its interpretation; 2) that the idea of the Kingdom has had *de facto* political applications for millenia (whether or not it *should* have had such applications is a separate question); 3) that some of the major political developments in the last few centuries—for example, American Manifest Destiny, South African Apartheid, Marxism, Nazism, Zionism, Latin American "liberation theology," Irish IRA and Orange factionism—are or have been buttressed by variant interpretations or misinterpretations of the concept of the Kingdom; and 4) that it may be of the utmost importance for the future of democracy to come to terms with the variant interpretations of the Kingdom, the question of their political applicability, and their specific implications for national and international democracy and "democratization."

In Chapter 4 of my *Paradox, Dialectic and System: a Reconstruction of the Hegelian Problematic*,[3] I discuss the Aristotelian contention that "dialectical" investigation of possible conflicting positions is an important prelude to philosophical analysis; I also examine dialogue as one important means of dialectical development of thought. My own systematic employment of dialectic in this book consists in interspersed dialogues between two characters, the idealistic and optimistic Cranston and the tough-minded and skeptical Turner, who tend to have roughly opposite viewpoints on many of the issues discussed, but are agreed on the importance of these issues and on the necessity of solving the associated problems. The pros and cons of some specific philosophical problems (formulated as questions in the chapter titles) will be developed in these dialogues, rather than woven into the chapters devoted to a more systematic, straightforward analysis, where they might detract from the tightness of the argumentation.

I am indebted to the Bradley Institute for Democracy and Social Values and to Marquette University for a combination of some initial funding for exploratory research, and a series of grants over the past few years which have made possible the research and writing of this book. I would also like to thank political scientist Siobhan Moroney of Marquette and theologian Dale Schlitt of St. Paul University–Ottawa in Canada for reading and critiquing the manuscript; the seven theologians at Marquette whose response to a questionaire that I sent to them forms the centerpiece of Chapter VII in this book; and my research assistants over the past few years, Wayne Ferguson, Bob Abele, Steve Whitworth, Calvin Pafford, Colin Oakes, and Lance Richey.

Conventions: Shortened titles will frequently be used in footnotes. Full titles and publishing data are to be found in the Bibliography. Abbreviated authors' names are utilized, where this will not result in any ambiguities.

---

[3]Philadelphia: Pennsylvania State University Press, 1988.

I. A Dangerous and/or Useful Kingdom?

> To destroy everything in a captured city, save perhaps the precious metals, was regarded as an act of high devotion to Yahweh. The Israelites were not alone in practicing, or claiming to practice, this kind of piety. —*The Interpreter's One-Volume Commentary, p. 127.*

TURNER: I have just finished rereading the Old Testament. This will be my last reading. I can't stomach the constant approving recitation of acts of what we would now call "terrorism." My disenchantment surfaced as I read the book of Joshua, in which the indiscriminate slaughter of hundreds of thousands of Canaanites by the Israelites is recorded.[1] And it became even more pronounced as I became more and more aware of the not unimportant fact that all this carnage was done in the name of God and religion—I am speaking of course of the "ban" (*harem*), the divine command to slaughter men, women and children belonging to certain specific categories of unbelievers.[2] And then there are those passages in the Psalms that refer to bashing the heads of the children of unbelievers against rocks,[3] and so forth. I'm sure you are familiar with these scriptural highlights. I've actually read them many times, but for some reason the incidents depicted never really caused any sort of shock previously. Possibly the contemporary international atmosphere, in which terrorism, often religiously motivated, is rife, is behind my

---

[1] See *Joshua* 6:21, 8:24-25, 10, 11.

[2] See *Deuteronomy* 3:2, 7:2-5, 20:16; *Numbers* 2:34, 3:3; *Joshua* 6:21-2, 8:26-28, ll:20; I *Samuel* 15:3, 28:18; II *Samuel* 21.

[3] Ps. 137:9.

change of attitude. I no longer find it inspirational to read how the "Kingdom of God" was perpetuated.

CRANSTON: I wouldn't be concerned about any widespread negative influence of these narratives. Hardly anyone—aside from theologians and religious professionals—reads the Old Testament any more.

TURNER: I suspect that those who do, including fundamentalists of course, are also the ones most susceptible to being negatively influenced by the messages they find there.

CRANSTON: I'm sure you must know, Turner, that there is very little historical factuality in any of those incidents. Theologians and scripture scholars tell us that these are highly imaginative tales of sometimes mythical heroes often written down centuries after whatever factual foundations (e.g. the Hebrew settlement in Canaan) they originally had. They were inflated tales of great deeds, devised to build up the spirits and morale of later Hebrew generations, and to bolster the reputation of their God, Yahweh. So you needn't get worked up about the matter. I'm sure you've come across comparable scenes of violence in classical literature and modern novels.

TURNER: I don't recall any laudatory accounts of genocide in the literature I'm acquainted with. But that may be due to the limited nature of my leisure reading. In any case, I don't believe narrative factuality is of the utmost importance. The idea, as they say, is father of the deed. These stories at the very least reflect intentions, inspirations, ideals. The ancients didn't make the fine distinctions we make between fact and fiction, history and myth. Even if none of it actually happened, they were holding up these terroristic acts as models for themselves and their children.

CRANSTON: You're taking these things way too seriously. When we moderns can't even decide if pornography (whatever that is) has a detectable effect on attitudes and behavior of its consumers, can we presume to discern some quantifiable causal relationship between grandiose ancient religious power-fantasies and attempts to actualize these fantasies, then or now? Get a hold of yourself. Otherwise you may find yourself in the uncomfortable corner of

Plato, incensed at the purported pernicious influence of poetry on ancient Greek youths, and opting for censorship. Think of how many present-day admirers of Plato are saddled with the task of explaining these aberrations away.

TURNER: You miss my point. I'm not competing with Plato; neither am I advocating censorship. I am concerned about the immense power of religion, and about the fact that people may easily be impelled to do things they themselves find ethically repugnant, in the name of promulgating and promoting the "kingdom of God."

CRANSTON: Careful, you're using a New Testament concept. The notion of a kingdom of God, which is so pivotal and crystallized in Christianity, is much less definite and explicit in the Old Testament. Some would say the relationship is tenuous.

TURNER: No matter. It is precisely in Christianity that the destructiveness particularly begins to burgeon, after cessation of the persecution of Christians and their accession to political power. Crusades featuring indiscriminate slaughter of "heathens," the Inquisition, pogroms against Jews, witch-burnings—Protestants and Catholics have vied with each other to speed up the coming of the kingdom of God through such stratagems.

CRANSTON: Admittedly. But your pointed examples hearken back to eras in which religion and politics ended up in unfortunate collusions between their collisions. The separation of church and state, which is certainly a hallmark of American democracy, has quelled much of this.

TURNER: But church and state will always find ways to get together as co-conspirators. Need I go into the specifics? The collusion of Christians with Hitler, of the Orthodox church with Stalin, the brutal acquisition of power by Boer Christians in South Africa, the endless violence of the IRA and Orangemen in Ireland under the banner of denominational Christianity, the enthusiastic support of Orthodox Jews and other religious Jews for Zionistic oppression of Palestinians.

CRANSTON: You've made your point. But the fact that a concept is dangerous does not mean it is ill-begotten or dispensable. The experiments with complete abolition of religion in communist regimes did not produce any kinder, gentler profile than Christianity. Complete separation of church and state may likewise produce a valueless state capable of heights of inhumanity that would make the Inquisition pale in comparison. Here, as in other areas of good-intentioned conflict-resolution, there is a very real danger of "throwing out the baby with the bathwater."

TURNER: I don't know if you are aware of the fact that you're offering a kind of "utility of religion" argument—à la Voltaire, Rousseau, J.S. Mill and other champions of the Enlightenment. The approach goes like this: Forget about the intrinsic value of religion, and consider only whether it contributes any important and perhaps even indispensable benefits to good government, social order, etc. Even Stalin resorted to this type of calculation at certain periods in order to receive the cooperation of the church. In a somewhat similar ideological stance, we find some liberation theologians who offer us "utility of Marxism" arguments. But all such utilitarian approaches skirt over the main point: is religion intrinsically worthwhile? Intrinsically humane? Not bent on destructiveness?

CRANSTON: Your own question is also implicitly utilitarian. When you say, "intrinsically humane, not bent on destructiveness," you mean, "useful for bringing about peace, harmony, cooperation." But maybe religion is intrinsically worthwhile, even though it engenders conflict and war. Do you remember Jesus saying, "I have not come to bring peace, but the sword"?

TURNER: Your approach is the approach of the believer. Here we have to separate believers and skeptics like myself.

CRANSTON: At least we should be aware of just what it is that believers are committed to, and the political and social implications of these commitments.

TURNER: I am particularly interested in its implications for the future of democracy.

CRANSTON: So am I. But we must handle the topic with kid gloves, if we are to avoid the utility-of-religion syndrome.

II. Is There a Concept of the Kingdom of God?

> The notion of a people of God, called to live under the rule
> of God, begins [with the Exodus], and with it the notion of the
> kingdom of God. —John Bright, *The Kingdom of God*

CRANSTON: A theologian I know has admonished me that there is no "general concept" of the Judaeo-Christian kingdom of God, but rather a group of biblical terms which have "overlapping semantic fields."

TURNER: I've noticed that some theologians prefer to speak about the "symbol" or "metaphor" or "representation" or "theme" of the kingdom of God, or refer to it as a "term" or a "phrase"—which almost seems to imply that it is so mysterious as to be unconceptualizable.

CRANSTON: I think this is because they look upon "concepts" as embodying a great deal of precision. Thus, for example, Perrin argues against the use of "concept," and favors "symbol," in discussions of the kingdom of God.[1] His reasoning for this is that he takes "concept" to be tantamount to a "steno-symbol" like the symbol "π," which designates a specific mathematical operation.[2] Following Wheelwright, he then distinguishes "steno-symbols" further from "tensive symbols," which are highly connotative, and subject to multiple interpretations. He admits that in some cases the "kingdom of God" is a steno-symbol, especially when it is used in reference to concrete historical events, such as the apocalyptic descriptions of the coming of the Kingdom in the

---

[1]Norman Perrin, *Jesus and the Language of the Kingdom*, p. 33.
[2]Ibid., pp. 33, 30.

book of Daniel. But the more interesting and important cases, in his estimation, involve the use of tensive symbols.

TURNER: He is more sanguine about the precision of concepts than I am. I think that many concepts that lack anything like mathematical precision are meaningful and often connotative. But what he seems to be doing is just underlining his conviction that the kingdom of God is a myth or mystery which aids in the understanding of the human situation and invites people in all ages to come up with positive interpretations and applications not necessarily related to specific past historical events.

CRANSTON: If the Kingdom were an unconceptualizable myth or mystery, and philosophically inaccessible even with less-than-precise concepts, then we all would do well to keep silent about it, as Wittgenstein advises at the end of his *Tractatus* with regard to the "mystical." But let us not conclude a priori that we have here a subject impervious to philosophical investigation. If we conduct an examination of the symbols or terms connected with the mysterious kingdom of God in the Old Testament, I presume we will find out soon enough whether they obviate philosophical analysis, or not.

TURNER: If there is indeed some space where the symbols or terms overlap, or some place of intersection, then we have at least a "lowest common denominator," if not a "general concept" in the most desirable sense. Otherwise we will be constrained to give different names to the terms which don't overlap or intersect, or use subscripts—e.g. $KofG_1$, $KofG_2$, etc.

CRANSTON: I hope that will not be necessary. But it is difficult to pinpoint meanings when we are dealing with fluid "entities," influenced considerably by subjective factors—for example, when we try to define social states of affairs like conservatism or revolution, or intellectual systems like philosophy or theology. It's much easier to be concise and precise when we are dealing with stable objects with rather fixed features—like chairs and mountains and trees. To take philosophy as a case-in-point: philosophy for Plato meant a kind of passion for knowledge of the Good, for Aquinas and the scholastics a knowledge of all things according to self-evident first principles, for Descartes and the Cartesians a deduction from clear and distinct subjective certitudes, while the contemporary *Encyclopedia of Philosophy* defines it as "discourse about discourse." It might take a good deal of push and pull to extract a common-denominator meaning from this variety. And we face similar complications in any attempt to define theology: For Aristotle, theology in the strict sense meant "first philosophy" or metaphysics, for some of the Fathers of the Church it meant the ancient mythologies or cosmogonies, but in contemporary scholarship it has some different connotations: the "rational elaboration of revealed truths" or "systematic treatment of beliefs about God" or "dogmatics." For many moderns, theology is inseparably interconnected with certain methodologies of scriptural criticism. Augustine, for one, would be surprised, possibly shocked, if he had known what modern theologians would be engaged in.

TURNER: The problem will become even more acute if and when we get to defining the relationship between the kingdom of God and democracy. I hope that we will not end up speaking about the relationship of the $KofG_1$ with $Democracy_4$, etc.

CRANSTON: We may have no other choice. But we don't want to be in the position of that fellow that Hegel talks about, who never learnt to swim because he insisted on learning how to swim before he got into the water.[3] Let us at least try to clarify some of the essential elements connected with the concept of the kingdom of God in at least some of its applications.

TURNER: If I dared to ask you to define the essential elements of an "essential element," I suppose I would be in the position of that Hegelian fellow you just referred to. Very well, I'll try to cooperate in this enterprise of clarification.

CRANSTON: A good place to start would be with the meaning of "kingdom."

---

[3] G. W. F. Hegel, *Logic* (Part One of his 3-part *Encyclopedia of the Philosophical Sciences*, 3rd. ed., §41. Hegel used this simile in arguing against the position that we have to understand the nature of knowledge or the knowing processes before we actually proceed to know philosophically.

TURNER: You have already taken an implicit position in this regard by adopting "kingdom" as a translation of the Aramaic *malkuth* or the Greek *basileia*, rather than offering "reign" as a translation. The former term connotes a place, while the latter indicates a state of affairs, an actualized situation.

CRANSTON: Since the original terms can have either meaning, one has to make a choice. I chose "kingdom" because this is the term most commonly used. The English word, "kingdom," was sometimes used in Shakespearean times in the sense of "reign"; so this would have permitted our predecessors to reproduce the ambiguity of the original. But we moderns have to make a choice.

TURNER: Very well. If we concentrate on our own contemporary usage of the terms involved in the phrase, "kingdom of God," the first and major connotation seems to be that God rather than anyone or anything else is the ruler.

CRANSTON: I agree. And since "anyone else" would include other gods, monotheism would be implied; that is, the exclusion of other gods.

TURNER: I would say, not just the exclusion of other gods from the actual kingship (as if there could be other gods standing around but divested of political power), but the exclusion of the existence of other gods: in other words, *the* one God recognized as sovereign.

CRANSTON: Thus the kingdom of this God, not encountering any opposition from other gods out of other kingdoms, would also be conceived as universal—i.e., not just a sovereignty over a particular people at a particular place or time.

TURNER: Universality in time implies eternity. This would constitute another distinguishable element.

CRANSTON: As long as we are presupposing the traditional idea of a God who always was and always will be, this would be a corollary.

TURNER: It seems to me there is one other element worth isolating: Namely, that the kingdom of God, wherever and whenever it is, implies a cosmic situation in which everything is under control—that there are no potential crises or conflicts or entropic surges that would cause the Creator to lose control, and throw up his hands in exasperation, so to speak?

CRANSTON: I think so. But let's stop there, although there may be other elements that we haven't brought out. We have at least five elements: 1) Actual possession of power by God; 2) monotheism; 3) universal rule; 4) eternal rule; and 5) impossibility of subversion.

TURNER: I think we can immediately see that some of the major struggles in the Judaeo-Christian tradition are attributable to choices that had to be made in manifesting or expressing these five elements. For example, is the actual possession of power by God to be expressed by the direct influence of God, or by some intermediary (e.g. king, prophet, judge, priest, scribe, rabbi, pope, patriarch)? The resolution of this problem is still a major item on the agenda of Protestantism and Catholicism today.

CRANSTON: The element of monotheism has also been responsible for its share of theological conflict: Witness the battles in the Old Testament to wean the people away from allegiance to Yahweh's competitors, the "false gods"; and the battles in Christianity about whether Jesus as Son of God could be equal to the Father, how "three divine persons" could still be one God, etc.

TURNER: I don't believe all these questions have yet been solved to everyone's satisfaction (certainly not to mine). But the element of "universality" is even more controversial: Does the kingdom of God extend properly only to some elite group—e.g. a chosen people, or the "one true church," or the "twelve lost tribes of Israel," or the "144,000 saved" of the Apocalypse? There are still some intense contests in that regard.

CRANSTON: Universality in time is also a major problem, because an eternal kingdom eludes identification with any ephemeral, transitory political or ecclesiastical structure, and quite possibly has to be construed as transcending all of them, and all of time. Which leads to the question about whether the kingdom of God comes only at the end of time, or in some fashion develops in an inchoate way within time.

CRANSTON: A parallel conflict emerges in regard to the last element, i.e., whether the kingdom of God will be able ultimately to best all conflicts and keep the upper hand. Many say this can only be achieved in some other world, while the optimists look forward to the full assertion of the authority of God on earth. Again, some see the coming of the Kingdom as a resolution of all conflicts, while others see it as the catalyst which will bring all conflicts to a head.

TURNER: I can see we have our work cut out for us.

III. The Development of the Concept
of a Kingdom of God in the Old Testament

> It was by faith that Abraham obeyed the call to set out for
> a country that was the inheritance given to him and his descen-
> dants, and that he set out without knowing where he was
> going. By faith he arrived, as a foreigner, in the Promised
> Land, and lived there as if in a strange country, with Isaac and
> Jacob, who were heirs with him of the same promise. They
> lived there in tents while he looked forward to a city founded,
> designed and built by God. —Hebrews 11:8-10

> Wisdom delivered her servants from their ordeals. The
> virtuous man [Jacob], fleeing from the anger of his brother,
> was led by her along straight paths. She showed him the
> kingdom of God and taught him the knowledge of holy things.
> —Wisdom (The Wisdom of Solomon) 10:9-10

> Glorified and sanctified be God's great name throughout the
> world which He has created according to His will.... Establish
> His kingdom in your lifetime and during your days within the
> life of the entire house of Israel. —Kaddish (ancient Jewish
> prayer, possible source of the Christian "Lord's Prayer")

The phrase, "kingdom of God," appears only once in the Old
Testament, in the book of Wisdom, but the concept of a domain
characterized by the rulership of God is found frequently in the Psalms
and the prophetic books, and in the Pentateuch as well. According to St.
Paul's Epistle to the Hebrews, the vision of a kingdom of God as an
object of faith began with Abraham. But when we reflect that the book
of Wisdom is not considered a canonical book by either Jews or
Protestants, that most New Testament scholars reject Paul's authorship of
Hebrews, that some Old Testament scholars cast doubt upon the actual
existence of Abraham—we perhaps have the necessary and sufficient

15

motivation for beginning with a preliminary discussion of historicity, authenticity and interpretation:

The historical facts upon which the Old Testament is based may be summarized as follows: The era of the Patriarchs began in the 19th century B.C.   Some descendants of the patriarch Jacob emigrated to Egypt in the 17th century B.C., and remained there about 400 years until the "exodus" of the Israelites. Shortly thereafter they began a conquest of the land of Canaan. They were ruled by "Judges" until the formation of a monarchy in the 10th century. After about a century, the monarchy split into two kingdoms, the kingdom of Israel and the kingdom of Judah. After repeated invasions and subjection to exile by a succession of powerful empires, only a small remnant of the Kingdom of Judah remained in Jerusalem. This remnant, the Jews, which claimed ancestry from the original tribes of the patriarchal age, built a second temple to replace the original temple of Solomon, and entrenched themselves in spite of massive political losses to retain and perpetuate their ethnic and religious heritage.

Scripture scholars tell us that various narratives from both the kingdom of Israel and the kingdom of Judah were salvaged or rediscovered during that final period of retrenchment, and that the Jews undertook the massive task of editing these narratives. The editors are presumed to have been conscientious and as accurate as was possible in creating a literature out of the fragments of tradition; but they were also generally motivated to use what we would now call a mixture of history and myth for solidifying the consciousness of Jewry as a people and a nation and for providing moral lessons to their contemporaries. Thus, for example, in imitation of literary genres prevalent among other nations, they went beyond the immediate objective of writing the chronicle of a people to presenting a large-scale interpretation of the origins of the world, of mankind, and the various nations, in order to give added force and sanctions to their work; thus also they presented the five books of Moses (the Pentateuch) as a work authored by Moses himself, thereby transforming narratives which had to do with Hebrew origins into the word of Moses, and, since Moses was portrayed as God's spokesman, into the "word of God"; and, looking back upon the trials of the Israelites after the Davidic monarchy as punishments for establishing a monarchy "like all the other nations," they may have interpolated warnings about the dangers of monarchy in what seem to be historical narratives.[1]

---

[1] See e.g. 1 Sam. 10:19.

Thus, if we can trust the industry and methodology of twentieth-century scripture scholars, we can perhaps best portray the Old Testament as something like a jigsaw puzzle, which has finally been joined together in a recognizable pattern—a pattern of the development of a religious-ethnic heritage which reaches its zenith in the mighty Davidic monarchy, shortly thereafter begins to decline politically, but in the midst of bad times musters up the cultural and spiritual reserves that it has been able to preserve and pass on to subsequent generations.

It would seem, then, that an investigation of the concept of the kingdom of God in the Old Testament would be hopelessly over-optimistic if it aspired, e.g. to reconstruct the idea of the Kingdom as it was conceived, if it was conceived, by Abraham or Jacob or Moses or even David. But it is perhaps within realistic parameters for us to reconstruct some inchoate stages of the development of the concept which laid the groundwork for the redactions of later writers and the final spiritualized reinterpretations of the prophets of Israel and Judah. The reconstruction would have to take into account the following three distinguishable stages:

1) The *original concept* of a king of creation, king of the world. The myth of God as the "king of the world" under various titles ("Marduk," "Asshur," "Milhom," etc.) was common to all ancient Near East peoples, as Perrin notes.[2] The kingship-imagery which the Hebrews eventually associated with Yahweh is summed up eloquently in Psalm 93:

> Yahweh is King, robed in majesty.... You have made the
> world firm, unshakable; your throne has stood since then....
> Yahweh reigns transcendent in the heights.

This King of the World, for mysterious reasons, takes it upon Himself to grant special protection to the Israelites, the descendants of the patriarch Jacob. Jacob had been designated prophetically as the father of the twelve tribes of Israel after wresting some rights of inheritance from his brother Esau.[3] As a sign of continuing concern and protection, God shows "his might to his specially chosen people by giving them the lands of the nations,"[4] i.e. the fertile land of Canaan, even though it was already inhabited by numerous tribes and peoples.

---

[2]See Norman Perrin, *Jesus and the Language of the Kingdom*, p. 17.
[3]Genesis 28:10ff.
[4]Psalm 110

2) *Later accretions to the concept*: As the Israelites became more organized in the face of threats or perceived threats from other nations, they established a monarchy, in the glory of which Yahweh the King immediately came to participate. But an unavoidable ambiguity developed as to whether the king was sharing the glory with Yahweh, or Yahweh was sharing glory with the king. After the period of glory had passed, the ambiguity also disappeared, to be replaced by hard facts: The monarchy was divided after feuds and intrigues into the rival kingdoms of Israel (Samaria) and Judah; and inhabitants of both kingdoms were exiled into the lands of successive empires (Babylonian, Persian, Macedonian, Syrian, etc.). Only memories of the glory of the erstwhile earthly monarchy remained. Upon the return, by order of Cyrus, of a remnant of the Jewish kingdom to Jerusalem after the period of Persian domination, the idea of a special presence of Yahweh the King on Mount Zion, the former stronghold of the Davidic monarchy, began to emerge. In an apparent revision or adaptation of the covenantal promises made to Abraham and Jacob, the patrimony of Israel seemed to devolve once and for all on the traditional inhabitants of Jerusalem (the tribes of Judah and Benjamin). This remnant, the "Jews," for some time projected the possibility of the establishment by Yahweh of a future messianic rule of a Jewish king over the empires of the world:

> Yahweh addresses [the gentile nations]: "This is my king, installed by me on Zion, my holy mountain.... You are my son, today I have become your father. Ask and I will give you the nations for your heritage, the ends of the earth for your domain...."[5]

Such messianic hopes were particularly attached to the reign of King Zerubbabel, governor of Judah under Persian rule, who began the construction of the second Temple.[6] But when Zerubbabel in the last analysis did not give any indication of being the Messiah, and no possibility of legally restoring the Davidic monarchy was foreseeable, a gradual detachment of the idea of the "kingdom of God" from actual earthly kings began to take place. The warnings of the prophets that the kingdom of God was independent of any actual state, and could thrive

---

[5]Psalm 2
[6]Hag. 1:1-2; Zech. 4:9.

even in the midst of the political disintegration of the remnants of Israel, began to take root.[7]

3) *Final stages in the evolution of the concept*: If a faithful Jew gave credence to the prophecies that Israel was no longer to be identified with the kingdom of Judah, but also *continued to believe* that the promises made to his forefathers would still be fulfilled, in what direction might he turn? Three possibilities presented themselves[8]:

a) *A spiritual kingdom*, stripped of the trappings of worldly glory and political power, but nonetheless remaining and organizing for the accomplishment of God's purposes. This is the idea of a *Holy Commonwealth*, a quasi-church, inaugurated by the scribe, Ezra, together with the governor of Jerusalem, Nehemiah[9]. This is the concept of the Kingdom that was perpetuated under the leadership of the Pharisees, who expected that meticulous fidelity to the law would bring God's blessings down upon his people, in spite of any and all political vicissitudes. The formation of an opposing party of Sadducees during the Hasmonean dynasty represented a rejection of the "fine tuning" of the law by the Pharisees in favor of a return to the basic Mosaic law, and an advocacy of closer cooperation with the hierocratic hierarchy. During the client-kingship of Herod under Rome, the Pharisees lost much of the religious-political power they had possessed.

b) *A kingdom established by direct, miraculous, divine intervention:* This was another possible solution to the problem of furthering the kingdom of God amid the seemingly inexorable pressures from earthly empires. It was the vision of Daniel, who predicted to Nebuchadnezzar that

> ...in the days of those kings the God of heaven will set up a kingdom which shall never be destroyed, nor shall its sovereignty be left to another people. It shall break in pieces all these kingdoms and bring them to an end, and it shall stand for ever.[10]

---

[7]See e.g. Amos 5:18-20, 9:7; Jer. 29:10-14; Ezek. 11:16; Isa. 45:22-23, 56:7-8; Zech. 2:11; Mal. 1:11; Jonah 4:11.

[8]The following lines of analysis are suggested in John Bright's *The Kingdom of God*, Ch. 7.

[9]Cf. Ezra 7ff. and Nehemiah, *passim*.

[10]Dan. 2:44

This apocalyptic vision also became associated with the coming of a heavenly Son of Man, who would inaugurate the new order. Whether or not this Son of Man would be an earthly monarch after the pattern of David and Solomon was a matter of interpretation and dispute. In the aftermath of the Maccabean revolt, which eventually dashed expectations and renewed disappointments, the apocalyptic interpretation became rife in the separatist Qumran communities (Essenes). These communities existed up to 70 A.D., when the Jewish revolt was crushed by Roman legions.

        c) *A kingdom achieved by revolution*: Inspired by a tradition which told them that past military heroes like Joshua had overcome what had seemed to be overwhelming forces of enemies, some Jews were committed to the achievement of political-theological independence by military force. "Zion" in this interpretation was a future-revolutionary order to be established after military victories secured by Yahwist devotees of great discipline and purity. The "zealots" of Jesus' time were parties to this vision of Zion.

It is dimly conceivable that a syncretism of *all three* of these interpretations might take place—e.g. Yahweh's apocalyptic establishment of a new theocratic Zion to cap off the efforts of valiant revolutionaries (like the Maccabees). But in actual fact the three directions tended to branch off from one another rather than to dovetail; and this variety of visions fashioned the religious-political environment which prevailed during the last few centuries before the advent of Christianity.

IV. Is an Apolitical Kingdom of God Possible?

If the cultural or religious historian crosses the political boundaries he is aware that this is an abstraction from actual life, and he does not forget that the *political* unities, whether large or small, remain the conditions of all cultural life.... It is significant that the symbol in which the Bible expresses the meaning of history is political: "Kingdom of God," and not "Life of the Spirit" or "economic abundance." The element of centeredness which characterizes the political realm makes it an adequate symbol for the ultimate aim of history. —Paul Tillich, *Systematic Theology* III

CRANSTON: Recently a theologian, when I mentioned that I was researching the relationship of the concept of the kingdom of God to politics, congratulated me. He said it was important that people realize how essentially and irrevocably political that symbol is. But I'm disturbed by his unqualified support, because I'm not sure I want to go that far. It seems to me that if you make every interpretation of the kingdom of God "political," you run the danger of watering down the meaning of "political" itself. You might deduce, for example, that everything Christian becomes political—going to Catholic school, sending Bibles to Russia, doing missionary work.

TURNER: You have to admit the symbol *is prima facie* intrinsically political: It smacks of hierarchy, organization, power and sanctions, perhaps absolute authority.

CRANSTON: Certainly not if it is taken as future.

TURNER: Provided that the future is not taken as a criterion foreboding judgement on the present. Daniel's apocalyptic vision of the future kingdom of God inaugurated by the Son of Man was definitely politically charged.   King Nebuchadnezzar did not react to Daniel's vision[1] as a quaint, utopian, idealistic dream.

CRANSTON: But Daniel's vision did not pose any direct political threat to Nebuchadnezzar, and posed an indirect political threat only because of the king's reliance on visions of this sort. Many absolute rulers, then and now, would be able to take their apocalypse with a grain of salt. So apocalyptic versions of the Kingdom do not necessarily have any political entailments and mandate any political response.

TURNER: They are "political" only in the widest sense.

CRANSTON: Even less political, I would say, is the concept of the Kingdom as future in the sense of an "afterlife." Heaven as the kingdom of God seems quite removed from politics-as-usual.

TURNER: The idea of an afterlife in any form did not seem to be formulated in the Old Testament to any significant degree, if at all. But if the idea did occur, e.g. to the writers of the Wisdom books,[2] to the Psalmist,[3] to the prophets,[4] and during the time of the Maccabees[5], I think you are right: It would be stretching things quite a bit to regard this strictly heavenly (or partially purgatorial) vision of the kingdom of God as political in any important sense.

CRANSTON: Of course with the development in Christianity of the concept of an afterlife with choirs of angels and hierarchies of saints, the future Kingdom became politicized in a sense; and it might have held political implications for some Christians who were anxious to assure themselves of political privileges in the afterlife.

TURNER: But such conceptions would be "political" only in an analogous sense—the way that exercise can be "healthy," and a rosy

---

[1]See above, p. 19.
[2]Cf. e.g. Wis. 16:14, Ecclus. 7:17-19.
[3]Ps. 16:9-10.
[4]See Isaiah 26:19
[5]See 2 Macc. 12:43ff.

complexion can be "healthy." But we know that only a living organism can be "healthy" in the strict sense; so also, we know that only an actual, presently participated kingdom of God could be "political" in the strict sense of the word.

CRANSTON: So we might prudently search out strong and univocal political implications only in interpretations which construe the kingdom of God as something present.

TURNER: But are we to surmise that any attempt to relegate it to the present is political?

CRANSTON: I would think not, if we take the symbolism literally. It seems to convey the idea of a direct rule of God, and presumably not from a mountain top, or from a region of thunder in the sky, but from within—i.e., from within mankind, within consciousness, within the human spirit. In the later Old Testament era, when the prophets taught obedience to the spirit of God within man, this notion began to take root. Of itself, the idea is not political. It is when we start adding mediating agencies and external props, to help us "hearken to the voice of God" more perfectly, that it begins to take on explicitly political connotations.

TURNER: The prophets seemed to consider themselves the mediating instruments for communicating the word of God. I can't think of a religious system then or now that has ever dispensed with the need for intermediaries. Even the idea, which has appeared now and then in both Old and New Testaments, that everyone on earth will somehow be directly subject to the spirit of God, was conveyed and perpetuated and worked for by intermediaries who were presumably directly inspired themselves.

CRANSTON: One need not go to the prophets to find examples of inspired or charismatic persons or groups acting as intermediaries or channels. The "Judges" after Moses certainly were thought to perform that function, communicating the words of Yahweh, enforcing Yahweh's regulations, etc.

TURNER: There you have it. What begins allegedly as an inner contact, or joining of forces, with a transcendent realm, ends up as a system of education at best, indoctrination at worst; organization at best, regulation at worst; unification at best, mobilization at worst. Just like a political state.

CRANSTON: All this has to do with what we now associate with ecclesiastical structuring—a structuring which gives good *prima facie* evidence of being outside the political. If you disallow this, you risk overextending the term, "political," so that it can be applied not only to ecclesiastical structures but also fraternities and corporate stockholders' groups and senior citizens' self-help councils, as well. The organizing you're referring to is ecclesiastical—by definition outside of the political.

TURNER: I see you are edging towards a narrow definition of "political." Which is...?

CRANSTON: I think Aristotle put it very well in characterizing politics as the art of organizing and balancing all the diverse interests in a state. Clearly religious organizations would be one of the diverse interests that need to *be* balanced, *not* the balancing instrumentality.

TURNER: Unless the religious organization became identical with or coterminous with the state, or the power behind the state; or unless the state becomes just an extension of the religious community. I'm sure you are aware of the many historical instances of this phenomenon.

CRANSTON: I am. In fact, the Israelite religion during the time of Judges dovetailed more or less with the political state, becoming what Eric Voegelin calls a "theopolity."[6] But we must "bite the bullet" and consider whether there is not something in the very concept of the kingdom of God which leads necessarily, as it has led so often, to such phenomena.

TURNER: Not "necessarily," it would seem. We also observe in history sufficiently numerous instances in which a religious sect, because of convictions, sets itself up against the state. The later history of Israel, when the Jews under the Maccabees, deprived of political power, revolted for religious reasons against the

---

[6]*Order and History* I, p. 243n.

Hellenistic regime, is just one of many examples that could be cited.

CRANSTON: I don't think even the strongest religious motivations would make the Maccabean revolt apolitical. But what if they had not resisted? It occurs to me that a religious group persecuted and oppressed by a political state but not revolting, would clearly be existing in an apolitical fashion.

TURNER: Possibly forced into that mode of existence temporarily. But with a tremendous risk attached. For example, it is arguable that if Judas Maccabeus had not revolted, the Jewish identity would have endured irreversible assimilation, and the Judaism that we know as a religious-ethnic tradition in continuity with the past would not exist at present.

CRANSTON: I'm not so sure as you are on that surmisal. The Jews of the diaspora survived for centuries, often under oppressive political powers. The collective choice of the diaspora as a means of retrenchment and perpetuation of their traditions could have taken place earlier.

TURNER: I submit that only intense convictions coupled with a blocking of all other realistic responses could have led to a diaspora as a "solution." I doubt if there was that coupling in the time of the Maccabees.

CRANSTON: I agree that insurmountable political obstacles may be the all-important factors in decisions made by a highly cohesive religious group regarding their politicization or nonpoliticization.

TURNER: Perhaps we are now in a position to sum up some of the areas of consensus that we have arrived at, regarding the interconnection of the kingdom of God with politics: First of all, it seems that the first choice that has to be made is whether the kingdom of God is construed as present or future; a strictly future kingdom of God can be considered apolitical, in spite of various indirect and peripheral political consequences it might have. If it is characterized as present, however, the next choice is whether it is to be identified with a political state or not. Only when it is not so identified does the kingdom of God stand a chance of remaining apolitical, while still remaining an identifiable present community or church or movement or ideal (the question of how best to characterize a "present kingdom of God" must be left to later).

CRANSTON: "Choice" is extremely voluntaristic language to use to describe what in view of historical pressures often seem to be ineluctable collective responses. As we examine the political ramifications of the Old Testament concept of a kingdom of God, we see precisely such responses taking place.

V. The Vicissitudes of Theocracy in Israel

Some peoples have entrusted the supreme political power to monarchies, others to oligarchies, yet others to the masses. Our lawgiver [Moses], however...gave to his constitution the form of what—if a forced expression be permitted—may be termed a "theocracy," placing all sovereignty and authority in the hands of God. —Josephus Flavius, *Against Apion*

It was God alone ... who held sovereignty over the Hebrews, and so this state alone, by virtue of the covenant, was rightly called the kingdom of God, and God was also called the king of the Hebrews. Consequently, the enemies of this state were the enemies of God; citizens who aimed to seize the sovereignty were guilty of treason against God, and the laws of the state were the laws and commands of God. So in this state civil law and religion ... were one and the same thing.... Hence this form of government could be called a theocracy, its citizens being bound only by such law as was revealed by God. However, all this was a matter of theory rather than fact, for in reality the Hebrews retained their sovereign right completely.... —Baruch Spinoza, *Tractatus Theologico-Politicus*

Our first concern must be to build up the Land [of Israel], to foster its economy, its security and international status. But these are the whereby, not the end. The end is a State fulfilling prophecy, bringing salvation, to be guide and exemplar to all men. In the words of the Prophet is for us a truth perpetual: "I will give thee for a light to the Gentiles, that thou mayest be my salvation unto the end of the earth." —David Ben-Gurion, *Rebirth and Destiny of Israel*

Ben-Gurion rightly sees in the Messianic vision the second cornerstone of living Judaism. But this ... is in need of more concreteness. It is not enough to set "the redemption of Israel" side by side with "the redemption of the human race." The

27

> Messianic message is unique in the demand God makes upon
> the nations of men to realize His kingdom and in this way to
> take part in the redemption of the world.... Behind everything
> that Ben-Gurion has said on that point there lies, it seems to
> me, the will to make the political factor supreme. He is one
> of the proponents of that kind of secularization which cultivat-
> ed its "thoughts" and "visions" so diligently that it keeps men
> from hearing the voice of the living God. —"Zionism True and
> False: Interview with Professor Mordechai Martin Buber," in
> Ehud Ben-Ezer (ed.), *Unease in Zion*

The term, "theocracy," was coined by the Jewish historian
Josephus (37-110 A.D.) to describe as precisely as possible just what
would be meant by a "Kingdom ruled by God," and to indicate how this
concept had been implemented to a high degree in Judaism. For Jews in
Josephus' time the concept of a kingdom of God connoted a realm of
peace, justice and freedom, standing in stark contrast with, and even in
contradiction to, the Roman Empire of the day. In our time, "theocracy"
has taken on connotations of hierocracy, i.e., high-handed rule over
secular life by religious leaders or ecclesiastics—as in e.g. contemporary
Iran, where the control of Islam over politics is direct and explicit. The
term, "kingdom of God," on the other hand, at least for Christians, has
taken on the same positive connotations it had in Josephus' era, although
in the present era it connotes an opposition to a somewhat different
species of secular kingdoms—totalitarianism, fascism, etc. But it is
important to note that in prevailing theological discourse the kingdom of
God is not identified with "theocracy."

The fact that theocracy has become in practice, if not in
principle, synonymous with hierocracy is itself an indication that the
implementation of those originally positive images and that liberating
vision from Josephus' time has been persistently problematic. As we
have seen,[1] even those committed or aspiring to a kingdom of God may
find themselves at odds in interpreting it as heavenly or earthly, future or
present, spiritual or political, ruled directly by God or through mediators,
whether they be religious mediators or political mediators. The difficulty
entailed in making these choices is illustrated by some milestones in the
socio-political development of Israel from ancient to modern times:

It is arguable that the closest approximation in Israel to theocracy
in the literal sense of "rule by God, not by men" is to be found during
the period of "judges" in the aftermath of the Exodus and the occupation

---

[1]Ch. 2 above.

by Israel of the land of Canaan. Eric Voegelin, to avoid the hierocratic connotations of "theocracy," follows Martin Buber in using the term "theopolity" rather than "theocracy" to describe the political organization which prevailed during this period.[2] Others refer to it as a "theocracy" in a non-pejorative sense.[3] The various segments of the Israelite people for a period of about two centuries after the conquest of Canaan were scattered throughout Canaan, often separated geographically by Canaanite towns and city-states, but joined spiritually and culturally in a "loose confederation of clans united to one another about the worship of the common God."[4] For the sake of historical comparison, it could probably be best described as "something like an amphictyonic league of formerly separate clans, under the name of Israel,"[5] analogous to the Greek amphictyonic leagues, such as the Delphic league. It would also be somewhat analogous to the American pre-Constitution confederation of colonies, banded together for mutual benefit and assistance, without sacrificing autonomy to any considerable degree. In lieu of highly structured, centralized administration, Israel was led intermittently by a system of "judges," i.e. charismatic, divinely inspired liberators, champions, who also occasionally became involved in what we would now designate as judicial and jurisdictional roles. The spiritual unity of these peasant clans, which included as members many indigenous Canaanites, was manifested and furthered by periodic common worship centered at the shrine of the Ark of the Covenant at Shiloh.[6] In times of crisis and danger, God was relied upon to raise up heroic "judges" who would mobilize the clans militarily as well as help the confederacy to maintain its economic stability and strength. All in all, one might credibly maintain that this highly decentralized religious confederation was the most suitable way to implement the ideal of a "kingdom of God" in which God alone, through timely and powerful inspiration of men and women "of the hour," would rule the Israelites, freeing them from the necessity of having to submit to any of the multitude of surrounding empires and kingdoms and chiefdoms and the multitude of alien totemic gods.

---

[2]See *Order and History* I, p. 243n.

[3]See e.g. Dale Patrick, "The Kingdom of God in the Old Testament," p. 74.

[4]John Bright, *The Kingdom of God*, p. 31.

[5]Eric Voegelin, *Order and History*, I, p. 167.

[6]I Sam. 1-4.

A major challenge to the viability of this application of the theocratic ideal was encountered by the Israelites with the intrusion of a world-class imperial force into Canaan—the Philistines, highly organized and equipped with the latest developments in military technology. The Philistines aimed a blow directly at the heart of Yahwism by capturing the Ark of the Covenant from the shrine at Shiloh, killing the priests in charge, and destroying Shiloh. No intermittent charismatic "judge," no matter how filled with zeal for Yahweh's honor, was equal to countering such forces, combined with the other formidable local forces that the Israelites were habitually facing. The Israelites found themselves at a crossroads: either revise and update the rather idyllic notion of being "ruled by God alone," or risk almost certain loss of their religious/ethnic identity as the "people of God" in the wake of a massive foreign invasion.

Prior to the emergence of the Philistine threat, there had been an attempt to promote one of the more renowned "judges," Gideon, to the status of kingship over a rather limited area (Ophrah and adjacent towns).[7]   Gideon had replied to his constituents that he would not rule over them but rather God alone would rule over them. Some interpreters have taken this as a sign that Gideon refused the kingship altogether, in deference to God's sovereignty; others have maintained that he accepted the kingship but was simply trying to make it clear that it would be only God ruling through him; still others have suggested that he was only rejecting the name of "king" while accepting what amounted to a chieftainship. The story does seem to be based on fact, rather than being the imaginative imposition of anti-monarchical sentiments upon a legendary character by writers from later centuries, disillusioned with experiences with monarchies. If the account is indeed based on fact, any and all of the interpretations just given suggest a certain ambivalence concerning the idea of an earthly monarchy, or, more strongly, a definite conviction that an actual king would seriously compromise the religious idea of commitment to the kingship of Yahweh.

The ambivalence characterizing the Gideon narrative is of a piece with the later ambivalence characterizing Israel's transition to a full-scale, world-class monarchy on par with the Philistines: As Israel faced up to the imminent Philistine threat, Samuel, the last of the line of "judges," was urged to anoint a king who might be able to mobilize all the tribes of Israel and mold them into a united fighting machine against the invader. Samuel in compliance anoints Saul, but with great reluctance

---

[7]Judges 8:22.

and misgivings about the potential resultant spiritual harm to the Israelites.[8] Samuel's fear was that the election of the first king of all Israel would be tantamount to a rejection of Yahweh. Thus King Saul ascended the throne of Israel amid clouds of uncertainty about whether this was the right sort of thing for Yahweh's "chosen people" to be involved in.

As King David and King Solomon succeeded to the throne in a rather surreptitious manner to the throne in what initially had the earmarks of an hereditary monarchy, they tried to calm all misgivings concerning the crucial issue that began to emerge: whether Israel was just a kingdom like other kingdoms that come and go, or was indeed the theocracy that it was apparently chosen to be. Officially consecrated as God's anointed representatives, these new monarchs took pains to give signs to their subjects that they were doing God's work. For example, David "offered burnt offerings" dressed in a linen ephod, which was a priestly garment, when the Ark was brought up to Jerusalem[9]; Solomon offered burnt offerings and burned incense before God when worship began in the Temple[10]; and both David and Solomon blessed the people, a function which was supposed to be reserved for the priests[11]. David also moved the recaptured Ark of the Covenant, formerly of Shiloh, to his citadel in Jerusalem, Zion, and made several of his sons priests,[12] as if to give further concrete evidence of the union of the monarchy and the priesthood in this new "city of God."[13]

In this "golden age" of Israel, the "promised land" was almost completely in the hands of Israel, and successive generations of both Jews and Christians have looked back upon this era as one of unparalleled glory and success for the Yahwist religion. The Davidic monarchy is also frequently referred to as a "theocracy." But if we compare the political organization under David and Solomon with that which had prevailed just a few generations earlier, it quickly becomes evident that a sea change had taken place: No longer was "charismatic" leadership under "judges" in force; rather, hereditary monarchy, frequently subverted by intrigues and assassinations, became the established order. Solomon was chosen not because of his charisma, but because David had decided

---

[8]I Sam. 8-12.

[9]II Sam. 6:14-18.

[10]I Kings 9:25.

[11]I Sam. 6:18; I Kings 8:55-61.

[12]II Sam. 8:16-18.

[13]Ps. 46:5.

this particular son out of a multitude of sons would have the ability to hold together his massive empire. And with Solomon's accession to the throne, the influence of religious authorities on politics becomes a variable rather than a constant. Yahwism under Solomon became a state-supported, established religion; and rather than receiving admonition from priest or prophet, Solomon dismissed the priest Abiathar for holding opinions contrary to his own.[14]

The main theocratic question posed by the new monarchy was, as John Bright phrases it,

> Would all the hope of Israel, and all her sense of destiny, be transferred bodily to the Davidic state and find its fulfillment in terms of it? In short, would the kingdom of God be made equal to the Kingdom of Israel?[15]

After the death of Solomon, a splitting of the kingdom into the Northern Kingdom (Israel) and the Southern Kingdom (Judah) took place. The former lasted about two centuries; the latter almost twice as long. But after several monarchical successions on each side, the answer to the "theocratic question" began to become obvious: Neither the Northern nor the Southern Kingdom, in spite of spasmodic attempts to reactivate their "favored nation" status with Yahweh, approximated in any significant way to the kingdom of God. Some thought that if only the spirit of the monarchy of David, who was considered to be especially favored by God, could be recaptured, the kingdom of God would not be far behind; but others—especially the prophets—began to view the monarchy itself as something like the fabled Tower of Babel: an affront to God, the substitution of an earthly kingdom for the establishment of God's kingdom, and the reliance on human resources to accomplish what only could be accomplished in God's good time and in God's way.

Final reinterpretations of the theocratic problem began to take place after the irreversible fall of the kingdom of Israel (Samaria) to the Assyrians in 722; and after the fall of the kingdom of Judah in 586 with the sacking of Jerusalem by the Babylonians and the destruction of the Temple built by Solomon. Finally, in the wake of the return of a remnant of the kingdom of Judah with the permission of Cyrus, one of a procession of conquering emperors, the indomitable Jews, sobered and chastened, were once again ready to try their hand at concretizing the

---

[14]I Kings 2:26-7.
[15]John Bright, *The Kingdom of God*, p. 45.

vision of Abraham and Jacob in a new way: Under the leadership of the scribe Ezra and with the help of a governor, Nehemiah, a new order sometimes referred to as the "postexilic theocracy" was inaugurated. The Torah (the written record of the divine King's laws) became a quasi-constitution for the "Holy Commonwealth" inaugurated by Ezra. Government by kings was replaced by the rule of high priests; the comparative dearth of prophets was repaired by the collaboration of scribes who would preserve and interpret the sacred writings and function as teachers of morality. Taxation and legislation was through the aristocracy of high priests. In short, the reformed interpretation of theocracy amounted to a hierocracy, in which the reins of executive, judicial and legislative power were held by religious leaders. A temporary return to a monarchical framework took place after the formation of the Hasmonean dynasty following the success of the Maccabean revolts against Hellenic culture: the Hasmoneans eventually added the title "king" to that of "high priest."

By the time that Flavius Josephus came to reflect on the history of Israel and Judah, and to develop his concept of a theocracy, a final change took place—due no doubt to collective experience of the excesses of hierocracy, but also to the historical fact that with the destruction of the second Temple by the Romans in 70 A.D. sacrifice by the priesthood was no longer feasible—from hierocracy to nomocracy. The government of God's chosen people was no longer entrusted to judges or kings or priests, but to rabbis—or rather, one should say, to the law itself, promulgated and preserved and applied by the traditionally scholarly class of rabbis. Josephus' nomocratic "theocracy" was the product of an age in which the hard facts of dispersion (diaspora) were addressed through the building up of close-knit religious/social/economic communities. This Jewish nomocracy was an ingenious solution to the problem of maintaining a theocracy in the absence of a) a homeland and b) access to political power.

In comparison with Josephus, Philo Judaeus (20 B.C.-50 A.D.), a "devout Jew" and "an older contemporary of Christ," proposed a more ambitious, utopian theocratic ideal, which could be called "theocratic ecumenic futurism."[16] His vision is reminiscent of the universalism of deutero-Isaiah:

> Yahweh has spoken.... "It is not enough for you to be my servant, to restore the tribes of Jacob and bring back the

---

[16]Dante Germino, *Political Philosophy and the Open Society*, p. 104-108.

> survivors of Israel; I will make you the light of the nations so
> that my salvation may reach to the ends of the earth."[17]

Philo foresaw an ecumenical world order ruled by the law of Moses
rather than Rome, with an elected federative monarchy, a system of
judges throughout the world, and a government based on law. This
regime was the Messianic order to be established by God.

We can perhaps perceive in Philo's utopian vision of a worldwide, republican, federative extension of a rabbinical system the seeds of
the various Zionist movements which gathered momentum in the
nineteenth century and resulted in the creation of the state of Israel in the
twentieth—except that in the latter there is a decisive emphasis on
physical repossession of David's citadel, Zion, as a geographical center
from which the Judaic influence might radiate. Encountering persecutions and pogroms in country after country over the centuries, even Jews
who were inclined towards assimilation and even Jews of a non-religious
orientation began to consider a return to the "homeland" as the only
possible solution to the problems of the diaspora.

Given that the Nazi holocaust provided the necessary and
sufficient emphasis for world-wide sympathy for the Zionist movement,
can we say that the state of Israel, having now been officially established
by the United Nations, is in any way a fulfillment of the original idea of
the Kingdom, as some visionaries (like the quasi-religious, quasi-secular
Ben-Gurion) have maintained? Orthodox Jews initially opposed the
founding of the state of Israel, on the grounds that its establishment was
an unwarranted attempt to anticipate the inauguration of a final messianic
order on earth; but at present only a small minority of dissenters in Israel
maintain this stand. In fact many religious Israelis support a "militant
synagogue" strategy rather than passive expectation of a Messiah, and the
Gush Emummim look forward to the total forcible occupation of
Palestine as the condition for achieving the final stage in which Israel
will become a heavenly kingdom of priests and wise men, inculcating
morality in the rest of the world by its own fidelity to the commandments
of the Torah—a revival of Philo's vision from two millennia ago.

How would Josephus evaluate contemporary Israel, using his
criterion of nomocratic theocracy? Israel is officially a "secular" state,
but it is also officially committed to considerable intertwining of the
religious and the political: It is officially the "sovereign state of the
Jewish people" comprising the biblical territories of "Judaea" and

---

[17]Isa. 49:6.

"Samaria," forbidding (as did Ezra and his followers in the post-exilic reforms) intermarriage with gentiles, and zoning off 92% of its land as the "inalienable property of the Jewish people." Israel has no judges or prophets or high priests with a "direct line" of influence over the head of government, but on the other hand it has minority religious parties sitting in parliament, who can wield considerable power through coalitions. Established under duress like the Davidic monarchy, and rising to a position of great national power and prestige, it is now beset, as were David's successors, with the problem of maintaining territory won in battle and warding off threats from outlying groups of Palestinians (no doubt including many descendants of the original "twelve tribes of Israel"!) who have opposing claims to territory and sovereignty, and who associate Palestine with Haifa and Jaffa rather than Judaea and Samaria.

Josephus, in response to the hypothetical question about theocracy, might answer with a comparison of the modern state of Israel with the ancient Davidic state: namely, that both were created under duress by a motley group of religious and not-so-religious Israelites, that both attained considerable wealth and prestige and worldly power, and that modern Israel seems to be in the same uncomfortable position that the successors of David found themselves in—surrounded by hostile forces unable to summon up great sympathy with the ideal of Zion, an ideal which is still regrettably remote from the internationalism of deutero-Isaiah. And he might fault them both for their establishment of, and power over, religion: no longer do charismatic judges or inspired prophets or their modern equivalents have a status transcending the state, so that they might operate as moral/religious checks without controlling the state in hierocratic fashion.

Whether Christians have done any better in interpreting their even more explicit vision of a kingdom of God remains to be examined.

VI. New Testament Conceptualization of Messianic Fulfillment

This is what Jesus taught them:....."Do not swear at all, either by heaven, since that is God's throne; or by the earth, since that is his footstool; or by Jerusalem, since that is the city of the great king." —Matthew, 5

"How do you know me?" said Nathanael. "Before Philip came to call you," said Jesus "I saw you under the fig tree." Nathanael answered, "Rabbi, you are the Son of God, you are the King of Israel." —John 1

"Jesus of Nazareth," they answered, "...proved he was a great prophet by the things he said and did in the sight of God and of the whole people; ...our chief priests and our leaders handed him over to be sentenced to death, and had him crucified. Our own hope had been that he would be the one to set Israel free." —Luke 24

Having met together, they asked [the risen Jesus], "Lord, has the time come? Are you going to restore the kingdom to Israel?" He replied, "It is not for you to know times or dates that the Father has decided by his own authority...." —Acts 1:6-8

It does not matter if a person is circumcised or not; what matters is for him to become an altogether new creature. Peace and mercy to all who follow this rule, who form the Israel of God. —Galatians 6:15-16

What you have come to is Mount Zion and the city of the living God, the heavenly Jerusalem where the millions of angels have gathered for the festival, with the whole Church in which everyone is a "first-born son" and a citizen of heaven. —Hebrews 12:22-3

The phrase, "kingdom of God," or its synonym, "kingdom of heaven," occurs over a hundred times in the Christian gospels. It is widely considered by theologians to be the most important message of the gospels, the pivotal idea on which everything else hinges. It is a distinctive Judaeo-Christian ideal; nothing quite similar to it is found in the other great world religions. It contrasts sharply with the *Nirvana* of Buddhism, with *Samahdi* in Hinduism, with the *Tao* of the Chinese religious tradition. But the positive content of the idea of the "kingdom of God" is not easily arrived at. For example, from the context in which Jesus spoke of the kingdom of God, one could not be certain which of the three interpretations of the kingdom prevailing at the end of the Old Testament era[1] was actually favored by Jesus: One might surmise that Jesus leaned towards *the apocalyptic interpretation*, since he is reported to have referred to "The Son of Man" frequently, and talks about the imminent end of the world "in this generation"[2]; but it also seems that he adopts the *Holy Commonwealth interpretation*, when he says, for instance, that he has not come to abrogate the law, and is reported to have spoken about the founding of a "church"[3]; and one cannot completely eliminate the *revolutionary interpretation* since he also speaks about coming not to bring peace, but the sword, and about "spreading fire on the earth"[4].

The multitude of references to the kingdom of God by Jesus can probably best be sorted out and categorized in terms of ostensible present and future reference:

   a)*References which seem oriented towards the present*

            1> Among present-oriented statements, some emphasize the *presence of the kingdom of God on earth* here and now. When Jesus tells the disciples to tell the people of Israel that "the kingdom of heaven is close at hand"[5] as they cast out devils and diseases, and when Jesus challenges his critics with the assertion that "If it is through the Spirit of God that I cast devils out, then know that the kingdom of God has overtaken you"[6], he is not referring to some future event, but to the present,

---

[1]See p. 19 above.
[2]Mk. 8:38, Lk. 9:26, and elsewhere.
[3]Matt. 16:18.
[4]Matt. 10:34; Lk. 12:49.
[5]Matt. 10:7-8.
[6]Matt. 12:28.

and is implying that the kingdom of God is where the Spirit is and operates. And when Jesus tells a Scribe about the two great love-commandments, and the Scribe comments, "well spoken," etc., and Jesus answers, "You are not far from the kingdom of God!" here Jesus is obviously not informing the Scribe that he was just about to die and go into the afterlife, but is referring to some present development in which the Scribe may conceivably participate.

2> Other present-oriented texts seem to emphasize some *present organization*. When Jesus set up his headquarters in Capernaum[7] and chose the twelve apostles as twelve new "patriarchs" to assist in the spread of the Kingdom,[8] he was manifestly endeavoring to create a new community independent of ties of blood. And when Peter, after confessing the divinity of Christ, is given the "keys of the kingdom of heaven" for binding and loosing[9], the appropriate image to summon forth is not that of Peter at the "pearly gates" in the afterlife, but Peter with some sort of jurisdictional power comparable to that of the rabbis, with authority to interpret the Law, and to interpret the extent to which the law is binding. Explicit mention of a "church" is found in two places in the gospels.[10] But even among those who maintain that Jesus' idea of the Kingdom involved a present organization, there is still dispute as to whether this present organization was intended by Jesus to entail what we now call a "church."

3> Finally, there are also to be found some general references to the fact that a *New Covenant* is now the present state of affairs: When Jesus is asked about John the Baptist, and states, "Among those born of women there has arisen no one greater than John the Baptist; yet he who is least in the kingdom of heaven is greater than he,"[11] he is not making the rather jejune

---

[7]Lk. 4.

[8]Ibid. 5-6.

[9]Matt. 16:19.

[10]Mt. 13:41 and Lk. 22:29.

[11]Matt. 11:11; Lk. 7:28.

and irrelevant observation that departed souls in heaven are in a superior state than the still-living John the Baptist, but pointing out that a New Covenant had now replaced the Old. John the Baptist, being in Jesus' estimation the major transitional figure marking the end of the old dispensation, partakes in the incompleteness and indefiniteness of that dispensation.

b)*References which seem oriented towards the future*

1> *Apocalyptic references*: The text that seems to be cited most frequently as an example of Jesus' apocalyptic bent is: "Truly I say to you, there are some standing here who will not taste death before they see the Son of Man coming in his kingdom."[12] On the other hand, the advent of the Kingdom before the death of many of Jesus' contemporaries (disciples as well as enemies) is sometimes interpreted as a reference to *Pentecost*; and it is interesting to note that Thomas Aquinas in his *Catena aurea* cites interpreters who read this same passage as a reference to the "*transfiguration*" which, in all three of the synoptic gospels, follows immediately after this text.[13] In other words, according to the interpreters cited by Aquinas, Jesus was referring to a future visionary experience of the three apostles who were to witness his Transfiguration! Less ambiguous are Jesus' invocation of the apocalyptic images of the Book of Daniel, e.g. when he answers "yes" to the high priest's question about his Messiahship, and then adds that "you will see the Son of Man seated at the right hand of the Power."[14]

2> *Eschatological* interpretations: References to the Kingdom as a possibly more distant future (the "end of the world," the last judgement, the final separation of the just and condemned) are also found. A few of the references are found in parables in which the kingdom of God is presented as an idea that grows like a seed or some leaven in the hearts of the "subjects of the king-

[12]Matt. 16:28; Mk. 8:39; Lk. 9:27.
[13]See Thomas Aquinas, *Catena aurea in quatuor evangelia* I, Cap. XVI, 7; Cap. VIII, 5; II, Cap. IX, 5.
[14]Mk. 14:62.

dom," who do not give up under persecution, and who are not overcome with worldly worries and the lure of riches. Alongside these subjects are the "subjects of the Evil One," sowed by the Evil One and remaining among these until they are separated at the "end of time."[15] A definite reference to the future is also obvious when Jesus relies on a comparison to the ancient destruction of Sodom to instruct his disciples concerning what they should say to those who refuse to listen to them: "[Tell those who reject you:] 'Be sure of this: the kingdom of God is very near.' I tell you on that day it will not go as hard with Sodom as with that town."[16]

3> *The Afterlife*: Some future references, on the other hand, are simply allusions to an "afterlife." When, for example, Jesus speaks of Abraham, Isaac and Jacob being in the "kingdom of God"[17], there is no overt or covert allusion to an "end time" or "last judgement"; and neither is there any such allusion during the crucifixion when the good thief says, "Lord,*" remember me when you come into your kingdom," and Jesus answers, "*Today* you will be with me in paradise."[18]

It goes without saying that Jesus' idea of the kingdom of God does not seem to fit neatly into any one of the above categories. Even his disciples seemed to be confused about the present or future nature of the kingdom of God. Thus after the crucifixion and resurrection, the disciples who do not yet recognize the risen Christ walking by their side say, "our own hope had been that he would be the one that set Israel free." It is probable that these disciples spoke for a multitude of Jesus' followers, and that this multitude had been looking forward to some kind of present establishment of a kingdom, although they were not completely clear as to the exact nature of that kingdom. Jesus certainly disappointed the hope of the three traditional Jewish factions: the zealots, the apocalyptics, and the architects of the "Holy Commonwealth" of fidelity to law. He seemed to identify most with the "suffering servant" of Isaiah—and this was a scandal to most Jews.

---

[15]Matt. 13.
[16]Lk. 10:12
[17]Lk. 13:28.
[18]Lk. 23:42.

The fact that Jesus included a zealot like Simon as well as a tax-collector like Matthew among the twelve apostles might be taken as a symbol that Jesus himself was willing to tolerate, perhaps even encourage, different interpretations (revolution *vs.* cooperation) of the kingdom of God—at least insofar as the kingdom of God was to be considered as *present*.[19] In other words, it is possible that Jesus was willing to leave it up to his disciples to determine the exact concrete profile of the present kingdom of God, even in regard to some important political policy-orientations, or in regard to whether its present mission should be purely spiritual/ecclesiastical, or not. But the numerous clear references of Jesus to a future kingdom of God instigate doubts at the very least about how the present *and* future kingdom of God are to be coordinated, and at most about whether what seem to be *prima facie* references to a present kingdom of God should not really be reinterpreted in terms of the future. Certainly Jesus did not leave it to his disciples to choose between a present and a future kingdom of God, or, with respect to the future kingdom of God, to choose between possible future interpretations. Or did he? It almost seems that he did, if we examine the history of Christian interpretations.

---

[19]Cf. Langemeyer, *Menschsein in Wendekreis des Nichts*, p. 76.

VII. Is an Alternative Messianic Scenario Conceivable?

TURNER: It occurs to me that the political twists and turns of the "kingdom of God" in history have been dictated by a motley group of necessities—the fact that the Israelites had to eventually build their own monarchy to resist the empires of the day, the later fact that after the disintegration of their monarchy the Jews could not aspire to an earthly kingdom but only a spiritualized one, the still later fact that the Christians had to try to make sense of the Kingdom after their hoped-for king had been crucified, etc.

CRANSTON: I wouldn't call these necessities, since that connotes something like fate or destiny, submerging our freedom. Historical contingencies emerge, and we need to respond (freely) to them. But sadly there are no rules for doing this in a creditable manner, and what one generation looks upon as a necessary or inevitable response may be understood by a later generation as idiosyncratic or even a mistake.

TURNER: The very "need" to respond implies a necessity. But of course it's a hypothetical necessity: if you want to attain such-and-such a goal, then it is necessary for you to respond to the "contingencies" in such-and-such a way. And here is where the conceptualization of the kingdom of God looms as important. If the Israelites in David's time had visualized the Kingdom as something spiritual, no monarchical buildup would have been needed; if Jesus had visualized the Kingdom as earthly, he would have felt it necessary to resist in some forceful manner the efforts of Jews and Romans to silence him.

CRANSTON: So what we learn from all this is that the concept of the kingdom of God is very malleable, and has been hammered into shape by a host of historical circumstances.

TURNER: I would say that it was hammered into rough shape by Jesus and the early Christians. Further interpretations and applications to "historical contingencies" might be expected to be in continuity with that vision.

CRANSTON: That early Christian vision seems to be primarily affected, and I might even say infected, by the historical contingency that Jesus was not accepted as Messiah by the Jews and was executed by the Romans. Thus we have a whole theology of the redemption of the world from "the sin of Adam" by the crucifixion, of the attainment of beatitude by suffering and death, of the postponement of the separation of the saved and the damned until the Last Judgement, etc. But it *could* have been otherwise. The Jews could have accepted the messiahship of Jesus entering Jerusalem on a donkey on Palm Sunday; Pilate could have taken Jesus into protective custody and shipped him off to Rome.

TURNER: But the acceptance of Jesus by the Jews was the primary *desideratum*—God's "Plan A," if you like. What actually happened is the "Plan B" version of the Kingdom.

CRANSTON: My point is that under Plan A, and the different applications of the vision that would have been made under it, there would also have emerged a completely different Christian theology. Jesus would have been accepted as the Messiah, the king of Israel. Presumably it would have been a spiritual kingship that did not threaten the Roman Empire. Presumably Jesus would have established his headquarters in Jerusalem, or perhaps Capernaum, and sent his disciples out to spread the message of the coming of the Kingdom. And then what? He couldn't have died a natural death, since death is supposed to be a punishment for what we would today call 'original sin,' which he was not guilty of. Would he have passed on the leadership to Peter or somebody and ascended into heaven? Or stayed on for countless generations like that Indian guru, Babaji, who is supposed to have lived on in a physical form for thousands of years in the Himalayas?

TURNER: You have the makings of a good novel, there, but of the fantasy variety. In order for your story to be more realistic, you'd have to bring in the Roman Empire as the antagonist. It would be completely unrealistic to portray the Empire as smiling benignly upon the appearance in Judaea of a new King of the Jews, not appointed through the proper channels, and offering no obeisance to Caesar.

CRANSTON: Novels aside, there would be a whole new theology. No Catholic reenactment of Jesus' death in the Mass, no Protestant redemption from sin through Jesus' death, no Christian expectation of the future *parousia*—because Jesus would not have been crucified.

TURNER: Speculative questions like that are outside the range of theology.

CRANSTON: Tell that to Augustine, who speculated at length about what might have been if Adam and Eve hadn't eaten that forbidden fruit in the Garden of Eden.

TURNER: That sort of theologizing is out of vogue now. Theology is concerned with what is, not with what might have been.

CRANSTON: I realize that. Nevertheless, I thought it might be interesting to get some reactions from theologians on the "what might have been" aspect. I sent a questionnaire around to about twenty theologians, and raised the following question:

> In all of the Christian interpretations, the events of Christ's passion, death and resurrection are presupposed as in some way inaugurating the Kingdom. But if there is free will, certainly it was not foreordained that the Jews had to reject Jesus; nor was it foreordained that the Romans would have to enter into complicity with the Jews in executing Jesus. So what would have happened to the kingdom of God if the Jews in the spirit of Palm Sunday had continued to accept Jesus? and what would have happened if Pilate in defiance of Jewish demands and political expediency had decided to take Jesus under his protection, perhaps sending him to a more secure place temporarily or permanently?

Here is a sampling of the responses I received:

> **Theologian A**: Without failure, without death and resurrection, I do not believe the incarnation would have taken place at all.... The hopes for the return of the exiles in 539 B.C. and of the setting up of the kingdom in the book of Daniel in 164 B.C. are very much of a continuity with the New Testament hopes, yet they were ultimately dashed; they depended on an earthly kingdom; they depended on making the metaphor a literal reality. It is only in retrospect that we find it was a metaphor at all. So it remains a metaphor. Any "what if?" that tries to take it out of that category is theologically a non-question, and so ultimately of no interest.

TURNER: Notice his preference for the term, "metaphor," instead of "concept." We've already noticed[20] that other theologians have shown this same tendency, referring to the "symbol" of the Kingdom or to "the phrase, "kingdom of God," etc." They seem to be intent on emphasizing that it is just a matter of faith, and outside the range of conceptual investigation—at least for theologians.

CRANSTON: A second response I received is even more emphatic about the avoidance of speculation:

> **Theologian B**: The "what if" of your queries ... implies the merely relative significance of the historical, in the sense that inasmuch as the decisions which put Jesus on the Cross were free, they are in principle reversible, and consequently to lend to them the absolute value which they have in the history of salvation is to take contingencies far too seriously.... Christianity ... affirms that the life, death and resurrection of our Lord dominates and gives objective meaning to all that is, without limit or reservation. Therefore, what is past is irrevocably past, not to be recalled or played again.

---

[20]See p. 9 above.

TURNER: This should help dispel any image people might have of contemporary theologians as less than hard-headed and scientific. They are interested in actualities, not possibilities.

CRANSTON: But even scientists are interested in possibilities; and the consideration of alternative possibilities, even of possibilities that never took place, is important in the development of scientific theories. So also, it seems to me, the notion of a kingdom of God, which in Christianity has been conditioned and concretized by the fact of the crucifixion, might have a wider, more important meaning that has been lost track of through this concretization. I referred earlier to Augustine. Augustine, in raising the question about "what might have happened" if Adam and Eve hadn't disobeyed the divine command, helps set the stage for his very influential theory about just what the specific effects of that disobedience in our world are. Augustine's contemporary, Julian of Eclanum, raised the same question and came to a completely different conclusion—that Adam's sin caused death of a spiritual sort, and was not the cause of earthly suffering and labor and deformities and death. It is interesting to conjecture what changes in the Christian worldview might have resulted if Julian's theory had taken root among Christians.

TURNER: It's unfortunate that Augustine had Julian declared a heretic. The furtherance of theological debate on that question could have been beneficial.

CRANSTON: Precisely. Actually, I did find a third theologian who reluctantly agreed to consider my "what if" question about the alternative non-crucifixion scenario. **Theologian C**'s response was that if the Jews had accepted Jesus, the Kingdom would have been established with Jesus' installation as Messiah, and the world as we know it would have simply come to an end.

TURNER: So your alternative scenario would spell the end of theology, along with all of history.

CRANSTON: When I realized that, I posed a question to the same theologian about that other scenario in which Jesus is not accepted as Messiah by the Jews, but is taken under the wing by Pilate and given protective custody by Rome.

TURNER: You were possibly straining the limits of his tolerance at that point.

CRANSTON: Yes, but he did venture one last response. He said this scenario could never take place, because "protective custody" or a reasonable facsimile would have been out of the question. Jesus, he said, was so committed to Judaism that he would never have accepted protection from Rome. Jesus saw Rome as the epitome of evil.

TURNER: If that is the case, there is an interesting parallelism between Jesus and Socrates. Socrates identified so thoroughly with Athens that, when he was offered a choice between death and exile from Athens, he chose death.

CRANSTON: Yes. And Jesus' parallel *identification with Judaism* is, I think, a facet that has been definitely clarified by my posing the "what if?" question. I've also been led to reconsider the common notion that Jesus was "rejected" by the Jews. We tend to view the Christian idea of the Kingdom in terms of Jesus' rejection by the Jews, but this could be a serious mistake. A fourth theologian brought this to my attention, writing:

> The Jews *did* accept Jesus in Palestine, Antioch, and the whole of the Mediterranean basin. They became the core of the early Christian communities and their synagogues were the bases from which Christianity grew.

TURNER: We tend to look upon Christianity as a new religion after Judaism. But Jesus, the disciples and the early Christians did not consider themselves Jewish heretics and did not seem to have any intention of starting a new religion.

CRANSTON: If Jesus was really so committed to Judaism, that puts the debates between Paul and the other apostles about the perpetuation of Jewish dietary laws and rituals in a new light. If the Christian church were to be in any way an extension or continuation or anticipation of *Jesus'* vision of the Kingdom it would have to be much more Jewish than it is now.

TURNER: A Catholic might reply that his church is more Jewish than contemporary Judaism itself, since it has the sacrifice of the Mass, which is a prolongation in time of "Christ's sacrifice on the cross," while in Judaism there has been no sacrifice and no priesthood since the destruction of the Second Temple in A.D. 70. Sacrifice seemed to be central in Judaism up to that time.

CRANSTON: One wonders what sort of sacrifice would have come to prevail under "Plan A."

TURNER: I have a suspicion that that **theologian** C projected an apocalypse just to get out of answering that question.

VIII. Did Jesus make a Major Mistake?

Like that whole apocalyptic generation, Jesus expected the kingdom of God, the kingdom of justice, freedom, joy and peace, in the *immediate future*.... Was he not in fact mistaken if, as it seems from the undoubtedly authentic material, he expected an early end to the world?... In the light of today's perspectives we have to say that what is involved in this immediate expectation is not so much an error as a time-conditioned, time-bound world view which Jesus shared with his contemporaries. —Hans Küng, *On Being a Christian*

[On the other hand:] If, as is widely held today, Jesus was in error in the *main emphasis* of his message, if he was mistaken as to the *central purposes* of his mission—to proclaim and to prepare men for an imminent end of the world—it is difficult to understand how the other elements in his religious message remain trustworthy.... [It is also difficult to understand] how the present signs and powers of the future Kingdom can retain any validity or worth. They would be signs produced by a delusion and therefore must themselves be illusory. To imagine that one sees on the horizon the rosy blush of the breaking dawn and in its faint light sets out upon a journey only to wander in the darkness of midnight is utter deception. —George E. Ladd, *The Presence of the Future*

TURNER: What I find remarkable in examining the various references to a kingdom of God in the gospels is that no one ever seemed to ask Jesus, "Master, just what do you mean by the kingdom of God?"

Cranston: But his attempt to explain it in so many parables—the parable of the mustard seed, of the leaven, of the bridesmaids, etc.—is presumably a response to questions that were asked, but not recorded as being asked.

51

TURNER: Or responses to questions that his disciples did not ask, but should have asked. It seems clear that most of his disciples were expecting a messianic restoration of Israel, involving political liberation from Roman domination. This presupposition was so strong that he was trying to prepare them little by little for their inevitable disillusionment.

CRANSTON: That is possible, but I would expect that various shades of the then-prevalent interpretations—including spiritual, apocalyptic, and eschatological interpretations—were espoused by his disciples and the apostles. In any case, Jesus' interpretation may have differed from any of the prevailing interpretations, and it is important to get at the core meaning of the historical Jesus' own interpretation, if that is possible.

TURNER: To get at this meaning, it would seem one would have to choose between the two *prima facie* alternatives, present or future, unless you believe that the apparent present and future references can somehow be coordinated, without coming into contradiction with each other. In other words, do you want to go in the direction of a both/and or an either/or?

CRANSTON: I notice that you present the "both/and" and "either/or" in terms of an "either/or," since you use the disjunction—both/and "*or*" either/or.

TURNER: I can't conceive of a logical arrangement in which a conjunction and a disjunction could be both conjoined *and* disjoined. That's double-talk, and makes me shudder.

CRANSTON: Perhaps double-talk, or perhaps just extremely paradoxical. I suppose you hope to avoid paradox by insisting on the choice of the both/and or the either/or. But either choice will involve immense complexity, and perhaps even self-destruct: If one chooses, for example, the connotation of "present" in preference to "future," then all the apparent future connotations of the kingdom of God have to be reinterpreted in terms of covert present meanings; and vice versa, if one sees the future as the preeminent interpretation, then the ostensible present connotations have to be reinterpreted as future.

TURNER: My personal preference would be the both/and. I think the traditional philosophical distinction between "potency" and "act" would help to bolster this interpretation: Why couldn't we say that Jesus saw the kingdom of God as a potentiality developing slowly in the present, and finally at some juncture in time emerging into full bloom, after the manner of an evolutionary process?

CRANSTON: The problem with that approach is that the end result should be the eternal kingdom of God, but time doesn't flow easily into eternity. Even from the viewpoint of contemporary physics, if the law of entropy runs its course, time should come to a standstill rather than merging with eternity. The final, eschatological idea of a kingdom of God seems to transcend time. Your social-evolution-style approach also implies that human effort and a lot of hard work will pay off in the long run with the construction of the Kingdom. But many of the references to the kingdom of God in the gospels seem to imply that it will be a pure gift of God, and its coming will be an unpredictable, possibly instantaneous, and certainly miraculous event.

TURNER: Since I don't believe in miracles, I still find only an evolutionary approach worth considering seriously. But I will try to follow along in your line of thinking, which I take to represent traditional Christian thinking on the matter: I would say that the stickiest problems would seem to result from coming down strictly on the side of an interpretation in terms of the future. Because then, of course, a mistake on the part of Jesus is implied. And one would not expect mistakes on the part of someone who is taken to be God incarnate.

CRANSTON: This turned out to be a particularly acute problem in the early church. The early Christians considered it important and obligatory to uphold and defend the divinity of Christ. And it seemed highly unlikely that a divine person could have some serious lacuna of knowledge.

TURNER: Jesus himself indicates that he has such lacunae when he states that only the Father knows the day and the hour of the end of the world, not the Son.[1]

CRANSTON: Many scholars interpret this statement as a later addition, added by the evangelical writers after it became clear that there was not going to be an imminent apocalyptic event after Jesus' crucifixion and resurrection.

TURNER: I've noticed that the lists of "authentic sayings of Jesus" keep changing. The last I heard, the 200 American biblical scholars of the "Jesus Seminar" who meet in Sonoma, California, every year have ruled out the authenticity of 80% of the words attributed to Jesus in the Gospels. If he didn't make the statement about not knowing "the day or the hour," maybe he didn't make those other statements predicting the imminent apocalyptic end. That would at least help solve the problem about Jesus' reputed "mistake." But in any case, scriptural authenticity and canonicity doesn't seem to depend on whether Jesus or Moses or David or Isaiah really said the things that are attributed to them. Is it all that important whether Jesus said it or not?

CRANSTON: It certainly seemed so to Augustine and other Fathers, and medieval theologians. I find it interesting to read St. Thomas Aquinas' summary of the various patristic opinions concerning that very statement about not knowing "the day or the hour"[2]: Some of the fathers concluded that Jesus was making what we would call a "mental reservation"—e.g. Chrysostom stating that Jesus simply did not want to tell the Apostles about the exact hour; Jerome saying that although Jesus knew, it wasn't expedient for the Apostles to know; and Augustine explaining that Jesus knew, but not in such a way as to pass on this knowledge to others! Others came up with similarly ingenious explanations: Origen says that since the church is the body of Christ, Christ could not definitively say that he "knew" the day and the hour until the whole "mystical body" of believers knew it, and Basil offers the opinion that when Jesus says that only the Father but

---

[1]Matt. 24:36.

[2]See Thomas Aquinas, *Catena aurea in quatuor evangelia* I, Cap. XXIV, 35-36.

not "the Son" knows, he is referring not to the only-begotten son (Jesus) but to the adopted sons (Christians). This is just a sampling. What is most interesting in all this is the fact that none of these authorities seems to consider the possibility that Jesus could really have the lack of information that he claims to have.

TURNER: They were obviously trying to present a united front against heresies like Arianism, which tried to downplay or relativize the "divine nature" of Jesus. I have to say here that I sympathize with these attempts at apologetic. I am personally not sure that God exists; but if he does, and has to go through a learning process like the rest of us, that would be a damper for me. I would expect more from a bona fide God.

CRANSTON: I would, too. But here we have a special case of an incarnate God. Christians believe that Christ had both a divine nature and a human nature, to put it in terms of the traditional formula. While some gaps in knowledge might not jibe well with the idea of God, such gaps might be unavoidable in a God-man.

TURNER: What about a resurrected God-man? In the account of post-resurrection events in John's Gospel, Jesus tells Peter that he wishes "the beloved disciple" to remain "until I come"—which certainly seems to imply that the resurrected Jesus was still thinking of an imminent eschaton. One would think that with the resurrection any "blind spots" in Jesus' human knowledge might be overcome.

CRANSTON: That is a text that is still open to a wide variety of interpretations. For my part, I find it gratifying to think that even a resurrected God-man would not know the future. It enhances my sense of freedom. I think many would feel intimidated if they contemplated the possibility of voluntarily and spontaneously following a son of God who already knew what their "spontaneous" acts would be.

TURNER: My suspicion is that there has been some widespread misinterpretation of that phrase, "son of God." The phrase was commonly used for kings in those days, when monarchs were thought to be somehow chosen by, and representative of, the deity. Hans

Küng says it just meant Jesus had a title to rulership over Israel,[3] not that he was a sort of superhuman being with superhuman knowledge.

CRANSTON: Rulers don't generally rise from the dead.

TURNER: And gods don't generally end up in untimely deaths.

CRANSTON: Good analogy, but extend it a little further: God incarnate would be limited both with respect to his control of external circumstances and with respect to his knowledge of external circumstances.

TURNER: OK, but if Jesus *knew* the limitations of his knowledge, why did he apparently make such certain statements? Just "calling the shots" as he saw them?

CRANSTON: Yes, or perhaps the evangelists took general statements and overspecified them.

TURNER: He also seemed to be mistaken about the Scriptures, maintaining that the Scriptures cannot be rejected.[4] In our day there is a scientific rejection by theologians of much that is recorded in both the Old Testament and the New Testament—even including Jesus' statement about the non-rejectability of the Scriptures.

CRANSTON: The theologians maintain that they are only rejecting a literal and historical reading of the Scriptures, in order to bring out the true significance; and that one of the main contributions of modern theology and scriptural studies has been to highlight the bona fide humanity of Jesus—weaning Christians away from the "superman" tradition in the portrayal of Jesus.

TURNER: I have no trouble with any of that. I accept both the historicity and the humanity of Jesus. What I have problems with is divinity.

---

[3]*On Being a Christian*, p. 390.
[4]Jn. 10:35.

CRANSTON: The belief in the divinity of Jesus hinges, of course, not so much on those references to him as the "son of God," but on his raising himself from the dead.[5]

TURNER: Must we take as proofs for the historical factuality of the resurrection these same doubtful Scriptures, whose literal and historical meaning is always to be taken under consideration with a prudent skepticism?

CRANSTON: At this point we're getting into a matter of faith—which could never be derived from some sort of scientific certitude about the historical fact of a resurrection. I can see you're not ready to make the "leap of faith."

TURNER: No, I'm the "doubting Thomas" of legendary infamy. I insist on looking before I leap.

---

[5]John 2:18-22.

IX. The Dialectics of Christian Interpretation

The Kingdom—Present & Future: [Jesus] says, "He that breaketh one of the least of these commandments, and teacheth men so, shall be called least in the kingdom of heaven: but he that doeth and teacheth thus shall be called great in the kingdom of heaven." (Matt. 5:19) We must understand in one sense the kingdom of heaven in which exist together both he who breaks what he teaches and he who does it, the one being least, the other great; and in another sense the kingdom of heaven into which only he who does what he teaches shall enter. Consequently, where both classes exist, it is the Church as it now is, but where only the one shall exist, it is the Church as it is destined to be when no wicked person shall be in her. Therefore the Church even now is the kingdom of Christ, and the kingdom of heaven. —Augustine, *The City of God*

The Kingdom—Future: Weiss showed that the kingdom of God is not immanent in the world and does not grow as part of the world's history, but is rather eschatological, i.e., the kingdom of God transcends the historical order. God will suddenly put an end to the world and to history, and He will bring in a new world, the world of eternal blessedness. —Rudolph Bultmann, *Jesus Christ and Mythology*

The Kingdom—Future: Jesus never means by "kingdom" God's continual rule over Israel and the world, but always the future rule at the consummation of the world. —Hans Küng, *On Being a Christian*

The Kingdom—Present: While Jesus employed the traditional symbolism of apocalypse to indicate the "otherworldly" or absolute character of the Kingdom of God, He used parables to enforce and illustrate the idea that the Kingdom of God had come upon men there and then.... The Sacrament of the Eucharist...may be described as a sacrament of realized eschatology.... Each Communion is not a stage in a process by

> which [Jesus'] coming draws gradually nearer, or a milestone
> on the road by which we slowly approach the distant goal of
> the Kingdom of God on earth. It is a re-living of the decisive
> moment at which He came. —C. H. Dodd, *The Parables of the
> Kingdom*

There is general agreement among theologians and scripture
scholars concerning the importance of the doctrine of the kingdom of
God. But it is one thing to be convinced of its importance, and quite
another to get at its meaning. As Clayton Sullivan observes,

> Students of Christian origins are of one mind in contending
> that the kingdom of God was central in Jesus' teaching.
> Curiously enough, however, scholars have never been able to
> agree on what Jesus meant by this expression. Across the
> years, the phrase, "kingdom of God" has been semantic
> putty—pulled, shaped, and squeezed in all directions.[1]

The disagreements in question are not caused merely by the
inveterate stubbornness and opinionatedness of theologians, but have a
substantial foundation in the difficulty and complexity of the topic and
the terminology. An initial problem is that the idea of a kingdom of God
in the New Testament, while building upon the Old Testament tradition,
differs in some important respects from its genealogical antecedents: for
one thing, it is more universal in that it does not differentiate the spiritual
destiny of Jews and gentiles;[2] branching out from Judaism, it is expressly
organized for taking root in the gentile world. For another, it is
concerned more with the internal aspects of the Kingdom than with
externals,[3] being ready to sacrifice elements of the letter of "God's law"
when these seem to be inimical to the spirit of the law. But even when
these unique New Testament connotations are recognized, problems still
remain insofar as the term, "kingdom of God," or its synonym, "kingdom
of heaven," is used in the gospels in an apparent multiplicity of senses

---

[1]*Rethinking Realized Eschatology*, pt. VII; see also Georgia Harkniss,
Understanding the Kingdom of God, p. 9.

[2]See Dale Patrick, "The Kingdom of God in the Old Testament," pp.
76-7.

[3]This contrast with the Old Testament concept is examined in detail
in John Sanford's *The Kingdom Within*.

(Sanders counts 6 primary meanings, while Sullivan, following C. H. Dodd, lists a total of 28 distinguishable meanings.[4])

A number of peripheral but not insignificant controversies are related to translation issues: Some maintain that the Greek, *Basileia*, translated usually as "kingdom," is almost always used in a spatial sense, i.e. to designate a realm in time and place;[5] while others maintain that it is not used in the sense of locality, but in the more active sense of "rulership" or "reign."[6]   Many exegetes, from patristic times to the present, have interpreted "the kingdom of God is within you"[7] to mean something spiritual and individual;[8] while most contemporary scholars maintain it means something quite communal, perhaps best rendered as "among" rather than "in" or "within";[9] many have thought that "my kingdom is not of this world" means the Kingdom is rather indifferent to the world, whereas the meaning in context seems to be that it comes down to the world from heaven;[10] and many have taken Matthew's circumlocution, "kingdom of heaven," to be a reference to the afterlife, whereas the phrase in its cultural setting seems to be just an alternative way of referring to the coming down of the divine kingdom to earth.[11]

The most substantial controversies, however, have traditionally emerged, and still do emerge, in the context of the choice between a present *vs.* a future interpretation of the Kingdom. Conflicting interpretations are to be found even in early Christianity. It would seem that prior to St. Augustine's era, a future-oriented interpretation of the kingdom of God predominated, no doubt influenced to some extent by the political debility and earthly miseries of Christians under the Roman Empire, as well as by the ever-prevalent apocalyptic interpretations in the Judaeo-Christian tradition;[12] but portrayals of the kingdom of God as a present Christian society on Earth are also to be found in the works of

---

[4]Sanders, *Jesus and Judaism*, Chapter 6; Sullivan, *Rethinking Realized Eschatology*, pp. 45-6.

[5]See e.g. Clayton Sullivan, *Rethinking Realized Eschatology*, p. 48.

[6]See e.g. Hans Küng, *On Being a Christian*, p. 215.

[7]Lk. 17:21.

[8]A recent example is John Sanford's *The Kingdom Within*.

[9]See e.g. Viviano, *The Kingdom of God in History*, p. 69.

[10]Ibid., p. 19.

[11]Ibid.

[12]Clayton Sullivan, *Rethinking Realized Eschatology*, Chapter 1.

Irenaeus, Clement of Alexandria, Origen, Tertullian, Victorinus, Gregory Damascus, Hilary, and Ambrose.[13]

St. Augustine's *City of God* is usually taken as the watershed marking a transition (often considered with disfavor by contemporary theologians) from a future-oriented to a decisively present-oriented interpretation of the Kingdom, insofar as Augustine characterized the Church as the present Kingdom. But Augustine's view was actually more nuanced, as is indicated by the epigraph beginning this chapter, and also by his exegesis of the parable of the darnel seed growing together with the good seed until the darnel is finally gathered out of the Kingdom by the harvesters (angels). Concerning this parable Augustine comments:

> "They shall gather out of His kingdom all offenses...." Can [Jesus] mean out of that [future] kingdom in which there are no offenses? Then it must be out of His present kingdom, the Church, that they are gathered.[14]

It is noteworthy that 20th century exegetes sometimes offer interpretations of the darnel seed parable similar to Augustine's.[15] But most contemporary exegetes, even if they tend towards a "present kingdom" interpretation, would hesitate to identify the Kingdom with the *Church*.

The knotty perennial problem of the two alternatives presents itself in the 20th century largely in the guise of a choice between "consistent [future-oriented] eschatology" and "realized [present-oriented] eschatology":

"Consistent eschatology" portrays New Testament references to the kingdom of God as consistently future-oriented and apocalyptic, envisioning a sudden and miraculous coming of the Kingdom as a pure gift of God, not attainable by the most ardent initiatives and endeavors on the part of Christians.[16] This particular interpretation was "rediscovered" by Johannes Weiss[17] in the aftermath of the era of 18th and

---

[13]Henry Herrick, *The Kingdom of God in the Writings of the Fathers*, Vol. 1, pt. 3, pp. 100-106.

[14]*The City of God*, 10:9.

[15]See for example *The Interpreter's One-Volume Commentary* on Matthew 13:39-41.

[16]Viviano, *The Kingdom of God in History*, p. 29.

[17]*Jesus' Proclamation of the kingdom of God* (1892). In the last two pages of this book, Weiss opts for a more liberal interpretation of the Kingdom. But he insists that a distinction is to be made between this

19th century liberal German Protestantism in which the kingdom of God allegedly came to be identified largely with Christian bourgeois society and culture.[18]   Albert Schweitzer and Rudolf Bultmann in the 20th century led the way to the widespread acceptance, especially among European theologians, of this approach to interpretation. Proponents of this approach see its major contribution as a reemphasis on the eschatological and transcendental character of the kingdom of God[19]—distancing it from this-worldly aspirations and neo-Pelagian attempts to establish it by human efforts. But in the opinion of its opponents this approach has appeared not only to implicate Jesus in some large-scale and constant mistakes regarding an imminent apocalypse, but also to require a rather forced interpretation of many passages in the gospels in which the kingdom of God seems to be portrayed as present.

  Realized eschatology, proposed by C. H. Dodd,[20] sees the kingdom of God as a divine gift breaking into the present, rather than as future and apocalyptic: the kingdom of God is not something to be expected in the future, but has actually arrived on earth with the coming of Jesus. The key passage for advocates of realized eschatology is Jesus' response to the accusation by his adversaries that he is casting out devils by black magic. Jesus responds that Satan would have to be out of his mind to help depopulate the Satanic kingdom of devils, and then adds: "If I by the power of God cast out the demons, then the kingdom of God has come upon you!"[21] Thus realized eschatology portrays the Kingdom as a spiritual dynamism which has already been instilled into human affairs, forcefully dissipating evil. This interpretation, favored for several decades in the U.S. and England, was based on the "two document" theory concerning the origin of the synoptic gospels,[22] and has become less attractive to many scholars now that "form criticism," rejected by Dodd, has largely replaced the "two document" approach. Some scholars have registered strong objections to realized eschatology—e.g. R. Fuller, who writes:

---

liberal interpretation and the strictly future-oriented interpretation actually espoused by Jesus.

[18]Hans Küng, *The Church*, pp. 91-2.

[19]Hans Küng, *The Church*, p. 92.

[20]*The Parables of the Kingdom* (1935).

[21]Mt. 12:28; Lk. 11:20.

[22]The theory that the sources for their composition were Mark's account and a document called "Q."

The attempt of Dr. Dodd to explain the obvious future reference of [Mk. 14:25, Mt. 8:11 and 6:10, or Lk. 12:32], especially when he relegates Mk. 14:25 to the "transcendental order
beyond space and time" (a wholly nonbiblical, Platonic
conception!) is singularly unconvincing.[23]

St. Augustine, as we have seen, presented a two-tiered interpretation of the Kingdom, whereby the Church served as an intermediate
stage leading up to the final appearance of the kingdom of God in its
perfection at the end of time. Some contemporary theologians, although
shying away from Augustine's now suspect ecclesiology (identifying the
kingdom of God too closely with the Church), have tried to offer a
similarly *mediating approach* (present + future kingdom), *sans* the
ecclesiology.   Notable "mediators" would include Werner Georg
Kuemmel, Reginald Fuller, Oscar Cullmann, George Eldon Ladd,[24]
Jacques Schlosser[25] and the process theologian, Marjorie Suchocki.[26]
The best-known attempt at mediation is R. Morgenthaler's "D-Day"
simile, which argues that one has just as much reason to say the kingdom
of God is present with the coming of Jesus as to say that the allied
armies are "present on the Continent" in World War II, when actually
only a small group of commandos had landed on the coasts.[27]   But
Clayton Sullivan, viewing all such "mediating" approaches as misleading
and compromising, objects:

> The mediating theologians [bait] us with one conception of
> the Kingdom, that is, the conception of the kingdom as a
> curative power that was present in Jesus....   While still
> looking us in the eye and mesmerizing us with discussions on
> how *basileia* is to be understood in terms of *malkuth* [the
> Aramaic word for "kingdom" or "reign"], the mediating
> theologians go one step further and affirm, " and by the way,

---

[23]*The Mission and Achievement of Jesus*, p. 24.

[24]See Eldon Epp, "Mediating Approaches to the Kingdom: Werner
Georg Kuemmel and George Eldon Ladd."

[25]*Le règne de dieu dan les dits de Jésus*, Part II, pp. 676-7.

[26]*God, Christ, Church: a Practical Guide to Process Theology*, pp.
187-198.

[27]Cited by Gösta Lundström in *The Kingdom of God in the Teaching
of Jesus*. Epp (op. cit.) attributes this simile to Oscar Cullmann.

this kingdom we have told you was present, was also future."[28]

We might view such disagreements as an interesting example of
the staying power of ongoing scholarly debates (this debate now entering
into its third millennium). But if the proper interpretation of the idea of
the kingdom of God has important practical ramifications, such disputes
may be counterproductive at best and at worst an immense obstacle to the
Christian faith, since "If the trumpet gives an uncertain sound, who will
prepare themselves for battle?"[29]

As we come to trace out political ramifications of the concept of
the kingdom of God, it will be important to keep in mind which
interpretation of the Kingdom prevails in the context of which political
circumstances.

---

[28]*Rethinking Realized Eschatology*, p. 47.
[29]I Cor. 14:8.

X. Hermeneutical Circle, or *circulus vitiosus*?

The Greek vocational self-interpretation, as given in Aristotle's *Politics*, sees in the contrast between Greeks and barbarians the key to an interpretation of history, while the Jewish vocational self-interpretation, as given in the prophetic literature, sees such a key in the establishment of the rule of Yahweh over the nations of the world.... Which group and which vocational consciousness are able to give a key to history as a whole? Obviously, if we try to answer, we have already presupposed an interpretation of history with a claim to universality; we have already used the key in justifying its use. This is an unavoidable consequence of the "theological circle" within which systematic theology moves; but it is an unavoidable circle wherever the question of the ultimate meaning of history is asked. —Paul Tillich, *Systematic Theology* III

TURNER: Let us presume, in line with present scholarship, that many historical incidents in the Old Testament were imaginative reconstructions; that alleged "miracles" were often the result of a combination of legend and credulity, or of lucky occurrences of natural phenomena; that purported "prophecies" were actually predictions put into the mouth of revered ancestors by writers of subsequent generations who were privy to what actually happened in intervening generations. What is left of the "word of God"? Why should I attach any more importance, or give any more credence, to the Scriptures than, say, to Homer's *Iliad* and *Odyssey* or Virgil's *Aeneid*?

CRANSTON: I would have to answer with Kierkegaard that the greatest miracle is faith itself—not some dramatic external Cecil-B.-DeMille-spectacle like the parting of the waters of the Red Sea. The Scriptures are the "word of God" because they provide us with a narrative of the faith experience of early pathfinders in the faith community. Exposure to the Scriptures can both instigate a movement of faith, and corroborate the already existent faith of a believer.

TURNER: That answer is unsatisfactory since faith must be a faith in *something*, and—how can I put it?—one must presumably know something about that "something" in order for faith to be awakened in himself or herself. If you tell me, "well, of course, the object of religious faith, for us and for the ancients, is God"—that is still unsatisfactory, since it is one thing to have scriptures revealing something about God, and quite another to have scriptures narrating the development in people of a faith in God. The latter may be interesting to someone who already believes, but is hardly likely to inculcate faith in an unbeliever.

CRANSTON: You misunderstand me. I'm not saying that the Scriptures have to do with purely subjective experiences. The great significance of the Scriptures is that they give an objective account of the way that a group of ordinary, earthy and often unruly people received and responded progressively to a vision, and arrived at a remarkably high state of spiritual maturity as a result. Obviously God is not some object which could be revealed in an external fashion. If God is to be revealed at all, the revelation would have to be through effects, i.e., through His works. And in the Scriptures, we have documentation of God's most important works, which take place in human consciousnesses.

TURNER: Then although the historicity of the Bible is in general to be taken with a "grain of salt," we should have no qualms about accepting it as an authentic history of developments in consciousness of certain groups of people. Is that what you're saying?

CRANSTON: I would say that the Old and New Testaments both chronicle a history of successive developments of the vision of a kingdom of God, which was first concretized in Abraham and Moses, was later refined by Jesus and early Christians, and is still being refined and redefined, with reference to various social and cultural contexts, with reference to a progression of insights about the development of mankind and the world.

TURNER: So this history is the history of a vision, and the vision in question is a vision not of God, but of God's kingdom?

CRANSTON: I would say more precisely that the vision presented in the Bible is a vision of our spiritual ancestors' evolving relationship to God's kingdom.

TURNER: Then the Bible as the "word of God" is a history of the development of a vision of some kingdom which is attributed to a God who is revealed not directly but indirectly in this kingdom.

CRANSTON: That is the thrust of what I am saying. Various individuals may find much more than this revealed in the Bible, but I have been trying to focus on the minimum degree of revelation that anyone could expect to find there.

TURNER: On the one hand, I find this answer more acceptable than, say, the fundamentalist version of the "word of God"; but on the other, I think it can also lead to a vicious circle, if we (in this present investigation) hope to find clues as to the real significance of the kingdom of God *from the Scriptures themselves.* For you say the significance of the Scriptures is that they describe successive approximations to the vision of the kingdom of God; but we already have an idea in mind, possibly *not* derived from the Scriptures, of what the kingdom of God is, and we are selecting and evaluating these same Scriptures on the basis of our preconceived idea. For one thing, we eliminate at the very outset the scriptures of Hinduism, Buddhism, Islam, etc. from our discussion to concentrate on the "Judaeo-Christian" tradition.

CRANSTON: I would not "eliminate" Islam out-of-hand from consideration. Islam, with lines of derivation reaching to both Judaism and Christianity, does include a concept of a sovereignty of God in which earthly rulers participate,[1] and "rulership" is one of the "ninety-nine attributes" of God venerated by Muslims. But the scriptural and doctrinal emphasis on the "kingdom of God" found in Judaism and even more in Christianity is not noticeable in

---

[1]See the Q'ran 3:26.

Islam—possibly because the idea of the messiahship of a Son of God finds no place in Islam. For Muslims, Jesus is just a prophet, not an anointed ruler. With regard to Hinduism and other Eastern religions, I think it would be stretching things to attribute to them any concerted emphasis on the kingdom of God comparable to that in Judaism or Christianity. They tend to emphasize other aspects of the divinity. Thus I think we are justified in concentrating on the "Judaeo-Christian" tradition, if we can use that term as a kind of shorthand.

TURNER: Are we equally justified in our selectivity with regard to the Bible? We are quite probably choosing only those portions of the Bible which correspond to our preconceived idea. Possibly we are unconsciously rejecting other portions which may present a totally different idea of the Kingdom, or give clear evidence that there is no important idea of a Kingdom at all.

CRANSTON: This "idea" is not just derived from personal experience or history or extrapolations of the present into the future; it is an object of faith. It is entirely possible that the faith which moves me to adopt this idea as more than an interesting hypothesis is substantially the same faith that led others before me to the idea.

TURNER: For you it may be an object of faith; but for me, I'm afraid to say, it is just an interesting hypothesis.

CRANSTON: In any case, it should be kept in mind that we are not merely trying to get at the original meaning, as if that would give us the key to understanding what it is all about, whether it has been rightly applied, etc. We are reexamining it and reevaluating it for the purpose of redefining it. Consider, for the sake of analogy, the problem of defining democracy: We go back in history to ancient Greece to investigate the origins of democracy, but we always focus on Athens rather than Sparta, although Sparta had some of the mechanisms for democracy—election of the Assembly, an elective Senate and Ephorate, sharing of power between two monarchs as a block to absolutism, means of dismissing unwanted monarchs, constitutional government, etc.

TURNER: And also a wide reserve army of slaves.

CRANSTON: As did Athens. But we don't identify with the austerity and regimentation of Sparta, we don't connect it with the styles of constitutions we are familiar with in the democratic West. Thus we eliminate it at the outset from our investigation.

TURNER: You don't seriously suggest that we go back to Sparta for a model of democracy?

CRANSTON: They have some elements which we might do well to try to incorporate—e.g. the ephorate as a check on the power of the chief executive, procedures for preventing excessive inequalities in property between citizens. But no, I would not suggest Sparta as a paradigm. In refraining from this, however, I am taking my own idea of democracy, derived from personal experience, knowledge of history, etc. and applying it to the original concept. A kind of dialogue between ancients and moderns takes place when we do this. We go back to the original insight with all its imperfections, reexamine our own more complex structures to see if we have maintained that original insight, and possibly redefine the idea, enhancing the original inspiration and perhaps even occasionally dropping what is widely accepted and/or technologically advanced when it militates against the original inspiration. Or we might even decide that the original idea was misguided, and be led to revise it in a radical way. This is not a "vicious circle" but the kind of circularity taking place in a dialogue, where the circle of discussion leads to augmentation of insight rather than an impasse.

TURNER: If I follow your analogy, you seem to be implying that later generations, like our own generation, might produce some constructive revisions of the Judaeo-Christian idea of a kingdom of God. I'm not so sure how God might feel about that. I would presume He might consider it his "baby," so to speak—not to be tampered with.

CRANSTON: There may be an important subjective factor in the idea of the Kingdom. If God created human beings endowed with freedom, it's quite conceivable to me that he might leave room for humans to redefine what is meant by the kingdom of God, at least in some of its aspects.

TURNER: Would this extend to politics? How tolerant do you think God is?

CRANSTON: There can be no doubt that Jesus was apolitical. But this apoliticization is not necessarily a mandate for his followers. He may, for example, have relegated the potential political aspects to others.

TURNER: There can be no doubt that many of his followers have interpreted their mission precisely in that way, often with results that one would think would be undesirable to God, as well as to the masses. The history of Christian political theology gives proof of a lot of experimentation with such interpretations.

XI. Political Milestones: Three Romes, Three Reichs, Three Kingdoms, and a "Holy Roman Empire"

After a tranquil and prosperous reign [Emperor Constantine I] bequeathed to his family the inheritance of the Roman empire; a new capital, a new policy, and a new religion.... At the festival of the dedication [of the new capital], an edict, engraved on a column of marble, bestowed the title of SECOND or NEW ROME on the city of Constantine. But the name of Constantinople has prevailed over that honorable epithet, and after the revolution of fourteen centuries still perpetuates the fame of its author. —Edward Gibbon, *The Rise and Fall of the Roman Empire*

Attend to it, pious tsar, that all the Christian empires unite with your own; for two Romes have fallen, but the third stands, and a fourth there will not be. —Phiofei of Pskov, letter to Prince Vasily III of Moscow, ca. 1511

What should be more natural than that the first Napoleon, when he wanted to raise himself above the rank of "consul," should style himself "emperor" and should confer on his son and heir the title "King of Rome," which had been borne by candidates for the medieval Western office of "Holy Roman Emperor" until they were crowned at Rome by the Pope (a consecration which many of them failed to achieve)? As for the second (*soi-disant* third) Napoleon, he actually wrote, or caused to be published under his name, a life of Julius Caesar. Finally Hitler paid his tribute to the ghost of a ghost by establishing his country residence on a crag overhanging [the purported] enchanted Barbarossa's holy cave at Berchtesgarden and by accepting the regalia of Charlemagne, stolen from a Hapsburg museum. —Arnold Toynbee, *A Study of History*

The "Kingdom of God" [for Protestants in America] was ... the rule which, having been established from eternity, needed to be obeyed despite the rebellion against it which flourished

73

in the world. —H. Richard Niebuhr, *The Kingdom of God in America*

  In the first few centuries A.D., the Christian religion, growing amid frequent persecutions in the alien environment of the Roman Empire, was fairly bereft of nationalism and political ambition. As Voegelin observes, early Christian idealism presented a striking contrast with the Jewish messianism from which it had emerged:

> Yahweh had become the *summus deus* of a cosmological empire, while Israel had merged into an empire people under a Pharaonic mediator from the house of David.... [But in Christianity] the Son of God, the Messiah of Yahweh, was no longer the head of a Judaite clan; and the cosmic god no longer presided over a mundane empire. The house of David had been transformed into the house of God the Father, to be built with man as the material, by the Son.[1]

  Ancient Christianity was becoming an international religious diaspora, a community in the strictest sense of the word. Tertullian in his apologetic for Christianity describes the life and mores of the Christians to Roman critics of Christianity:

> We are a society with common religious feeling, unity of discipline, a common bond of hope. We meet in gathering and congregation to approach God in prayer, massing our forces to surround Him.... Every man once a month brings some modest coin—or whenever he wishes, and only if he does wish, and if he can.... They are not spent upon banquets nor drinking-parties ... but to feed the poor and to bury them, for boys and girls who lack property and parents, and then for slaves grown old and shipwrecked mariners.... We, who are united in mind and soul, have no hesitation about sharing property. All is common among us—except our wives. At that point we dissolve our partnership, which is the one place where the rest of men make it effective.[2]

  But intermingled amid this exemplary communality and altruism there was the ever-present ideal of Israelite theocracy—that God would

---

[1] *Order and History* I, p. 309-10.
[2] Tertullian, *Apologeticus*, XXXIX, 2-12.

indeed be king over all. And like the Jews in powerless exile, the Christians looked back upon the Davidic monarchy as a moment of theocratic glory, when God was honored or feared on earth and the true religion was respected by all the nations. What might happen if the worldly dynamics shifted, and what was formerly a persecuted religion once again had direct access to political power? What if a King David *redivivus* appeared on the scene, combining at just the right time and right place an indomitable and unflagging religious zeal with extraordinary political acumen and boundless ambition? If political opportunity knocked, would the door be answered?

Opportunity did knock with the accession to the Roman throne of Constantine I ("the Great"). Reportedly converted by a vision of the cross of Christ which led him to victory in the battle of the Milvian Bridge in A. D. 312, he became a protector and defender of all things Christian. Christianity at last had an emperor on its side. Although not actually baptized until his deathbed, and having quite a few skeletons in his family closet (including the still unexplained execution of his son and wife), he emerged as an unofficial vicar of Christ, even convening and participating in the first universal council of the Church at Nicea. Shortly after the council he dedicated the city later called Constantinople (Byzantium), and dubbed it *nova Roma* ("the New Rome"). He moved to this new capital in A.D. 330 and presided over the inauguration of a new, officially Christian empire, the *"Second Rome,"* a resurrected version of the then-disintegrating Rome of Augustus. This empire, in which Christianity became not just a state religion, but, in those days when the idea of "separation of church and state" was inconceivable, a combination of state and church,[3] continued expanding progressively both to the north and the west of Constantinople, even as it began to weaken politically.

Technically, the Byzantine version of the "Second Rome" continued to exist even after the deposition of Constantine VII (reigned 780-797), on account of the subsequent election of Charles I as the next successor of Constantine I. But the Western Empire, which had come to an apparent end in A.D. 476 after the reign of Romulus Augustus, was resuscitated artificially through the coronation by Pope Leo of Charlemagne in A.D. 800; and this grafted branch, portrayed as the legitimate succession (called the "translation," from the Latin, *transfero*, "to transfer") from Constantine, constituted the first German "Reich," in which Christendom achieved an acme of worldwide political power. The

---

[3]Hans Küng, *The Church*, p. 90.

transformation of this German Reich into a "Holy Roman Empire" was an extraordinary feat of human creativity, since the ties with Rome were non-existent, the imperial title for most of Charlemagne's successors, with the exception of the period from 962 to 1176, was honorific at best, and the claims to holiness were always in doubt—unless one equates holiness with ecclesiastical power. Some historians date the origins of the Holy Roman Empire from Charlemagne himself, but others date it from the accession to power of Otto the Great, who officially inaugurated the Holy Roman Empire with some credible claims to imperial power in 962, and was followed by other German contenders for universal power in succeeding generations.

If the post-exilic Jewish theocracy had been able to reach a point at which the high priests and scribes would be able to consecrate kings and inspire them to expand the borders of the kingdom of God through political maneuvering and military conquest, the result would have been something like what actually happened in the aftermath of Charlemagne's reign. After the struggle between papacy and Empire had been resolved largely in the papacy's favor, the popes consecrated the purported successors of Charlemagne, became heavily involved in politics, and either instigated or accepted the mobilization of the multiple Crusades to combat Jews, heretics and pagans, and in particular to liberate the Holy Land from the Muslim overlords who had first come to power in regions formerly held by monophysite Christian heretics. But the constant extensions of papal power paved the way for the "equal and opposite" reaction of the Protestant Reformation, which began to infiltrate into the bones and sinews of the Empire, now under Germanic control and subject to the power-brokerage of German Electors.

After the Reformation, the extension of the kingdom of God continued to take place under Catholicism—but in a less overtly militaristic manner—through a worldwide missionary organization that was partially dependent on, and cooperated with, the major monarchies remaining in the wake of the weakening Holy Roman Empire. Missions to the "heathens" of Latin America proceeded in conjunction with the Portuguese and Spanish empires. The less successful missionary adventures in China and Japan may perhaps be attributable to a lack of political-military sponsorship of the missionary activities, although fascinating questions remain regarding how successful Matteo Ricci might have been in China if he had been allowed by his Jesuit superiors to continue in his uniquely non-violent approach to conversion, which involved assimilation with Confucianism and Mandarin culture.

In the meantime, however, a *Third Rome* had arisen from the ashes of the Eastern Empire, which came to a close with the fall of

Constantinople to the Turks in 1453.　In 988, the ruling dynasty in Moscow adopted the Christian faith from Byzantium; and from that time the eastern implementation of the Empire became the concern of the Grand Dukes of Muscovy, who tried to recreate Caesar both in name ("Czar") and in the realities of political power.　The closest approximation to Caesarean imperialism in the Third Rome was no doubt to be found in the reign of Peter the Great (1682-1725), who reasserted once and for all the power of the crown over the church, by prohibiting the election of the patriarch.　Practices of appointment of bishops and patriarchs by Peter the Great's successors, and even of the jurisdiction of Emperors in matters of faith, continued for the next two hundred years, until the overthrow of Czardom by the Russian revolution of 1917. During these two centuries the Orthodox Church identified with the East, adopted strong ties to the Czar, and was ultra-hierarchical, its underclass being made up of many impoverished married priests who were a drain on the economy.

The "Third Rome" was of course finally superseded by the Third International of communism.　At first suppressed in the newly emerging Soviet regime, the Orthodox Church was readmitted to existence as a cooperative arm of the state under the Patriarch, Metropolitan Serguis, who in 1927 declared his loyalty to the Soviet state, and whose official installation was permitted in 1943 by Stalin.

In the West, the *Holy Roman Empire*, which had already splintered into various focal points of light as it gave way to the "divine right" of kings, finally came to an official close at the outset of the nineteenth century.　In 1806, Francis II of Hapsburg, claiming to be the successor to Augustus, Constantine, and Charlemagne, as well as Maximillian, renounced his authority, after some urging from Napoleon, to pave the way for Napoleon's own empire.　But the old empire was not about to be easily buried.　Napoleon considered his own empire the secularized successor to the Holy Roman Empire, and as James Bryce, writing in 1871, observed, there were quite a few unsuccessful nineteenth-century attempts to resuscitate the Empire:

> It would be an instructive, if it were not a tedious task, to examine the many pretensions that are still put forward to represent the Empire of Rome, all of them baseless, none of them effectless.　Austria,... Bonapartean France [have made such claims]....　Professing the creed of Byzantium, Russia

claims the crown of the Byzantine Caesars.... The Greek races
[make similar claims]....[4]

In the very year that Bryce's book was published, the Second
Reich, taking up where Charlemagne had left off, was established in
Germany with the installation of Wilhelm I as the new Caesar (Kaiser)
over the new German empire and Prince Otto von Bismarck as its first
chancellor. This attempted resuscitation of the golden age of the Western
Empire lasted until 1918 with the end of World War I. It remained for
Adolf Hitler in 1933 to make one final attempt to reestablish a worldwide
German Empire, with the inauguration of his "thousand year Reich," a
Third Reich, terminated abortively in 1945. Benito Mussolini's subsequent attempt in 1935 to reinaugurate the ancient Roman empire simply
seemed to constitute almost the logical/illogical conclusion to all such
abortive endeavors to recapture past glories.

In the meantime, in the *Protestant world*, an alternative to all
three Romes and all three Reichs was emerging. As Protestantism
developed in the context of the ascendancy of German Elec-
tor/Magistrates in an ever-weakening Holy Roman Empire, the idea of the
kingdom of God loomed as even more important doctrinally for the
Protestant than for the Catholic.[5] For the Protestant the kingdom of God
meant not only the rule of God in opposition to the rule of worldly
monarchs, but also the rule of God in contrast to the rule of the Pope and
the worldly ecclesiastics of Catholicism. In contrast to the political
conservatism of Luther himself, some other Protestant pathfinders
interpreted the kingdom of God in terms of political revolution as well
as ecclesiastical reform. Thomas Münzer published a pamphlet dedicated
to Christ as Duke and King of Kings, and led the Anabaptist rebellion of
1525; the Dutch Anabaptist, John Beukels, established a "New Zion" in
Münster with Christian communism, until the bishop's men were able to
regain control; Martin Bucer (1491-1551) in his *On the Kingdom of
Christ* developed a blueprint for an all-encompassing political implementation of the kingdom of God.

The major Protestant countries with missionary objectives after
the Reformation were England and Holland. But the missionary activity
of these two countries did not proceed after the pattern of Spain and
Portugal. Celibate missionaries were not sent to foreign countries in
conjunction with military conquerors or colonists; but Protestant

---

[4]James Bryce, *The Holy Roman Empire*, p. 368.
[5]H. R. Niebuhr, *The Kingdom of God in America*, pp. 18, 21.

settlements were established under British protection, and their religion became an important part of the culture they were determined to transmit to their new environment. English settlements in Ireland, beginning even before the Protestant Reformation, began after the Reformation to enforce Anglicanism, and prohibit the practice of Catholicism; and with even greater zeal, the descendants of the Dutch Boers who settled South Africa in the seventeenth century came to see themselves as a new Israel, chosen to inhabit a new Canaan and to bring the discipline and blessings of the pure Calvinist faith to the land and its natives.

A similar pattern emerged in the English settlements of North America, but without the extreme religious intolerance that characterized the settlement of Ireland, and without the extreme exclusivism that characterized the Dutch settlement of South Africa. The Puritans of the Massachusetts Bay colony, fleeing from oppression in the mother country, saw themselves as a new Israel chosen to establish the kingdom of God in a new "promised land," a constitutional theocracy subject to the rule of God rather than humans. William Penn established Philadelphia, the "City of Brotherly Love," as the "'holy experiment' of building the nearest possible human approach to the kingdom of God on earth."[6] John Adams summed up the sentiments of many settlers when he wrote in 1765:

> I always consider the settlement of America with reverence and wonder, as the opening of a grand scene and design in Providence for the illumination of the ignorant and the emancipation of the slavish part of mankind *all over the earth.*[7]

In a similar vein, John Winthrop's sermon, "A Model of Christian Charity", calls for the Christian community to serve as a model for the world: "wee must Consider that wee shall be as a Citty upon a Hill, the eies of all people are uppon us...."

Niebuhr discerns three significant phases in the development of the ideal of the kingdom of God in America:

> In the earliest phase, *the sovereignty of God* was emphasized. The task of the American Protestant settlers was not to "build" or "establish" the kingdom of God, but rather to be the

---

[6]George Eddy, *The Kingdom of God and the American Dream*, p. 5.
[7]Ibid.

exception to the rebellion against God's authority which was
rife and rampant in the world.[8]

In the second phase, *the reign of Christ* became the watchword,
and Christianity took on evangelical characteristics. One byproduct of
this outlook was the nationalistic presumption of "manifest destiny":

> The old idea of American Christians as a chosen people who
> had been called to a special task was turned into the notion of
> a chosen nation especially favored.... As the nineteenth
> century went on, the note of divine favoritism was increasingly
> sounded.... It is in particular the kingdom of the Anglo-Saxon
> race, which is destined to bring light to the gentiles by means
> of lamps manufactured in America.[9]

Inspired by this evangelical fervor, Elisha Mulford in the late nineteenth
century spoke of the nation as a "moral organism," moving towards
freedom and peace; of our religious calling to realize righteousness and
freedom, or the redemption of humanity; and of the vindication of Christ
as the Lord of history.[10]

The third phase, according to Niebuhr, has been characterized by
an orientation to the establishment of the *kingdom of God on earth*—an
orientation which led to the turn-of-the century "social gospel" movement, which, with a touch of neo-Pelagianism, supposed that by
intensified human effort the "second coming" of Christ on earth could be
accelerated. Thus Walter Rauschenbusch, a leading figure in the German
Baptist social gospel movement, theorized in the manuscript of his first
book, *The Righteousness of the Kingdom*, only recently published, that
"He [Christ] will appear the second time when the fullness of time shall
have come. When that will be, depends largely on us."[11]

It is noteworthy that in its interest in the kingdom of God,
American Protestantism is not anomalous, but has simply given added
emphasis to a long-standing tradition in Protestantism. For up to the

---

[8]H. Richard Niebuhr, *The Kingdom of God in America*, p. 56.

[9]Ibid., p. 179.

[10]See Eisha Mulford, *The Nation; the Foundations of Civil Order and
Political Life in the United States* (Boston, 1881), pp. 16, 17, 23; *The
Republic of God: An Institute of Theology* (Boston, 1881), p. 128.

[11]Walter Rauschenbusch, *The Righteousness of the Kingdom*, M.
Stackhouse ed. (Nashville: Abingdon Press, 1968), p. 107.

present era there has traditionally been a greater emphasis on the
kingdom of God in Protestantism than in Catholicism, where it is just one
truth among others and a goal secondary to the attainment of the "vision
of God."[12]   Tillich suggests that this phenomenon may be due to
proportionally greater sacramental emphasis in Catholicism, concerned
more with the consecration of the natural world than with the establishment of God's rule in the social world.[13]   It might be more accurate to
say, however, that there has been a long-standing interest in Catholicism
in the Augustinian concept of the "*City* of God," which had rather
different ecclesiastical connotations than the "kingdom of God" in
Protestantism, and in Catholicism took precedence over the latter. In any
case, this characterization no longer holds true. Both Catholic and
Protestant theologians in recent decades have shown an equal commitment to the overarching importance of the idea of the kingdom of God
in Christianity.

---

[12]Niebuhr, *The Kingdom of God in America*, p. 21.
[13]Paul Tillich, *Systematic Theology* III, p. 357.

XII. Catholic Political Theology:
The "Two Cities" and "Two Swords," and Beyond

Two cities have been formed by two loves: the earthly by the love of self, even to the contempt of God: the heavenly by the love of God, even to the contempt of self.... In the one, the princes and the nations it subdues are ruled by the love of ruling; in the other, the princes and the subjects serve one another in love, the latter obeying, while the former take thought for all.... Of the two first parents of the human race ... Cain was the first-born, and he belonged to the city of men; after him was born Abel, who belonged to the city of God.... It is recorded of Cain that he built a city, but Abel, being a sojourner, built none. For the city of the saints is above, although here below it begets citizens, in whom it sojourns till the time of its reign arrives, when it shall gather together all in the day of the resurrection. —St. Augustine, *The City of God* 14:28, 15:1

There are two things in particular by which this world is ruled: the sacred authority of the popes and royal power. In this jurisdictional division, the priestly burden is all the greater when there is a necessity to render an account at the Last Judgement even for the very kings among men. —Pope Gelasius I, letter to the Emperor Anastasius.

We are instructed by the very words of the Gospel that there are in the fold of Jesus Christ two swords, the spiritual and the temporal. For when the apostles said to the Lord, "Behold we have two swords here [that is, in the Church]," Our Lord did not respond, "that's too much," but rather "that is enough...."[1] Both swords, the spiritual and the material, are in the power of the Church. But the latter is to be exercised *for* the Church, the former *by* the Church. The former is to be wielded in the

---

[1]Luke 22:38.

83

hand of the priest, the latter in the hand of kings and sol-
diers—but at the nod, and with the consent, of the priest.
—Pope Boniface VIII, in the papal bull, *Unam Sanctam*.

The term, "political theology," is an "umbrella" term which
includes the classical political theologies of Augustine, Bossuet, and
others, as well as writings by German theologians such as Jürgen
Moltmann and Johannes Metz, and the "liberation theology" advocated
by Segundo, Gutiérrez, and other contemporary Latin American theologians.[2] Classical political theology, according to Löwith,[3] is the distant
progenitor of the speculative "philosophy of history"—a term coined by
Voltaire (who was vitally interested in supplanting the theological
approach to the interpretation of history) but undergoing still further
transmutation since Voltaire (Voegelin, for instance, identifies it with
political science).[4]

Augustine's *City of God*, as the first major attempt at the
development of a comprehensive political theology, is apologetic in its
motivation, concerned with responding to accusations that the deteriora-
tion afflicting the Roman Empire was attributable to the rise of Christianity. After arguing that the disintegration of the empire was easily
traceable to other causes—e.g. the barbarian incursions—Augustine
begins in the second half of the work to trace the evolution of the "city
of God" from its beginnings in the early Old Testament eras.[5]

The term, "city of God," in Augustine's usage is meant to be
synonymous with "state of God" or "kingdom of God."[6] However, there
is some divergence in emphasis and connotation between the two terms,
"city of God," and "kingdom of God." From a literary vantage point,
"city of God" constitutes the use of synecdoche—the use of a part to
designate the whole. Just as we can speak of "Washington" and
"Moscow" to designate the nations of which these are the respective
capitals, so too "city" in *The City of God* has the connotation of an elect
and elite central grouping, which in the Old Testament eventually found
a geographical foothold in the citadel of Zion in Jerusalem, from which

---

[2]Paul Lakeland, *The Politics of Salvation: The Hegelian Idea of the
State* (Albany, NY: State University of New York Press, 1984).

[3]Karl Löwith, *The Meaning of History*, pp. 58-9.

[4]See Eric Voegelin, *The New Science of Politics*, p. 1.

[5]*The City of God*, Books 11ff.

[6]E. Hendrikx, "Die Bedeutung von Augustinus 'De Civitate Dei' für
Kirche und Staat," p. 80.

radiated all the derivative concatenations of God's kingdom. Thus it is hierarchical in its thrust. Content-wise, Augustine's "city" of God as the new Zion is the remnant of Israel, in spiritual communion with the angels and the saints of all eras, developing in time in the Church Militant under the headship of its king, Christ, the Son of God.[7]

The ancient genealogy of the city of God, in Augustine's estimation, was spelled out quite explicitly in the Old Testament: On the one side, the line of the elect and the blessed is traced from Adam's descendant Abel through Noah and Noah's sons Shem and Japeth, to the patriarchs Abraham, Isaac and Jacob, thence through Job (a non-Hebrew) and Israel, to Moses, Joshua, and David to the emergence of the Messiah, Jesus Christ, and the new dispensation. On the other side, the line of the city of man traces its ancestry from Adam's descendant, Cain, through Noah's son, Ham, then through Ishmael, Esau, and the various ungodly people opposed to Israel—the Caananites, Assyrians, Babylonians, etc. The promises of God to Abraham were fulfilled in two stages: The first half of the promises, "Go into a land that I will show thee, and I will make of thee a great nation," "was fulfilled through David, and Solomon his son, whose kingdom was extended over the whole promised space; for they subdued all those nations, and made them tributary."[8] But the second half of the promises, "And in thee shall all tribes of the earth be blessed," had to wait for its fulfillment in the universal church, for "[Abraham] is the father, not of the one Israelite nation, but of all nations who follow the footprints of his faith."[9]

Augustine could be characterized as a precursor of the "mediating theologians" already referred to.[10] He, like they, was concerned with bringing together the apparent future and the apparent present aspects of the kingdom of God in a complementary, non-contradictory fashion. But the extremes between which he was trying to mediate had quite distinctive profiles in his day. On the one hand, the futurist extreme, exemplified by Augustine's contemporary, St. John Chrysostom, was oriented toward patient waiting on the part of a purely spiritual and purely voluntary community, for the eschatological appearance of the Kingdom. On the other, the newly emerged political extreme, exemplified by Constantine's court theologian, Bishop Eusebius, saw God's providence working in a special way in the Roman Empire and looked

---

[7]*City of God* 14:13, 16:2, 19:23.

[8]*City of God*, 17:2.

[9]*City of God*, 16:16.

[10]See above, p. 64.

with ardent longing for the establishment of God's kingdom on earth—perhaps even through the agency of the contemporary Emperor Constantine I himself.

In contrast with Chrysostom, Augustine theorized that the Church was a "present" kingdom of God developing on Earth, the Kingdom of Heaven now being gathered together for a future and eternal life. The "millennium" for Augustine was not some future state in which Christ would appear for the second time and bring God's kingdom into order, but was precisely identical with the Church. The Church *was*, in fact, the millennium, the interim process spanning the period between the 1st and 2nd comings of Christ.[11] But, in contrast with politically overoptimistic theorists like Eusebius, Augustine held that the Church was to remain above any direct involvement in the political state, which, as long as it was performing its proper task of preserving peace and order, could expect the cooperation of the Church:

> The heavenly city,... while it sojourns on earth, calls citizens out of all nations and gathers together a society of pilgrims of all languages, not scrupling about diversities in the manners, laws, and institutions whereby earthly peace is secured and maintained, but recognizing that, however various these are, they all tend to one and the same end of earthly peace. It is so far from rescinding and abolishing these diversities, that it even preserves and adopts them, so long only as no hindrance to the worship of the one supreme and true God is thus introduced. Even the heavenly city, therefore, while in its state of pilgrimage, avails itself of the peace of earth, and, so far as it can without injuring faith and godliness, desires and maintains a common agreement among men regarding the acquisition of the necessaries of life, and makes this earthly peace bear upon the peace of heaven.[12]

The Church, on Augustine's view, is thus a transcendent institution, wending its way circumspectly amid the temporal institutions set up by various governments, cooperating with them and benefitting from them, but not assuming any earthly jurisdiction over them.

Although Augustine may not have intended to support a visible church, identical with the institutional and hierarchical ecclesiastical

---

[11]Henry Martyn Herrick, *The Kingdom of God in the Writings of the Fathers*, pp. 100-106.

[12]*City of God*, 19:17.

organization, he did on occasion use language which connoted such visibility, offering some ammunition to later medieval ecclesiastics who looked to Augustine for legitimation of visible and substantial power.[13] In any case, even if Augustine's Church was to be strictly invisible, in no way was it to assume the autonomous stance that we moderns have come to associate with the "separation of church and state." Rather, the Church was the necessary basis, without which the Ciceronian ideal of virtuous, republican government could not be attained.[14] And the state was an unfortunate necessity for the Church, not only for material sustenance and protection of civil rights, but also for the enforcement of doctrinal orthodoxy.

This latter dependency on the state in Augustine's theory was the result of a major change of position on the part of Augustine, who in the earlier stages of his bishopric had opposed the use of force in compelling doctrinal uniformity. In a treatise Augustine wrote on the Church, he gave his reasons for the change:

> There are two volumes of mine which I have published under the title, *Against the Donatist camp*. In the first of these volumes I had said that it was not acceptable in my view to force schismatics into communion with us in a violent way by compulsion applied by any secular power. Actually, such use of force was not acceptable to me at that time due to the fact that I had as yet experienced neither the enormous capacity of the schismatics for evil nor the great potential of disciplinary diligence for converting them to that which is better.... Kings insofar as they are kings serve God, if in their reign they command good and forbid evil, not only with regard to human concourse, but also with regard to the divine religion.... But it is better (who can doubt it?) for men to be led by doctrine to divine worship than to be forced by suffering or fear of punishment.[15]

As Elaine Pagels observes,[16] Augustine's final position regarding the use of force in imposing ecclesiastical conformity was a quite consistent byproduct of his growing conviction about the infection of human nature by original sin. The original *fomes peccati*, manifested in

---

[13]Louis Berkhof, *The Kingdom of God*, pp. 22-23.

[14]*City of God*, 19:21.

[15]*De corpore Christi, quod est ecclesia*, Cap. IX, §§1400, 1403, 1411.

[16]*Adam, Eve, and the Serpent*, Chs. 4-5.

uncontrollable sexual impulses and other rebellious tendencies in all humans, so weakened human nature that the judicious use of force was inevitably needed at times to compel the recalcitrant to the good. In defense of the doctrine of original sin, Augustine collaborated with the priest, Orosius, against Pelagianism, which extolled the natural power of humans to do good without supernatural grace; and was eventually successful in attaching the stigma of heresy to Julian of Eclanum, who maintained that suffering and death were not punishments for original sin but natural concomitants of human life, and that baptized Christians had the freedom and the power to build the non-political "Christian society" advocated by Tertullian.[17]

Once Augustine's theses about the interdependence of church and state, and about the prevalence of original sin in all men (including temporal rulers) are granted, the step to a further thesis concerning the primacy of the spiritual (and those in charge of the spiritual) over the temporal seems quite logically consistent. This step would be facilitated by the traditionally strong influence on Christians of the Old Testament ideal of the jurisdiction of priests and prophets over kings, the paradigmatic instance of which has always been the Samuel-Saul relationship.[18] This primacy was elaborated with subtlety by Pope Gelasius in the fifth century:

> There used to be convergences before the coming of Christ, whereby certain people figuratively, though also operating corporeally, existed simultaneously as kings and priests, as Sacred Scripture indicates was the case with the holy Melchisedech.... But now that the true king and pontiff [Jesus Christ] has come upon earth, neither does the emperor claim the title of pontiff any more, nor does the pontiff claim royal prerogatives, although the members of this true king and pontiff, according to their participation in his magnificent nature, may be called by both titles, as they perdure as a royal and priestly race[19].... Thus spiritual action should stand apart from carnal pursuits, and "he who is fighting for God should involve himself only minimally in worldly affairs",[20] and correspond-

---

[17]*Ibid.*, Ch. 6.

[18]Voegelin, *Order and History* I, p. 245.

[19]1 Peter 2:9.

[20]2 Timothy 2:4.

ingly he who would be involved in worldly matters should not
be seen to preside over the divine....[21]

This theological defense by Pope Gelasius of his "Two Swords"
theory is in continuity with Augustine's "Two Cities": There are two
parallel, equal jurisdictions, each of them ruled by Christ, one concerned
with eternal salvation of all souls (including the souls of temporal rulers),
the other concerned with temporal salvation. But Gelasius' clear
statement of the supremacy of the spiritual authority, the papacy, over the
temporal authority was a call to revolutionary reversals, in an age when
emperors still expected to be the supreme authority in their empire.

The theory took several centuries to begin to be applied "across
the board." The major catalyst was Pope Leo's consecration to imperial
supremacy of the faithful Charlemagne, who "delighted in reading the
books of St. Augustine, especially those which are entitled *The City of
God.*"[22] The realization of the ideal of extending the kingdom of God
on earth, which Bishop Eusebius thought he saw in Constantine in the
Eastern Empire, now seemed even closer to implementation through
Charlemagne in the Western Empire, leading Alcuin of York, Charlemagne's counselor, to write to him:

All the faithful pray that the empire be extended to your great
glory, so that the catholic faith in unanimity may be impressed
on all hearts, to such a degree that by the grace of the highest
King the selfsame unity of holy peace and perfect charity may
rule and protect everyone everywhere.[23]

In the midst of the ebb and flow of Western, German, "holy"
imperial power after Charlemagne, strong popes such as Gregory VII,
Innocent III and Boniface VIII helped remove for almost two centuries
any lingering doubts about primacy in the empire. Although compromises
were made regarding investiture protocol, the papacy was able to

[21]S. Gelasii Papae Tractatus IV, ll. Cited in Andreas Thiel, *Epistolae Romanorum pontificum genuinae et quae ad eos scriptae sunt*, Tomus I, p. 567-8.
[22]Quoted from Eginhard, *Vita Karoli*, Cap. 24, by Bryce in *The Holy Roman Empire*, p. 93.
[23]Cited from Waltz, *Deutsche Verfassungs geschichte* ii, 182, from an unprinted letter of Alcuin, by Bryce in *The Holy Roman Empire*, p. 96.

maintain an upper hand and eventually free Italy from subjection to the Empire by 1250, with the death of Frederick II.

St. Thomas Aquinas, writing during the peak of papal power, elaborated a strictly hierarchical interpretation of the relation of spiritual and temporal realms (it is noteworthy that Aquinas draws a somewhat different conclusion than did Pope Gelasius[24] from the "conjunction of priesthood and kingship" in Christ!):

> The Roman Pontiff can rightly be called "king" as well as "priest." For if our Lord Jesus Christ is so called, it does not seem incongruous to give His successor the same title.... The corporeal and temporal depend on the spiritual and the perpetual, just as the operation of the body depends on the power of the soul. And so, in the same way that the body has its power and operation through the soul, so also the temporal jurisdiction of princes has its power and operation from the spiritual jurisdiction of Peter and the successors of Peter.[25]

In the context of this extremely hierarchical thinking, and on the grounds that spiritual evils were even more heinous than criminal acts, Aquinas justified and advocated the practice of handing heretics over to the secular authorities to be executed.[26]

But countercurrents to such hierarchical, strong-arm approaches to coordinating the spiritual and the temporal were already emerging before Aquinas' time. Most notable was the "three stage" theory of Joachim of Fiore (1131-1202), who theorized about the abolition of clergy and hierarchy in a coming "age of the Holy Spirit":

> The mysteries of Holy Scripture point us to three orders (states, or conditions) of the world: to the first, in which we were under the Law; to the second, in which we are under grace; to the third, which we already imminently expect, and in which we shall be under a yet more abundant grace... The first condition is in the bondage of slaves, the second in the bondage of sons, the third in liberty. The first in fear, the

---

[24]See p. 88.

[25]Thomas Aquinas, *De regimine principum* Lib. III, Cap. X.

[26]*Summa theologiae* 2-2, q. 10, 8; q. 11, 3c.

second in faith, the third in love. The first in the condition of
thralls, the second of freemen, the third of friends.[27]

Aquinas vigorously opposed Joachim's theory, or at least the rather
simplified versions of Joachim's "third stage" prevailing in Aquinas'
milieu.[28] But some of Joachim's fellow Franciscans actually tried to put
Joachim's idea of a charismatic, non-hierarchical "third-stage" community
into practice.[29] And Joachim's somewhat arcane insight into the "three
stages" had considerable influence in later centuries, directly on
Lessing[30], indirectly on Fichte and other German idealists,[31] possibly
also on Comte and Marx[32] and on Hitler.[33] Friedrich Schelling (1775-
1854), influential among Catholic romantics, developed the idea of a
dritte Reich, the age of the Holy Spirit, independently of Joachite
influence, but was later delighted to discover the parallel with Joachim's
theory.[34]

    Further opposition to Aquinas' view emerged in the fourteenth
century in Marsilius of Padua's polemical defense of a purely secular
state in *Defensor Pacis* and in the political writings of John of Paris, who
argued against the view that the Papacy as supreme ruler should have
jurisdiction over temporal affairs.[35] John Wycliffe's position was equally
opposed, but evangelically motivated: he accepted the general Augustinian characterization of the "two cities," but wanted to base all social
organization on the Bible, which is ideally suited "for the government of
the people, by the people, and for the people."

    But the main opposition, of course, came later with the advent
of Protestantism, almost as one more attempt to implement Joachim of
Fiore's vision of non-hierarchical freedom of the spirit. Whether
Protestantism has been any more successful in this endeavor than
Catholicism will be examined in Chapter XIV.

---

[27]*Concordia novi ac veteris testament*, Venice 1519, Lib. V, 84, 112;
translated by E. Benz, *Erasmos-Jahrbuch*, 1956, pp. 314f.

[28]Summa theologiae I-II q. 106, a. 4.

[29]Karl Löwith, *The Meaning of History*, Ch. 8.

[30]Karl Löwith, *The Meaning of History*, p. 208.

[31]Jürgen Moltmann, op. cit., p. 208.

[32]Ibid.

[33]Karl Löwith, op. cit., Ch. 8.

[34]F. W. J. Schelling, *The Philosophy of Revelation*, lecture #36.

[35]Benedict Viviano, *The Kingdom of God in History*, p. 79.

The body-soul analogy utilized by Aquinas to elucidate the relation between church and state gives us an indication of the prevailing medieval perspective: What in our view reeks of heavy-handed hierarchical domination appeared to the medieval theoretician to be a natural, quasi-organic relationship, something like the Aristotelian form-matter, soul-body relationship. Just as the soul gave life and form to the body in which it was concretized and externalized, so too did the Church ensoul the body politic and make it into a living reality. This organic metaphor, which also corresponded very well with the Pauline doctrine of Christians as the "mystical [communal] body" of Christ, eventually came to be associated with a grandiose vision of a universal "Christian Republic," reminiscent of Philo's ancient utopian projection of a worldwide zionist commonwealth.[36] According to Kantorowicz, the idea of the "mystical body of Christ" (the Church) began in the Middle Ages to be extended to the "mystical body of the Republic," by Vincent of Beauvais, Godfrey of Fontaines, and others.   Some even used the Christian metaphor of the "marriage" between a bishop and his flock to describe the relationship between the supreme secular ruler and his "flock".[37]   In the fifteenth century, Andres Diaz de Escobar at the Council of Basel used the same metaphor:

> The Church is a kind of mystical body, and a kind of republic
> of the Christian people....   That most holy republic is the
> universal Church... and therefore it is a common affair of the
> Christian people.[38]

The idea of a "Christian republic" was not always a vote against the hierarchical *sacrum imperium*. Englebert in the fourteenth century, for example, sees it as simply an extension of the Augustinian idea that there can be no true republic without Christianity.[39] And it needs to be kept in mind that in medieval Christianity the relationship between church and state was so close, that the "Holy Empire" became tantamount to the "visible church."[40] Indifference—let alone hostility—to Christian-

---

[36]See p. 34 above.

[37]Kantorowicz, *The King's Two Bodies*, ch. V, sect. 2, "*Corpus Reipublicae Mysticum*."

[38]William Johnson Everett, *God's Federal Republic*, pp. 71-72.

[39]See James Bryce, *The Holy Roman Empire*, p. 98.

[40]Ibid., p. 326.

ity was simply forbidden.[41] But in some versions an effort to modify the "two swords" theory was noticeable. Thus Dante, who propounded the vision of a messianic prince, the mystical DVX, savior of Italy and leader of a Christian empire,[42] also propounded something like an Averroist version of Pope Gelasius' "two swords" doctrine, in which the division is not between pope and emperor, but between philosopher and emperor.[43] And Roger Bacon, although basing his idea of a universal Christian Republic on Augustine's *City of God*, conceptualized it as a commonwealth concerned (unlike the Church) strictly with temporal well-being, and eschewing (unlike the State) purely nationalistic interests, although utilizing the wisdom of clerics and Christian savants to defend the Christian Republic against pagans and infidels and to extend the boundaries of Christianity.[44]

Probably the best-known attempt to actually inaugurate a Christian Republic was the fifteenth-century experiment in theocratic republicanism by the Dominican friar, Jerome Savonarola, who, inspired by the Joachite Movement and by Aquinas' treatise on prophecy in the *Summa*, decreed the establishment of a republic ruled only by Christ the King in Florence. (The decree has never been formally rescinded.) Savonarola's expectation that Charles VIII of France would restore Christendom was abortive, however; and he himself was burnt at the stake as a heretic.[45] A happier ending was in store two centuries later for another Dominican, Tommaso Campanella, who did not actually try to establish a Christian republic, but wrote *The City of the Sun*, portraying a utopian society influenced by Plato's *Republic* and controlled by philosopher-priests under the governance of the Pope.[46]

In the seventeenth century, the Jesuit bishop, Jacques Bossuet, to whom it occurred that Augustine's *City of God* was in serious need of updating, wrote the *Discours sur l'histoire universelle*, a new essay in the theology of history, concerned most specifically with history from the time of Augustine to Charlemagne. This book, which was used for the instruction of the son of Louis XIV, concluded that the French monarchy was heir to the Roman and Holy Roman Empires.

---

[41]John Baillie, *What is a Christian Civilization?*, p. 14.
[42]Christopher Dawson, "The Kingdom of God in History," p. 208.
[43]Barry Cooper, *The Political Theory of Eric Voegelin*, p. 69.
[44]Etienne Gilson, *Les metamorphoses de la Cité de Dieu*, pp. 81-2.
[45]Viviano, *The Kingdom of God in History*, Ch. 4.
[46]Ibid.

As will be shown in Chapter XVI, such endeavors in the theology of history were eventually superseded for the most part by a new branching-out of philosophy into the "philosophy of history." But efforts specifically in the theology of history have not completely died out. In the twentieth century, Paul Tillich's *Systematic Theology* is primarily a systematic analysis of the way in which the "kingdom of God" has applied and should apply to the development of society; and the voluminous analyses of world history by Christopher Dawson and Arnold Toynbee include significant speculative attempts to interpret history in terms of the development of Christianity.

In the aftermath of the discovery of the theory of evolution and attempts to formulate theories of social evolution, evolutionary theories of the "Christian republic" mold have developed in modern times. The Jewish philosopher, Henri Bergson, who describes himself as having a "moral commitment to Catholicism," foresaw a possible but not inevitable evolution of society to a World State which would emerge by a "lateral revolution" (expanding from a spiritual cluster of mystically-inspired persons), and which would prevent democracies from being engulfed in the wars emerging in the instinctive "closed" societies where *homo homini lupus* prevails.[47] Influenced by Bergson, the Catholic theologian Joseph Bonsirven has interpreted the kingdom of God in terms of a Bergsonian evolution of affectivity in mankind.[48] The best-known evolutionary synthesis is that of the Jesuit paleontologist, Pierre Teilhard de Chardin, another disciple of Bergson, who projects an evolutionary process towards a final communal social consciousness beyond all present political forms, leading eventually to the transcendent parousia traditionally associated with the second coming of Christ.[49]

Mainstream contemporary Catholic theology has shown a tendency to steer clear of all such evolutionary approaches to the development of the kingdom of God, and in general of all attempts to associate the Kingdom with a visible political order or even with the visible Church. Thus Küng faults any theory which presupposes a continuity from stage to stage of the Kingdom[50] and any theory which compromises the transcendent (and essentially invisible) character of the

---

[47]Dante Germino, *Political Philosophy and the Open Society*, pp. 165-6.

[48]*Le règne de dieu*, pp. 101ff.

[49]*The Phenomenon of Man* (NY: Harper, 1959), pp. 254ff.

[50]Hans Küng, *The Church*, p. 96.

Kingdom.[51]. And Schnachenburg, after a thorough treatment of the Old-Testament and New-Testament treatments of the kingdom of God, concludes a) that Augustine made a major mistake in identifying the kingdom of God on earth with the Church, and b) that the Kingdom is a purely religious concept, although it may have indirect socio-political consequences.[52]

But the commitment of the Catholic Church to the purely religious/transcendent profile favored by many Catholic theologians is not steady and unwavering. When Pope John XXIII in *Mater et Magistra* (1961) points to the "shared responsibility of wealthy industrialized nations for the plight of less privileged countries" and when Pope Paul VI in *Populorum Progressio* (1967) deplores "a type of capitalism which has been the source of excessive suffering, injustices, and fratricidal conflicts," some present and quite visible interpretation of the Kingdom seems to be involved. And when the Vatican II document *Gaudium et spes* (1965) insists that the Church has the right and the duty to pass judgements on political matters, the subjection of worldly immanence to transcendent criticism is implied. Theologians such as Edward Schillebeeckx[53] and Adolf Holl[54] have also emphasized the centrality of the mission to the poor in Christianity.

The Latin American Episcopal (CELAM II) conference in Medellin, Columbia in 1968, represented a reaction against traditional political/religious ambiguity. There the wheels were set in motion that led to a reexamination of the Church's relationship to the politico-economic sphere, to the initiation of a "Christians for Socialism" movement in Latin America (in which the compatibility of Christianity and Marxism was averred), and the eventual crystallization of these initiatives in what is now called "liberation theology."

Liberation theology is an anomalous "theory," insofar as it faults theorizing and insists on the direct and necessary connection between any theoretical position it enunciates and actual practice. Concern has been aroused among many mainstream Catholic and Protestant theologians, not only by the controversial positions taken by liberation theologians regarding the dangers of capitalism and of dependence on the United States, regarding the specially privileged place of the poor, and regarding the dispensability of ecclesiastical hierarchy; but also by the practical

---

[51]Ibid., p. 92.

[52]Rudolph Schnachenburg, *God's Rule and Kingdom*.

[53]*In Search of the Kingdom of God*, pp. 121-2.

[54]*Jesus in Bad Company*, Chapter 6.

founding of communal socio-economic-religious organizations and the devising of tactics for dealing with vested interests. But a considerable number of Catholic theologians, along with a much smaller number of Protestants[55] and even Jews[56] have developed liberation theology into a comprehensive and multi-faceted system in the last two decades.

The sharp disparities between liberation theology and traditional mainstream theology may be illustrated by José Miranda's refutation of the traditional positions that the kingdom of God is future (or even present *and* future, in the sense of the "mediating-theologian" interpretation) and apolitical and oriented towards nonviolence:

> To maintain that the kingdom is in the other world is equivalent to denying the very content of the gospel. And to say in escapist desperation that the kingdom is "partly in this world and partly in the other" is to launch a thesis totally without support in Jesus' teaching.... The kingdom is made ready in heaven, or resides temporarily in heaven, but its final destination is earth....[57] No single historical fact about Jesus of Nazareth is more demonstrable than this one: that he engaged in revolutionary political activity.... The sign that Pilate ordered attached to the head of the cross of Jesus (INRI) specifies political delict as the motive of the punishment of this particular crucified criminal....[58] *Jesus explicitly approves the use of violence.* Note that in order to defend honor paid to one's parents against the compromising interpretations of the scribes and Pharisees, Jesus could have simply cited "Honor your father and your mother" from Exodus 20:12. But no, he draws on a different chapter of Exodus, and adds: "And who curses his father or his mother shall die without mercy...." These executions were carried out by the entire people. Here we have sure documentary evidence, which no pedantry will manage to escape. Jesus explicitly approves and defends the use of violence.[59]

Although there are differing opinions among liberation theologians regarding the use of violence, there is general agreement among

---

[55]E. g., Rubem Alves, José Bonmo.

[56]E.g. Marc Ellis, author of *Toward a Jewish Theology of Liberation.*

[57]José Porfirio Miranda, *Communism in the Bible*, p. 15.

[58]Ibid., p. 70.

[59]Ibid., p. 75.

them that the kingdom of God is meant to be a quite visible kingdom established on earth, characterized by social justice and fellowship, and involving a new, spiritually charged approach to politics. Frequent appeal is made in liberation theology to the Exodus of the Israelites from Israel as a prefigurement of the situation of the "Church of the Poor" in Latin America and elsewhere: The "base communities" of the poor constitute a new Israel, in the process of being liberated with divine assistance from centuries of oppression. Nicaragua under Sandinista control was not just a new Marxist satellite but the pilot political experiment in building the kingdom of God on earth,[60] with the specialized assistance of a representative number of liberation theologians, some of them holding political office.

Most of the pivotal works in liberation theology were published before the recent collapse of Marxist regimes in Europe and also in Nicaragua. One may expect that some will interpret the downfall of Nicaragua as attributable to U.S. financing of "contra" rebels, forcible capitalist restriction of normal Nicaraguan trade, etc. But the reaction to the involvement of theologians in liberation movements in Nicaragua and elsewhere may depend on the degree of their Marxist commitment. According to one account, CELAM, the organization which presided over the birth of liberation theology, responding to the "signs of the time," is now vigorously promoting a "theology of reconciliation" as a more acceptable alternative to, and indeed a reaction to, liberationism.[61]

The intertwining of liberation theology with Marxism ("scientific socialism") has been, on the one hand, a natural offshoot of its commitment to building up a visible and politically sophisticated Christian socialism; but on the other hand, an almost insuperable obstacle to its acceptance by theologians (or the Church) at large, in view of the fact that atheism is not just an option but an essential and indispensable feature in Marxism (the proletariat, according to Marx, must be weaned away from the "opiate of religion" before they can rise to a revolutionary consciousness). The majority of liberation theologians—including Gustavo Gutiérrez, Jon Sobrino, Enrique Dussel, and Juan Segundo—explain that Marxism is for them "just an instrument"—the Archimedean lever which happens to be available for the poor of the world to reverse the state of oppression in which they find themselves.

---

[60]See Conor Cruise O'Brien, "God and Man in Nicaragua," *Atlantic*, August, 1986.

[61]Kevin P. O'Higgins, "Liberation Theology and the 'New World Order'," *America* 163:16, Nov. 24, 1990, p. 389.

Most of them would shy away from the effusive Marxist sympathies of theologian Leonardo Boff who, on returning from the Soviet Union, proclaimed it a "healthy, clean society," one that led his group to think of the "kingdom of God" as being realized.[62] However, some, such as José Miranda and Otto Madura, see Marxism as an essential ingredient in their blueprints for Christian communism.

Various arguments have been offered by liberation theologians and by Marxist scholars to show how "Christian Marxism" might not, after all, be a contradiction in terms—e.g. that *non-bourgeois* Christianity would not be the type of Christianity that Marx had in mind, that Christianity along with politics and ideology in general would change when the material conditions of life are changed, that Christianity's orientation to the poor can only be honored in conjunction with the one ideology oriented specifically to the proletariat of all nations, etc.[63] But for theologians who, like the medieval advocates of the "Christian Republic" ideal, wished to establish the "mystical body of Christ" in this world, but, unlike the medievals, did not want any semblance of a "two swords" approach or privileged hierarchies, the highly organized and ideologically egalitarian Marxist philosophy may have presented itself as the logical ideology- or "instrument-" of-choice.

Liberation theology is important at the very least for once again "moving the question" regarding the *visibility* of the kingdom of God. Are the mainstream theologians who maintain that the Gospel notion of the kingdom of God is strictly eschatological, not incorporated in any church, and lacking any specific political agenda, really "escapist" as José Miranda alleges? Is liberation theology, in amalgamating politics with religion, risking the loss of the transcendent, spiritual aspects of religion, as Cardinal Ratzinger has alleged?[64] Is liberation theology simply blind to the truth that traditional theology at its core is not an ivory-tower occupation but intrinsically liberating, as Hans Küng asserts?[65]

In response to criticisms, liberation theologians who wish to remain and work within the Church have clarified or modified a number of their positions to such an extent that Arthur McGovern in his 1988 report on the status of liberation theology observes that

---

[62]Arthur F. McGovern and Thomas L. Schubeck, "Updating Liberation Theology," p. 33.

[63]See Denys Turner, *Marxism and Christianity*, Chapter 10.

[64]Benedict Viviano, *The Kingdom of God in History*, pp. 144-5.

[65]*Theology for the Third Millennium*, p. 283.

Earlier this year, Enrique Castillo Moralles, adjunct secretary of C.E.L.A.M., declared publicly "that the problem with liberation theology has passed for Latin Americans, that the two declarations of the Vatican (1984 and 1986), along with the letters of the Pope to the bishops of Brazil and Peru, had achieved a "balance" that had been lacking.... In Brazil, Nicaragua and El Salvador, several liberation theologians we interviewed spoke enthusiastically about Pope John Paul II's new encyclical, *Sollicitudo rei socialis*.... [And] even several critics of liberation theology acknowledge that Gustavo Gutiérrez's work, *La verdad los hará libres* (*The Truth will Make You Free*)... answers effectively most of the objections raised against his views in respect to their orthodoxy.[66]

In their emphasis on the visible Church and the presence of the kingdom of God in the Church, the liberation theologians seem to be more in accord with traditional Catholic and Augustinian thinking than many "mainstream" theologians; but in view of their radical interpretation of the "preferential option for the poor" (comparable to Marx's proposal to create a classless society by putting the proletariat in the leadership), one suspects McGovern's and Schubeck's report is over-hasty and over-optimistic, since liberation theology is nothing less than a new interpretation of the Church.

---

[66]Arthur F. McGovern and Thomas L. Schubeck, "Updating Liberation Theology," p. 34.

XIII. How Visible can a "City of God" be?

[One thing which keeps me in the Church is] the name itself of Catholic, which, not without reason, amid so many heresies, the Church has still retained; so that, though all heretics wish to be called Catholics, yet when a stranger asks where the Catholic Church meets, no heretic will venture to point to his own chapel or house. —Augustine, *Against the Epistle of Manichaeus called Fundamental*

The Kingdom is inseparable from the Church, because both are inseparable from the person and work of Jesus himself. He established the Church to be the revelation and instrument of the Kingdom. It is not possible therefore to separate the Church from the Kingdom as if the first belonged exclusively to the imperfect realm of history, while the second would be the perfect eschatological fulfilment of the divine plan of salvation. Nor can the Kingdom be considered a purely interior or spiritual reality, in contrast with the Church considered as a historical and social realization of Jesus' intention to establish a community of faith and salvation. —Pope John Paul II, quoted in *L'Osservatore Romano*, English Edition, April, 1989.

CRANSTON: Many theologians in our time seem to be anxious to distance themselves from what they perceive to be "Augustinianism." They associate Augustine with the idea that the Church is a present and visible kingdom of God—a position which, they say, invests too much power in a fallible Church, and diverts attention from the strictly eschatological Gospel-meaning of the "kingdom of God." But it seems to me that Augustine does a good job of mediation. He coordinates the present and the future Kingdom without confusing the two; and he tempers the "visibility" of the Kingdom with the awareness that the true beauty of the Kingdom can never appear on earth.[1] Of course, he made a mistake in shifting from a policy of persuasion to the utilization of force in his campaigns against heresy. But that simply provides us with one more lesson in history about the dangers of intertwining religion with the enforcement powers of the state.

TURNER: When Augustine speaks of "the Church that even the heretics can recognize," and refers to its institutions and organization, he is certainly giving the impression that this present "City of God" is visible. But he doesn't do this consistently. Berkhof observes that he gives even more attention to the invisible aspect[2]—as one might expect in view of his admission that the Church contains many members from that "other city" that began with Cain.[3]

CRANSTON: Augustine's zeal for making the "City of God" even more visible perhaps explains his ultimate decision to press for punishment of doctrinal deviation by civil authorities.

TURNER: No, the fundamental explanation for that move is his doctrine of original sin. If it were not for the presupposition of an original cussedness that leads some people willy-nilly off the deep dark end, Augustine would no doubt have maintained his commitment to noncoercive methods, geared to elicit free assent and create consensus among believers—as did most of his predecessors.

CRANSTON: I think the rumors of the Augustinian "invention" of original sin are greatly exaggerated. The outlines of the doctrine are found in the epistles of St. Paul, which declare that all men had sinned in Adam[4] and that there is a law in our members that works against the spirit.[5] But we don't even need scriptures and texts to prove original sin. The fact of original sin is empirically observable. Every day, one encounters in the newspapers or on TV, or even sees for himself, such barbarous cruelty and

---

[1]Augustine, *Retractiones*, II, 18.
[2]Louis Berkhof, *The Kingdom of God*, pp. 22-23.
[3]See above, p. 85.
[4]Romans 5:22.
[5]Rom. 7:23.

inhumanity that it takes no astute theological speculation to conclude that something has indeed gone awry with human nature.

TURNER: I don't believe you are fully aware of what you are saying. It's one thing to talk about moral problems and criminality, but quite another to hypothesize an "original sin," passed on from some proto-humans to all their descendants; so that every baby at birth is stigmatized with it. As far as I'm concerned, "original sin" is a contradiction in terms. "Sin" by definition is something personal—deliberate, requiring consciousness and forethought and intention.

CRANSTON: Aside from our disagreement or agreement with such doctrines, it is interesting to see the practical implications that follow, once assent is given to a particular doctrine.

TURNER: That I can agree with. And of course the pivotal doctrine for the early Christian was the divinity of Christ, the man-God, whose every saying, including predictions of an imminent end of the world, had to be taken as the unquestionable word of God. So the great analytic intelligence of Augustine, to whom it never occurred for a moment that a man-God could make a faulty prediction, went to work on apocalyptic texts and came up with ingenious explanations to show how they really didn't refer to some imminent eschaton which didn't happen. He started out with premises about the absolute veracity of Jesus and the Scriptures, and drew the inevitable logical conclusions. His explanation of the millennium as the ecclesiastical interval between the First and Second Comings of Christ seems to me to be a good example of tortuous textual reconstruction.

CRANSTON: The connection with a millennium is just a corollary to his overall characterization of the Church as something like that field in the parable "with good grain but also weeds", which remains bogged down with the weeds until a final separation is made at the harvest.

TURNER: You're forgetting that some rather drastic and final separation of presumed "weeds" will have already been made by the interim harvesters like Augustine and their civil and ecclesiastical confederates.

CRANSTON: But I think we are agreed that this is just one possible approach that was developed in response to the question, "How do we deal with original sin?"

TURNER: The question, "How do we deal with original sin?" is still there for believers. Original sin, so far as I know, is still an important tenet of faith. I haven't heard of any retractions or downgrading of that doctrine.

CRANSTON: That's true.   But there is a major contextual difference between the situation in the medieval era wherein a "separate and independent" status for religion and state was unthinkable, and our own situation, in which the separation of church and state is axiomatic.   The separation of church and state obviates the possibility of hysterical believers trying to carry out preemptive warfare on original sin through surrogate or satellite civil governments.

TURNER: Why is it that I don't feel relieved at your soothing assurances? In any case, it is possible the main applications of theory to practice in ecclesiastical discipline have involved not theological tenets but philosophical ideas. In particular, I am convinced that the traditional idea of a soul-body relationship, with the soul lording it over the body, is the most important, although least obvious, theoretical position bearing on the issue of theological politics.

CRANSTON: The soul doesn't necessarily "lord it over" the body. There are more cooperative models available in the history of philosophy.

TURNER: It's important to know what model is operative.

CRANSTON: It would seem that many of those "mystical body of the republic" theories in the middle ages included attempts to employ a more cooperative model. The thrust of some of these theories was that the relation between the Church and the people should not be a hierarchical-administrative one with chains of command, but something like the harmony of the Aristotelian soul with the organic body which it informs—a union which gives life.

TURNER: It is interesting that their theoretical methodology was the opposite of Plato's. Plato in the *Republic* wanted to clarify the inner workings of justice in the psyche, so he looked to the macrosystem, the polity, where justice is "writ large," for a model which could potentially elucidate the problem of the psyche. The medievals, on the other hand, hoping for a theoretical breakthrough in the harmonization of their ecclesiastical-political milieu, looked to the microcosmic model of the individual body-soul relationship for inspiration and elucidation.

CRANSTON: They were trying to show what a present kingdom of God would look like—a functioning social homeostasis of spirit and matter.

TURNER: And they ended up in strange utopias, where the "body politic" and the "vivifying spirit" are in unreal harmony.

CRANSTON: You sound like you're edging into original-sin theory. If there is no original sin, as you maintained, what's wrong with expecting to achieve maximum social harmony with reasonable social planning? Utopias would be possible.

TURNER: You misunderstand me. I didn't say my doubts about original sin were based on a contrary belief in original innocence or universal immaculate conceptions. As I see it, human beings start out neither from original goodness nor original badness, but from original neutrality. As for all the disharmonies and inhumanities in the world, these can be sufficiently explained by personal sin or personal immorality. One doesn't need to resort to a hypothesis of original sin.

CRANSTON: Isn't what you call "original neutrality" just a mixture of good and evil?

TURNER: No. It's pure potentiality, which becomes actuated when people begin making choices.

CRANSTON: Any choice whatsoever?

TURNER: It would be tangential for us here to get into that traditional dilemma in ethical theory about whether someone could really choose evil, or whether any bona fide "choice" has to be good.

For the purposes of our present discussion, our presupposition simply has to be that if there is any moral good or evil, there has to be sufficient development of consciousness and freedom to make an authentic choice possible.

CRANSTON: Would you have any objections against taking your reconstructed and modified idea of the psyche—starting from original neutrality and developing in the direction of personal freedom and responsibility—as a model for a political system like the "Christian Republic?"

TURNER: It is probably inevitable that theorists will muster up such analogical models as one instrument for throwing light on problems. Some classical political philosophers[6] and even some contemporary democratic theorists[7] have utilized a model of the individual psyche to clarify mechanisms of democratic government. But I'm pessimistic about the usefulness of such models—because socio-political entities are, after all, not organic and ensouled, but composite structures resulting from the conglomeration of a multitude of individual units. Utopian portrayals of the "body politic" or the "mystical body of the Christian Republic," imbued with some magically unifying life-principle, tend to result from the psychic analogies.

CRANSTON: Would you consider liberation theology utopian?

TURNER: As utopian as Marxism, which starts with unreal premises about some mysterious collective consciousness which emerges in the international proletariat, and which carries them forward with inspired and unflagging determination to a never-ending quasi-paradisiacal state of human equality and happiness. The only difference is that in liberation theology, the hopes are centered around poor Christians rather than an industrial "proletariat." Rather similar revolutionary-utopian results are expected.

CRANSTON: A "realistic utopia" would be just as much a contradiction as "original sin," which you find objectionable.

---

[6]E.g., Rousseau, *The Social Contract*, 1:6-7.

[7]See e.g. Carl Cohen, *Democracy*, Ch. 1; Roberto Mangabeira Ungar, *Knowledge and Politics*, Part I.

TURNER: Correct. I think it would be best to part with utopias altogether.

CRANSTON: Would you consider an Augustinian model of the Church without the original-sin presupposition, and the compensating heavy-handed spiritual authority, to be non-utopian?

TURNER: Possibly. A purely voluntary organization, with a cautious optimism about what is obtainable by human nature with God's assistance and mutual spiritual support might have a good shot at becoming a visible "present kingdom of God." But there's no guarantee. There's always the lingering possibility that you'll end up with the likes of the medieval "church of Babylon" in the tenth and eleventh centuries, with the papal intrigues and murders, the wild Vatican orgies, the nepotism and extortion, etc.; or the sequel, "church of Babylon II," in the fifteenth and sixteenth centuries.

CRANSTON: Here we come back to the problem of the "visible" kingdom of God. And you should notice that the problem is similar to the one you mentioned at the very outset of our investigation in regard to the apparent atrocities of the ancient Israelites.

TURNER: Yes, it's hard to discern even the dim outlines of a "kingdom of God" emerging from all this. If it is there at all, it must be far in the background, hidden, invisible.

CRANSTON: I'm sure you've heard the phrase, "God writes straight with crooked lines." Excesses and abuses, even with regard to the implementation of the kingdom of God, lead to the downfall of the miscreants and often to important reform movements.

TURNER: The most important reform movement took place when the Protestants turned away from the ecclesiastical visible/present kingdom of God, which was far from inspirational in Luther's day.

CRANSTON: It would be more precise to say that the Protestants redefined the criteria for visibility of the kingdom of God. Rather than regal power, pomp and ceremony, and a massive bureaucratic-hierarchical organization as criteria of visibility, the Protestants focused on what they considered to be more essential aspects of

Christianity—consensus on the Incarnation, sacramental participation, Biblical literacy, etc.

TURNER: I'm not so sure that the Protestants differed in that respect from Augustine who, in his better moments, certainly emphasized such "Protestant" criteria for visibility.

CRANSTON: The Protestant reformers also had to sacrifice the title of "Catholic" (with the Capital "C" and the absence of qualifying adjectives), which in Augustine's estimation was certainly an important visible aspect.

TURNER: I think that most Protestants would say that that particular aspect of visibility has been voluntarily sacrificed for the attainment of other worthwhile goals.

XIV. Protestant Political Theology:
Beyond the "Two Kingdoms" and the "Two Regiments"

> We must divide the children of Adam and all men into two
> parts, the first belonging to the kingdom of God, and the
> second to the kingdom of the world. Those who belong to the
> kingdom of God are all true believers in Christ, and are subject
> to Christ. For Christ is the King and Lord in the kingdom of
> God.... All who are not Christians belong to the kingdom of
> the world and are subject to the law.   The world and the
> masses are and always will be unchristian, although they are
> all baptized and are nominally Christian.... It is out of the
> question that there should be a common Christian government
> over the whole world, nay even over one land or company of
> people, since the wicked always outnumber the good. —Martin
> Luther, *On Secular Authority*

> To the Catholic [in the 16th cent.] the Church was the king-
> dom of God on earth—*in via*.... The Reformers... against the
> Catholic view... set the apocalyptic vision of an apostate
> church, a harlot.... The true church was... the hidden saints who
> followed the teaching of the Bible.... —Christopher Dawson,
> "The Kingdom of God in History"

> The invisibility of the Catholic [sic] Church is due not only
> to the fact that no one society or nation of Christians can
> represent the   universal but also to the fact that no one time,
> but only all times together, can set forth the full meaning of
> the movement toward the eternal and its created image. —H.
> Richard Niebuhr, *The Kingdom of God in America*

References to the "visible" and "invisible" (or "hidden") Church
tend to be ambiguous. Any church, and even "the" Church, if it is
structured and organized at all, is visible in so far forth. The idea of an
"invisible" Church was born out of the recognition that membership in
a church is no guarante*e of inner commitment, and that those with the

inner commitment may because of various obstacles not be able to join. Augustine, in admitting that the Church contains a motley group of both saved and damned, is indicating that the group of the saved is relatively invisible.   But he also emphasizes some visible aspects—e.g. the worldwide unity in doctrine and discipline of the Catholic church.[1] Luther in opposing the corruption and abuses of the all-too-visible Catholic church had to call attention to the "hidden" congeries of true Christians and the invisible priesthood of believers; but he also felt it necessary to point out to potential joiners some visible marks by which this latter group could be recognized—for instance, the fidelity to the pure word of God, unadulterated with the glosses of Romish hierarchies.

The application of the qualifier "visible" to "church" is most relevant when the church in question is considered to be a present kingdom (or city) of God. If the "Church triumphant" (i.e., the heavenly kingdom) is meant, then of course visibility is at present out of the question; if the Church is defined as a mere "sign" or prolepsis[2] of an essentially future kingdom of God, then it is a visible sign, but the reality signified is invisible.

The real question of visibility, of course, is not regarding the visibility of the Church but regarding the visibility of the kingdom (or city) of God. From the point of view of the Protestant reformers, the question of the visibility of the kingdom of God in Catholicism boiled down to questions about the often shabby externals vs. the inchoate spirit, the frequently unworthy and scandal-ridden hierarchy vs. the true "salt of the earth," the ritually baptized membership vs. those baptized by the Holy Spirit.   In Protestantism, the question was more complex to formulate: In view of the fact that the Catholic church took itself to be the visible kingdom of God, Protestantism defined itself as the inner spiritual Kingdom, but lacking, at least temporarily, the visibility of Catholicism. But Protestantism as the "inner spirit" of Christianity would also have visible outer expressions, different from those touted by Catholicism.   But visibility is also a matter of degree. Some Protestant sects, e.g. separatist sects such as the Mennonites, differed from mainstream Protestants in their emphasis on the necessity of creating visible expressions of their faith in the world.

Luther, originally an Augustinian monk, produced an interpretation of the kingdom of God based on Augustine's political theology, but envisaging an even more radical opposition between the "two kingdoms"

---

[1]See the epigraph, Ch. XIII.

[2]Cf. Benedict Viviano, *The Kingdom of God in History*, p. 21.

than that discerned by Augustine[3]—to such an extent that any sizeable conversion of the wayward earthly kingdom was inconceivable. Outdistancing even Augustine in his perception of the waywardness of human nature, Luther leaves no room for hopes of building an earthly kingdom of God. Luther's idea of the Kingdom has been called "transcendental progressivism" by Paul Tillich, insofar as no relationship is discerned between a just life on earth and the justice of the kingdom of God.[4] Because of the transcendence of the Kingdom, revolutionary attempts to translate the justice of the Kingdom into a visible earthly reality are no part of God's plan. The state is a kingdom of wrath ruled by a prince who is often entrusted with the mission of administering divine wrath, and who is not to be lightly opposed by Christians simply on the basis of some misgivings concerning his methods or his intentions.

Although Luther accepted Augustine's idea of the "two kingdoms", he rejected the "two swords" theory with its traditional implications of papal supremacy. This traditional Catholic division of power was modified in Luther's hands into the distinction between the "two regiments"—one being the purely spiritual ministry of the Word and the sacraments on a voluntary basis for building up the invisible Kingdom within the souls of men, the other being the earthly regime, whose authorities (whether monarchical or non-monarchical) had a divine right to rule by force to maintain order and punish wrongdoers.[5] Luther's "two regiments" theory was complemented by a "two callings" theory, concerning the dual vocation of the Christian. The Christian in his visible aspects—in everyday secular life—had an obligation to demonstrate the Christian love and justice which was nourished and fostered by his religion.[6] This latter theory, of course, was in reaction to the compartmentalization of society into a Catholic hierarchy of official lay and religious callings, and the compartmentalization (as seen by Protestants) of Catholic daily life into perfunctory religious duties and unethical secular practices.

Luther's "second regiment" theoretically had no control over religion. But in practice Luther's efforts to gain advantages for his reforms led him to extremes. He demanded governmental protection for his own denomination, while at the same time urging strong government

---

[3]Benedict Viviano, *The Kingdom of God in History*, p. 89.

[4]*Systematic Theology* III, p. 355.

[5]W. D. J. Cargell Thompson, "Martin Luther and the 'Two Kingdoms'," pp. 34ff.

[6]Ibid., p. 50.

persecution of Catholics, Anabaptists, and "the Jews with their lies."[7] But the government could also expect extreme, unfaltering loyalty from faithful Protestants, who were admonished by Luther to offer unqualified obedience to their princes:

> I am called a clergyman and am a minister of the word, but even if I served a Turk and saw my lord in danger, I would forget my spiritual office and stab and hew as long as my heart beat.   If I were slain in so doing, I should go straight to heaven. For rebellion is a crime that deserves neither a court trial nor mercy, whether it be among heathen, Jews, Turks, Christians, or any other people; the rebel has already been tried, judged, condemned and sentenced to death and everyone is authorized to execute him. Nothing more needs to be done than to give him his due and to execute him.[8]

The conflicting loyalties among Catholics and Protestants, combined with the impulse to territoriality among princes, led to the unofficial compromise of letting the respective Protestant and Catholic princes decide on religious affiliation—*cujus regio, ejus religio*. This practice was officially elaborated in the Peace of Augsburg in 1555.

Although Protestants were of one mind in their opposition to Roman Catholicism and in their emphasis on Scripture, and almost of one mind concerning the priesthood of the laity and other matters, they evinced considerable variety in their formulations of church-state relationships. John Calvin, far removed from a pragmatic *cujus regio, ejus religio*, emphasized a kind of Christian socialism which entailed strict church control over the state, enforced by an inquisitorial board of discipline called the Consistory, made up of ministers and secular elders.[9] (Niebuhr, however, defends the Calvinist leaders against "the charge of absolutism," which "is possible only when the care with which Calvinist leaders limited their own claims is forgotten...."[10]) Thomas Münzer, resorting to revolution against all princely control because of the nearness of the "endtime," tried to implement his vision of the marriage

---

[7]Gerald Runkle, *A History of Western Political Theory*, p. 196. *Concerning the Jews and Their Lies* is the title of Luther's 1542 pamphlet.

[8]*Luther's Works* 46:81-2.

[9]Gerald Runkle, ibid., p. 189.

[10]H. Richard Niebuhr, *The Kingdom of God in America*, p. 40.

of "Duke Christ," the King of Kings with "his Bride, the Church of the Poor."[11]   On the other hand, John Locke suggested a state/church separation in terms of a "public vs. private" distinction, while the Puritans, "cutting the Gordian knot,"[12] opted for an institutionalized separatism from the corrupt world. In Germany, Pietist Lutherans, downplaying the utter separation between the "Two Kingdoms," emphasized an ethical activism geared to facilitating a partial realization of God's kingdom on earth.[13]

By the beginning of the nineteenth century, many Protestants may have wished for something like a Protestant Thomas Aquinas to come along and give direction and unity to Protestant thinking; and some think such an Aquinas redivivus did arrive in the person of the German idealist, G.W.F. Hegel (1770-1831).   Hegel while still a Lutheran seminary student, along with his friend, Hölderlin, was inspired by the possibility of establishing the kingdom of God on earth:

> By means of a new mythology, a new folk religion was to be created to establish the "kingdom of God" on earth and, once and for all, to do away with the allegedly fatal alliance of Christian orthodoxy and political despotism. The great aim was a society free of all masters. As the most significant obstacle along the way to its realization, the idea of a transcendent God had to be the first to fall.[14]

Hegel switched careers from the ministry to philosophy, and parted geographically with Hölderlin, who in a letter of 1794 suggested that their joint commitment to the kingdom of God could be a bond of union in their mutual absence.[15]   Hegel maintained this commitment. In a 1785 letter to his collaborator in philosophy, Schelling, Hegel writes: "May the kingdom of God come, and our hands not be idle!... Reason and freedom remain our password, and the Invisible Church our rallying point."[16] Hegel's later system, a synthesis of all branches of philosophy, was in Hegel's own estimation primarily just a fuller elaboration of the

---

[11]Benedict Viviano, *The Kingdom of God in History*, Ch. 4.

[12]H. Richard Niebuhr, *The Kingdom of God in America*, pp. 41-42.

[13]Paul Kuenning, "Two Kingdoms: Weighed and Found Wanting," pp. 24-25.

[14]Christoph Jamme, "Hegel and Hölderlin's Tübingen View," p. 362.

[15]Clark Buttler, *Hegel: the Letters*, p. 24.

[16]Ibid., p. 32.

truths of religion.[17]   In his political philosophy and philosophy of history, Hegel was influenced more by the Pietistic strand of Lutheranism, which emphasized the translation of the Christian spirit into the realities of ethical life, than by orthodox "two kingdoms" thinking. Protestant Christianity was, in Hegel's view, the necessary foundation for building a modern "free society" which would be the secular expression of the non-hierarchical Protestant view of the kingdom of God.[18]

Hegel's theory of church-state relations could almost be characterized as a new "two cities" theory—with Catholicism as the "other city." Hegel takes Catholicism as an object-lesson in how *not* to foster the Christian ideal of the kingdom of God.   He allows that Catholicism, as a form of Christianity, is in possession of "absolute spirit," *content*-wise; but accuses Catholicism of reducing this content to an unsuitable objectivized form—for example, God as the "host" worshipped in Catholic religious services,[19] and, in keeping with its objective orientation, organizing an *ecclesiastical* kingdom of God to stand alongside of secular governments in the world.[20]   And Catholicism, although quite public in its ritualized expressions, and quite worldly in the extension of its ecclesiastical kingdom, is "private" (in the pejorative sense) in its indifference to the necessary and indispensable expression in secular life of the ethical spirit of Christianity.[21]   Standing for all practical purposes as a separate kingdom in competition with secular governments, Catholicism instigates an unhealthy opposition between church and state in Catholic countries.[22]

This view of Catholicism, based apparently on some of the nadirs of medieval Catholicism and ongoing clashes of power in Catholic countries, sets the stage for Hegel's analysis of the chief virtues of Protestantism, which is the ideal foundation for a free state.   Like a Protestant Augustine, Hegel portrays the Protestant church as being the important present dimension of the Kingdom:

> For its individual members, the Church is ... a preparation for
> an eternal state as something future; .. but the Church has also

---

[17]Hegel, *Werke* (Suhrkamp ed.) 16:28.

[18]See H. Kainz, "Hegel, Democracy, and the 'Kingdom of God'," forthcoming in the *Hegel Jahrbuch*, 1993.

[19]*Werke* 10, §552.

[20]*Werke* 10:402.

[21]*Werke*, pp. 421-2; *Werke* 17:331.

[22]*Werke* 16:236-45.

the Spirit of God actually present in it, it forgives the sinner and is a present kingdom of heaven.[23]

In Protestantism, according to Hegel, Christianity arrived at self-consciousness, and through the power of self-consciousness the reconciliation of the opposites (which had been at odds with each other in Catholicism) took place—ecclesiastical and secular,[24] divine commands and the mandates of reason,[25] religion and morality.[26] In Protestantism, the principle of a coordination of church and state is present in an initial, abstract way,[27] and only needs to be put into operation.

Hegel's concept of church-state relations flows from his position regarding the reconciliation-function of Christianity. While the proper domain of the Christian church is the arena of particular subjectivity and the salvation of individual souls,[28] the Christian religion as the reconciliation of divine commands and ethics is the basis for the common ethical life (*Sittlichkeit*) of a people, and as the reconciliation of sacred and secular is the indispensable foundation for the ultimate extension of communality in the modern free state.[29] Thus the Protestant citizen, already effecting in his own psyche a reconciliation with the world and society through his faith, finds a natural expression for this faith in the political sphere; and it would be out of the question for him to split his loyalties between church and state:

> There cannot be two consciences—a religious and an ethical, the latter differing from the former in substance and content.... Religion is for self-consciousness the basis for ethics and the state. It has become the colossal mistake of our era to separate these inseparables from each other, and even to want to consider them as mutually indifferent.[30]

---

[23]*Werke* 12:414.

[24]*Werke* 12:343-344, 502; 10:364; 17:332.

[25]*Werke* 12:504.

[26]*Werke* 10:353ff.

[27]*Werke*, 16:242.

[28]Hegel, *The Christian Religion*, p. 260.

[29]*Werke* 10, §552.

[30]*Werke* 10, §552.

Thus, as Lakeland has pointed out,[31] the really important natural expression of the impulses of religion for Protestant Christianity is not found at all in any ecclesiastical institution, but in the state; and the state that results is, as it were, the "horizontal" correlate of the "vertical" relationship with the divine already brought about by faith—a state of affairs quite comparable in spirit with the Old Testament theocratic ideal of the kingdom of God.[32]

Hegel, in continuity with a long and respectable Protestant tradition emphasizing the presence of the kingdom of God in the "invisible Church," faced up to the problem: just where does the presence of the Kingdom become manifest? Banking on historical hindsight, he promptly eliminated the possibility of strictly ecclesiastical forms of manifestation, and projected a free and communally oriented Protestant state (a constitutional monarchy somewhat after the British pattern) as the logical locus of visibility. We, with our own late-twentieth-century historical hindsight, might tend to see such a close Hegelian intertwining of state and religion as at least stifling and at most dangerous. But as Theunissen observes, the considerable weakening of Luther's strong division between the "two kingdoms" in Hegel's theory is counterbalanced by the fact that, far from advocating a subjection of the kingdom of God to the kingdom of man, he gives a primacy to the kingdom of God over the state in his philosophical system (since religion is placed in the highest category, "absolute spirit").[33]

In the late nineteenth and early twentieth centuries, the ideal of an essential intermeshing between religion and the politico-social sphere maintained its thrust and attractiveness for some theologians, although it was broadly reinterpreted along lines Hegel never contemplated. In the Anglican church, Frederick Denison Maurice (1805-1872) in his *Kingdom of Christ* tried to provide a blueprint for a universal spiritual society in which the Church of England would play a major role, and advocated Christian socialism as a means towards realization of this society;[34] and the Baptist, Walter Rauschenbusch (1861-1918) emphasized in neo-Pelagian fashion the actual construction of the kingdom of God through

---

[31]*The Politics of Salvation*, pp. 89.

[32]Ibid., pp. 140-143.

[33]Michael Theunissen, *Hegel's Lehre vom absoluten Geist als theologisch-politischen Traktat*, pp. 373, 441.

[34]See Benedict Viviano, *The Kingdom of God in History*, pp. 118-119.

fulfillment of the Social Gospel.[35] Both of these visions were more "churchy" than that of Hegel, who idealized a strictly spiritual church implementing the Kingdom in "secular" ways in a "secular" sphere so permeated with Christian spiritual consciousness that the traditional boundary lines between "secular" and "religious" would no longer exist. Closer to Hegel's thought in our own time is Paul Tillich (1886-1965) who, reacting to an alleged overemphasis by Karl Barth and other theologians on the "transcendence" of the kingdom of God to the detriment of Christian responsibility and accountability, insisted on an immanent and quite visible implementation of the Kingdom in the form of religious socialism[36]—defined by him as a middle ground between orthodox Lutheran "church action" and liberal reformed secular action.

American Lutherans have long been split in their loyalty to the orthodox Lutheran doctrine of a rigid separation between the "two kingdoms." According to Kuenning, a sizeable group, downplaying Luther's expectation of an imminent eschaton and pursuing a prime commitment to social justice, are in continuity with the same tradition of German pietism that influenced Hegel.[37]

The trend towards a strictly eschatological and non-political interpretation of the kingdom of God among contemporary European theologians seems to be one of many by-products of the reaction against the monstrosity of the Third Reich—in the creation of which one factor would seem to have been the passive cooperation of German Christians in Hitler's attempt to recreate the Charlemagnean empire. But as Viviano observes, some theologians have gone to extremes in depoliticizing commitment to the kingdom of God into a naive indifference to the realities of power-engagement.[38] Another offshoot of the reaction to Nazism seems to be the opposition to Hegel by Karl Popper, who portrays Hegel as a proto-totalitarian,[39] and by Eric Voegelin, who

---

[35]See above, p. 80.

[36]Paul Tillich, *Systematic Theology* III, pp. 126, 129-32, 358f.

[37]Paul Kuenning, "Two Kingdoms: Weighed and Found Wanting," pp. 22-26.

[38]Viviano, p. 49.

[39]See *The Open Society and its Enemies*, Part II. Popper portrays Hegel as a champion of the monistic and authoritarian Prussian state of his day. But Hegel's political philosophy, elaborated in his *Philosophy of Right* was immensely liberal, including much that was not extant in the then-prevailing political system, such as trial by jury, freedom of the press, division of legislative and executive powers, rights of conscientious

accuses Hegel of neo-gnostic pretensions about having privileged information concerning the workings of the divine *Logos* in the world.[40] These anti-Hegelian views have some *prima facie* grounding in the fact that the Nazis used Hegel to support their mystical-organic view of the German folk-spirit, just as they used Nietzsche to prop up their anti-semitic theories of racial superiority.[41]   But the connection is only specious. For Hegel, who traced the modern concepts of freedom and respect for persons to Christian origins, would be as adverse to Christian passivity under Nazism as Nietzsche would be adverse to the "Arian" superiority touted by the Nazis.

On the other hand, might it not be the case that any theoretician who idealizes an inseparable union and harmonious cooperation between Christianity and the state is laying the ground, at least unintentionally, for the sort of misuse of "harmony" and "cooperation" that stood Hitler in such good stead? —However that question is answered, the Protestant problematic in the context of which Hegel worked and developed his theoretical stance still remains: *If* Protestantism wants to be Catholic in the sense of "universal," *and* a church in the sense of a present kingdom of God, *but* avoid building up a visible "ecclesiastical" Kingdom with hierarchies and papal-style chains of command, and *also* avoid being merely "private" and "spiritual"—what other course is available than the sort of direct and connatural expression of the Kingdom in secular, including political, life extolled by Hegel? In other words, Hegel seems to have brought a certain important conception of the Protestant vocation to its logical conclusion.

---

objection, provisions for the representation of citizens in parliament, and guarantees of civic rights not envisioned by the government in power.

[40]See *From Enlightenment to Revolution*, Ch. 11.

[41]See Peter Viereck, *Meta-politics: the Roots of the Nazi Mind*, Chs. 9, 13.

XV. Does Hegelian Political Theology have a Future?

Why did Hegel not become for the Protestant world something similar to what Thomas Aquinas was for Roman Catholicism?... We do not know whether the age of Hegel is in fact entirely past, even if we should, in all seriousness, consider it to be so as far as we ourselves are concerned. It was only in the course of centuries that Thomas Aquinas acquired the position at present accorded him in the Roman Catholic world. It may be that the dawn of the true age of Hegel is still something that will take place in the future.... Everything that seems to give theology its particular splendour and special dignity appears to be looked after and honoured by [Hegel's] philosophy in a way incomparably better than that achieved by the theologians themselves (with the possible exception of Thomas Aquinas).... In a most thorough fashion Hegel himself showed the disturbers of the peace, and not least the theologians who were capitulating to them, who was master. He produced a philosophy...in which theology seemed to be taken better care of than in theology itself.... Modern man, without knowing of a better unity than that proposed by Hegel, yet split himself once again, as oil and water separate, into the Christian and the man. The grip whereby Hegel sought to unite him in himself turned out to be premature, too strong, or too weak, even, to prevent the centripetal forces of both sides from once again shattering the unity. —Karl Barth, *Protestant Thought*

A future Christology may join Hegel in thinking in terms of a unified understanding of reality in which the world is not without God nor God without the world, but in which God is in this world and the world in this God. —Hans Küng, *The Incarnation of God*

TURNER: I am amused at the extraordinary resurgence of interest in Hegel in the last decade or so, after a half-century of comparative neglect. Every month one sees a new scholarly book appear

119

on some aspect of Hegel's thought. Even the popular press has gotten into the act: Witness the tremendous outpouring of articles in the *New York Times*, *Encounter*, *The Nation*, and other newspapers and magazines, and now books, in response to Fukuyama's article in *The National Interest* on Hegel and the "end of history."[42]

CRANSTON: That article simply gives one more example of the prevailing widespread misunderstanding of Hegel. If Fukuyama had read Hegel carefully, he would never have taken Hegel as a prophet of the final victory of liberal democracy. Hegel favored constitutional monarchy, opposed democracy as a form of government which doesn't go far enough in guaranteeing and stabilizing freedom, and specifically rejected the possibility of saying anything valid about "the end of history."

TURNER: In any case, it's interesting that a neo-conservative like Fukuyama would feel it necessary to appeal to Hegel to bolster his libertarian and anti-communistic position.

CRANSTON: There's a logic in that, since Hegel was also Marx's foil. If one is against Marx, it might seem logical to be for Hegel, whose political philosophy Marx was trying to overturn and replace.

TURNER: Do you think the critics of the "all-too-close" relationship between church and state in Hegel are involved in a similar misunderstanding of what Hegel actually said?

CRANSTON: No. Hegel actually did opt for an intertwining of Christianity with the development of a free society on the national level. Since Hegel's time, we have redefined "free society," and we refer to it with the generic umbrella-term, "democracy." But, given the differences in definition, I don't see Hegel as essentially off-base. There may just be an essential relationship between "democracy" (or a "free society") and Christianity. Has

---

[42]Francis Fukuyama, "The End of History?" *The National Interest* 16, Summer, 1989; see also Francis Fukuyama, *The End of History and the Last Man* (NY and Toronto: the Free Press and Maxwell Macmillan, 1992).

democracy ever flourished in a non-Christian, especially an atheistic, society?

TURNER: You're missing the point—which is: whether Christianity is in some way essential to buttress democracy and obviate tyranny. I think the twentieth-century phenomenon of the rise of Nazism with little resistance from an overwhelmingly Christian German nation (the theologian Karl Barth was a splendid but rare exception) should put to rest any pretensions about a magical synergy between Christianity and democracy.

CRANSTON: I would not argue that Christianity is *sufficient* to insure democracy; but I do think it may be *necessary* to pave the way for democracy in the modern sense—with the interdiction of slavery, and equal rights for all. I believe Christianity is necessary for full democratization, but I would not go so far as to claim that it is sufficient to guarantee democratization.

TURNER: You could say the same thing about capitalism. Has any successful democracy in the modern sense come about without capitalism? Why not maintain that capitalism is "necessary but not sufficient" for democracy?

CRANSTON: I wouldn't reject that thesis out-of-hand as outlandish. To some extent, both may be "necessary, but not sufficient."

TURNER: That thesis would be inexcusably speculative. I'm sure you are aware of Latin American countries which are both overwhelmingly Christian and capitalistic, and perhaps even have some mechanisms of "democracy," but have never caught the democratic spirit.

CRANSTON: This is simply an illustration of the fact that they are not sufficient for democracy. But the possibility for democracy is there; whereas, in lieu of Christianity, and possibly also capitalism, there would not even be the possibility of democracy.

TURNER: I don't think you realize the complexities involved in maintaining a thesis like that. For starters, who's a "Christian"? In West Germany, roughly 90% of the population declare themselves Christian, but only a minuscule portion of that number actively participate in church activities or attend church services. In

America, in contrast, those who declare themselves Christian characteristically participate more in a church. Is such participation essential for being a Christian? Or would you be satisfied with mere nominal affiliation with some Christian church?

CRANSTON: Of course, I can't give you an exact answer to that, since religious commitment is not measurable. But I would have to admit that the degree of commitment would be an important factor in the equation. There is an unavoidably subjective dimension in such characterizations.

TURNER: There is also an important objective obstacle: Where is "the Church"? Let's say that I became convinced about the truth of Christianity, and wanted to unite with other Christians in the "Christian church." Where do I go? I am confronted with innumerable churches and sects, all claiming the title of "Christian," but differing in their beliefs in some very important respects. What banner do I rally under? "The Church" is for all practical purposes invisible. All I see is churches.

CRANSTON: The "invisibility" of the Church has of course been accentuated by the necessity for Protestants to differentiate themselves from the all-too-visible Catholic church. And subsequent splintering of Protestant denominations and sects after Luther has increased the invisibility of "The Church."

TURNER: You've been associating "Catholicity" with visibility.[43] But the association is tenuous. The fact that you have a massive worldwide church with billions of members may simply mean ... that you've got one very effective organization, whose managerial methods might usefully be studied in our business schools. Comte, who was no Christian, suggested studying the organizational methods of the Catholic Church to foster the advancement of sociology.[44] Even if the Catholic Church is an organizational marvel, and by dint of its superior methods actually possesses the doctrinal and ritual uniformity that it claims to have, there would be no obvious connection of such accomplishments with the visibility of the Church as a "present kingdom of God."

---

[43]See above, p. 101.
[44]See p. 127 above.

CRANSTON: In using the word, "uniformity," you're making a prejudgment. The *unity* of Christians would certainly be an important factor in the visibility of the type of community they profess. "Uniformity" puts a bad face on this unity, saying in effect that it is superficial and/or external.

TURNER: The fact that sincere Christians are so disunited among themselves leads one to expect that there is something missing from that branch of Christendom which claims overarching unity.

CRANSTON: It seems to me that the differences in belief and practices among Christian denominations—even between Catholics and Protestants—are not as unbridgeable as they appear at first blush. Consensus is possible amid differences. Take, for example, the consensus of various ethnic and racial groups in American democracy regarding essential national goals. There has been a comparable consensus emerging among Christians as a result of the "ecumenical movement" during the last few decades. As this consensus becomes clear enough, a viable option regarding "visibility" might be to accept the multiplicity of major Christian denominations as a visible-but-pluralistic Church.

TURNER: If this obtained, there would no longer be any disparity between Catholicism and Protestantism. The "Pluralistic Consensus" you project would be the new, revised Catholicism.

CRANSTON: But pluralism itself is the very issue on which it would be hardest to get any consensus between Catholics and Protestants.

TURNER: Hegel would very likely roll over in his grave if he were privy to any projection of a consensus between Catholics and Protestants.

CRANSTON: His philosophical system is famous for extraordinary conjunctions of opposites. But for some reason he did not consider those two opposites of Christianity synthesizable.

TURNER: I tend to think that he was right and that you are overlooking the gargantuan hurdles involved in overcoming that opposition.

XVI. The Emergence of the Secular Kingdom of God

The ideal of modern science of mastering the forces of nature and the idea of progress emerged neither in the classical world nor in the East, but in the West. But what enabled us to remake the world in the image of man? Is it perhaps that the belief in being created in the image of a Creator-God, the hope in a future Kingdom of God, and the Christian command to spread the gospel to all the nations for the sake of salvation have turned into the secular presumption that we have to transform the world into a better world in the image of man and to save unregenerate nations by Westernization and re-education?...

The fundamental premise of the *Communist Manifesto* is not the antagonism between bourgeoisie and proletariat as two opposite facets; for what makes them antagonistic is that the one class is the children of darkness and the other the children of light. Likewise, the final crisis of the bourgeois capitalist world which Marx prophesies in terms of a scientific prediction is a last judgment, though pronounced by the inexorable law of a historical process.... It is ... not by chance that the "last" antagonism between the two hostile camps of bourgeoisie and proletariat corresponds to the Jewish-Christian belief in a final fight between Christ and Antichrist in the last epoch of history, that the task of the proletariat corresponds to the world-historical mission of the chosen people, that the redemptive and universal function of the most degraded class is conceived on the religious pattern of Cross and Reconciliation, that the ultimate transformation of the realm of necessity into a realm of freedom corresponds to the transformation of the *civitas terrena* into a *civitas Dei*, and that the whole process of history as outlined in the *Communist Manifesto* corresponds to the general scheme of the Jewish-Christian interpretation of history as a providential advance toward a final goal which is meaningful. —Karl Löwith, *The Meaning of History*

Christianity has relieved the brutal warring ardor of the German to a certain extent; but it has been unable to uproot it,

and when the cross, that talisman which enchains him, shall be broken, then will break loose again that ferocity of the ancient warriors.... When you shall hear the noise and the tumult, be on your guard, dear neighbors of France, and keep out of what we shall do in Germany, for evil might come to you....
—Heinrich Heine, *Zur Geschichte der Religion und der Philosophie in Deutschland*, 1833.

The idea of humans appropriating divine prerogatives and perquisites has a long and honorable history. In Western culture, it is embodied in the myth of Prometheus, who stole fire from the gods for the benefit of mankind. In the ancient gnostic *Gospel of Philip*, it is not just the fire of the gods, but divinity itself, that is appropriated—or rather reappropriated, since divinity, falsely projected upon "gods," had belonged to man in the first place.[1] In the European middle ages, the humanistic problem was not so much "how to get divinity back from the deity" but "how to get divinity back from the Church"—which represented the divinity and jealously guarded its divinely-bestowed prerogatives. The solution to this problem began to be elaborated by the *lumières* of the seventeenth century: Oppressive ecclesiastical domination over the minds and spirits of men could not be overcome simply by revolting against the Church as one would against a secular power, but by a subtle and stealthy process of substitution and disenchantment—substitution of rational and progressive doctrines and rituals for the dogmas and rituals of religion, and gradual disenchantment of the masses from religious superstition by enlightened, scientific exorcism of the "mysteries" of religion.[2]

The watershed of secularization appeared in the eighteenth century. The first decisive steps were taken: Replacing the belief in a heavenly reward to compensate for all the sufferings and injustices of this present life was the belief in the definite possibility of building with human ingenuity a respectable facsimile of heaven on earth. To facilitate the construction of this new terrestrial enterprise, the "philosophy of utility" was developed by Helvetius and Hume and Voltaire, and this process was complemented by the "utilitarianism" of Bentham, who calculated with scientific precision the procedures for bringing about the

---

[1] Elaine Pagels, *Adam, Eve, and the Serpent*, p. 65.

[2] Daniel Bell, "Return of the Sacred," pp. 189-90; see also H. Kainz, *Hegel's Phenomenology, Part II*, pp. 64ff.

"greatest happiness for the greatest number."[3] The replacement offered for the pious belief in Divine Providence was the virile belief in the latent power of mankind to control its own destiny and to progress ever and ever closer to the ideal of a just and harmonious society in which every individual would be satisfied. Religious millennarianism and apocalyptic visions of a final irruption of the Kingdom from heaven likewise gave way to utopian projections of perfect egalitarian or elitist societies.

To celebrate and concretize the new secular spirit, the emancipated individuals of the Enlightenment set about systematically creating new symbols and constructs which would prevent the vacuum left by religion from inducing distress. In place of the hallowed creeds and ancient rituals of Catholicism, Rousseau devised a system of "civil religion" with new dogmas propagated by civil leaders to forge national unity,[4] and Comte, substituting a dialectic between positivist intellectuals and industrial managers for the traditional "two swords" of church and state,[5] proposed making use of the already existent organizational shell of Catholicism for launching (in Notre Dame Cathedral!) a new secular religion.

The impetus towards inventing a new secularized religion was most radical at the inauguration of the First French Republic, when the *citoyens* devised a new calendar built around secular feasts to take the place of the former religious feasts, and devised new symbols such as the goddess of Reason to outshine the former symbols. In America the secularization process was more moderate, although no less serious. The founders of the United States replaced the Judaeo-Christian obligations of covenant with a constitutionalism geared to the recognition of persons and inalienable rights guaranteed in a social contract; "divine right" evolved into sacred constitution and investiture into the oath of office; and divine justice was translated into inviolable human rights.[6] The deity "gives the nod" to the new arrangements, and this is commemorated on the American dollar bill (*annuit coeptis*); but one also reads on the same dollar bill that it is the new, emancipated, secular man who creates the "new order of the world" (*novus ordo seculorum*).

---

[3]See H. Kainz, ibid., pp. 78-83.

[4]Jean Jacques Rousseau, *The Social Contract*, 4:8.

[5]Barry Cooper, *The Political Theory of Eric Voegelin*, p. 69.

[6]See Carl Friedrichs, *Transcendent Justice*, Ch. 1; Neal Riemer, *The Future of the Democratic Revolution*, Ch. 5; George Sherwood Eddy, *The Kingdom of God and the American Dream*, p. 252.

During the same eras in which the *sacrum imperium* of Charlemagne and Otto fell by the wayside, and Napoleon failed to successfully replace it with a secular version, and Bismarck's and Hitler's final efforts to fill Charlemagne's boots also petered out, a new and formidable political entity was coming to the fore—the nation-state, a secular leviathan claiming absolute sovereignty and inspiring absolute devotion from its patriotic adherents. Providing the unity no longer offered by the now weakened, disintegrating Church, the nation-state fulfilled the aspirations of Voltaire and his friend, Frederick the Great, who wrote to Voltaire in 1740 that the moment in which the rock in Nebuchadnezzer's dream[7] had struck the idol and shattered all the previous kingdoms, had arrived—namely, Frederick's own kingdom, which was about to destroy the last vestiges of the Holy Roman Empire with its Hapsburg monarch. A new political religion had emerged, rivaling the world's major religions, including Christianity, and with more than a touch of the "demonic" in it, as Tillich has observed.[8]

The secularization process found an ally in philosophy. Among philosophers, one of the first attempts to provide ideological support for the secularization processes was through the "philosophy of history"—a speculative approach to history which is now no longer in vogue (having in recent decades been largely replaced by the analytic, metaphilosophically-oriented, and value-neutral "critical" philosophy of history). Speculative philosophy of history supplanted the political-theology/theology-of-history which had prevailed from Augustine and Orosius to Bossuet.[9] The transitional figure in the development of the philosophy of history was Vico (1668-1744), who took it upon himself in his *New Science* to *demonstrate* the "historical fact" of divine providence.[10] Epistemologically at odds with Descartes, who thought we could have certain knowledge only of mathematical constructions, Vico maintained we could have maximal certainty about history, precisely because, like gods, we create it ourselves.[11] After examining world history for many years, Vico came to the conclusion that divine providence works itself

---

[7]Dan. 2.

[8]Paul Tillich, "The Kingdom of God and History."

[9]See above, pp. 93ff.

[10]Giambattista Vico, *The New Science*, T. Bergin and M. Fisch tr. (Ithaca, NY: Cornell University Press, 1948), §342.

[11]Ibid., §349.

out in a cyclical fashion in each nation: from necessity to utility to comfort, then to amusement and luxury and dissolution.[12]

Vico, like Milton in *Paradise Lost*, thought he was doing something to "justify the ways of God to men," but in reality, by allowing faith in Providence to be supplanted by certain knowledge, he was paving the way for a strictly and professedly secular treatment of human history. The new, speculative, secularized treatment was soon crystallized in the thought of Voltaire, who coined the term, "philosophy of history." Voltaire in his *Essay on the Manners and Morals of Nations*, determined to avoid the pitfall of giving too much attention to the "abominable history of the Jews,"[13] extended his analysis beyond the Judaeo-Christian world to encompass a larger view of world history which would include the oriental civilizations. And reacting vociferously against those who would interpret the great tale of mankind myopically in terms of its relationship to the fortunes of some petty, egotistic, ruthless "chosen people" and their successors, Voltaire arrives at the apparently modest prognosis of gradual progress for mankind as a whole.[14]

Other practitioners of the philosophy of history (although they did not always use that term) emerged in the late eighteenth century. Johann Gottfried Herder in his *Ideas for a Philosophical History of Mankind* (1784) analyzed the "spirit" of various cultures and emphasized their unity; and Kant in *The Idea of a Universal History from a Cosmopolitan Point of View* (1784) developed a concept something like what Hegel later called the "cunning of reason"—disparate events and self-serving motivations leading willy-nilly towards greater unity for mankind. The anti-religious element, so predominant in Voltaire, is absent in these other practitioners. Kant, although making a sharp distinction between faith and reason and assiduously avoiding making any assertions relying on religious faith, nevertheless held that the religious sphere was of the utmost importance, although not accessible through philosophical analysis.

Not so diffident about the reach of the philosopher were Schelling and Hegel. Schelling in his *Philosophy of Revelation*[15] analyzed the stages of world history in trinitarian terms: 1) the age of the Father was represented by St. Peter and embodied in Catholicism; 2) the

---

[12]Ibid., §1106.

[13]Löwith, pp. 106, 110.

[14]Löwith, p. 111.

[15]Friedrich Schelling, *The Philosophy of Revelation*, Lecture #36.

age of the Son was represented by St. Paul and manifested historically in Protestantism; but 3) an age of the Spirit, represented by St. John, was predicted to be on the way, in which mankind would attain the state of perfect religion. (Schelling later expressed delight in discovering that Joachim of Fiore[16] had devised a similar schema.) Hegel, making a similar distinction on the conceptual level between the "three kingdoms," did not try to trace out the lineaments of the three kingdoms in world history or the history of religion; but at the outset of his detailed and comprehensive lectures on world history, he leaves behind the skepticism of Voltaire and revives a Vico-like commitment to the religious significance of history and the possibility of certain knowledge about divine providence:

> Our earnest endeavor must be directed to the recognition of the ways of Providence, the means it uses, and the historical phenomena in which it manifests itself.... In the Christian religion God has revealed Himself—that is, he has given us to understand what He is; so that He is no longer a concealed or secret existence. And this possibility of knowing Him, thus afforded us, renders such knowledge a duty. God wishes no narrow-hearted souls or empty heads for his children; but those whose spirit is of itself indeed, poor, but rich in the knowledge of Him.... It was for awhile the fashion to profess admiration for the wisdom of God, as displayed in animals, plants, and isolated occurrences. But, if it be allowed that Providence manifests itself in such objects and forms of existence, why not also in Universal History?[17]

In keeping with this ambitious objective, Hegel traces out the workings of "Spirit" in the historical development from the Far East to Greek and Roman civilizations and the modern Germanic world, showing how Spirit brings about a gradual progression from the autocratic status quo where one man is free, to the attainment of freedom by a select group, and finally to freedom for all—a gift to mankind ultimately traceable to Christianity, which first awakened human subjectivity to its full potential. Hegel ends his philosophy of history with a broad conclusion about the providential operation of God in the world:

---

[16]See p. 90 above.

[17]G.W.F. Hegel, *The Philosophy of History*, pp. 14-15.

> That the History of the World, with all the changing scenes which its annals present, is this process of development and the realization of Spirit—this is the true *Theodicaea*, the justification of God in History. Only *this* insight can reconcile Spirit with the History of the World—viz., that what has happened, and is happening every day, is not only not "without God," but is essentially His Work.[18]

Speculative philosophers of history after Hegel include Auguste Comte, whose *Cours de philosophie positive* sees the world as evolving historically from theological to metaphysical to "positive" conceptions of reality, the culmination of which will be social science; and Herbert Spencer, who in his *Principles of Sociology* examined evolution from homogeneity to organic heterogeneity. Two of the most notable twentieth century practitioners are Arnold Toynbee, whose *A Study of History* is a study of the rise and fall of world civilizations, and Eric Voegelin, who equates the philosophy of history with "political science."[19]

Another major substitution bolstered by philosophy was the substitution of an ethical kingdom for the "kingdom of God." The transitional figure in this enterprise was Immanuel Kant (1724-1804), who devised as an ethical counterpart to the kingdom of God a "kingdom of ends" in which the moral goals of all self-legislating persons would be mutually coordinated,[20] and in his later philosophy of religion develops the idea of an ethical commonwealth or kingdom of virtue, which he calls a "church," in which he proposes that we work together with a trust in Divine Providence to produce a final completely ethical society.[21] According to Kant, this revised secular kingdom comes through a "universal religion of reason" pervading the earth, and becomes public, even though no actual state embodying the kingdom is instituted.

A similar attempt in Kant's generation to replace the religious kingdom with an ethical kingdom was made by Lessing, who explicitly derived his inspiration from Joachim of Fiore. Joachim's projection of a "third age" of the Holy Spirit was adapted by Lessing in his fragment

---

[18]Ibid., p. 457.

[19]Eric Voegelin, *The New Science of Politics*, p. 1.

[20]Immanuel Kant, *Fundamental Principles of the Metaphysic of Morals*, Section 2.

[21]Immanuel Kant, *Religion Within the Limits of Reason Alone*, Bk. 3, "The Victory of the Good Over the Evil Principle, and the Founding of the Kingdom of God on Earth."

on *The Education of the Human Race*, and reinterpreted as a stage in which the common education of the entire human race would take place, leading to full human self-realization and the reign of reason. Friedrich Schlegel likewise devised a non-Gospel version of the kingdom of God, designed to lead to the progressive education and moral betterment of the human race.[22]

Fichte, influenced by both Lessing and Kant, looked forward to a final regeneration of rational beings in and through a "church of consciences":

> [The] reciprocity amongst all rational beings for the purpose of producing common practical convictions, is called a *Church*, an ethical commonwealth; and that about which they all agree is called their *symbol* [creed]. Each one ought to be a member of the [ethical] church.[23]

Hegel, who is known as a philosophical synthesizer, also carried out a revisionary synthesis of multiple aspects of the secularization process taking place in his time. He not only propounded a more extensive and ambitious philosophy of history than his predecessors, but also, like Kant and Fichte, took pains to translate the religious idea of the Kingdom into its moral equivalent (*Sittlichkeit*, a communally-oriented morality designed to supersede Kant's *Moralität*), and in his political philosophy, in direct opposition to Kant's conscientious defense of a confederation of nations, became a foremost defender of that great secular institution, the sovereign nation-state. Thus many of the reactions to secularization in the last two centuries, pro and con, have been reactions to Hegel's philosophy.

Critics who have thought Hegel went too far have ranged from Kierkegaard, who countered Hegel's alleged submersion of the individual with an existential philosophy centered on the transcendence of the individual,[24] to Löwith, who discerns in Hegel a massive displacement of Christian transcendence in favor of this-worldly goals.[25] But even more numerous were the leftist-oriented philosophers who thought that Hegel had not carried his secularization far enough. Thus Ludwig

---

[22]*Athenäumsfragmente*, #22.

[23]Johann Gottlieb Fichte, *The Science of Ethics*, p. 248.

[24]See Robert Gascoigne, *Religion, Rationality and Community*, p. 265.

[25]Karl Löwith, *The Meaning of History*, pp. 57-59; and *From Hegel to Nietzsche*, p. 33.

Feuerbach in his post-Hegelian *Essence of Christianity*, taking a cue from Hegel's theme of the "Unhappy (alienated) Consciousness," claims like the author of the *Gospel of Philip*,[26] that all forms of religion and theism are the result of alienation, and that we must reappropriate our own essence, falsely projected onto a "God"; and Pierre-Joseph Proudhon considers Hegel's defense of Providence and of a "realized transcendence" particularly pernicious, an ideological obstacle to the necessary assertion by humankind of its own control over its own destiny.[27]

Karl Marx, strongly influenced by Feuerbach's critique of Hegel, brought the efforts of the "left Hegelians" to their logical and political conclusions: All forms of religious transcendence are detrimental to human progress; religion is the "opiate" of the masses, which prevents them from realizing and activating their own societal potential. And we must not only abolish religion but also the alienating socio-economic structures which have nourished religious alienation and allied themselves with religions; for while atheism is the negation of religious alienation, true socialism is required for the "negation of the negation"—the return to the true sensuous essence of man.

Marx distinguished his "scientific" socialism from the "utopian" socialistic schemes of Fourier, Owen and others, which did not take into account the necessity for complete overthrow of bourgeois capitalist structures along with the ideologies allied with them. Marx's socialism, like a secularist revival of the apocalyptic-revolutionary fervor of the Anabaptists of Muenster, called for nothing less than a complete overthrow of the present world social order to make way for a new "communist man" fulfilling his polymorphous potentialities to the fullest in a new communist order.

Marx's followers, looking to the community of workers rather than to the Church militant for salvation, substituting Marxist-Leninist works for the Scriptures, uniting in creed and ritual under new priestly guardians of orthodoxy, would precipitate by revolution the coming of the new and final "communist" stage of human and humane development. This stage—a cooperative, crimeless, stateless international community, about which Marx writes only a few paragraphs of idyllic descriptions—is a new secular kingdom of God, the accomplishment by a united mankind of the goals of social justice which Christianity had failed to achieve.

---

[26]See above, p. 126.
[27]See Karl Löwith, *The Meaning of History*, pp. 61ff.

The idea that even Christians might help to orchestrate this Herculean accomplishment led the Cuban Ecumenical Council leaders to proclaim that the "kingdom of God" is to be found in Marxism-Leninism, and that

> ...Marxism offers an effective methodology to carry out Christ's mandate to feed the hungry and clothe the naked. The only difference between Christians and Marxists is the additional belief on the part of the Christians in an afterlife.[28]

As Jürgen Moltmann has observed, Marx comes on the scene as just one more disciple, albeit of a secularist bent, of Joachim of Fiore, who also preached about the coming transition from the stage of necessity to the realm of true liberty.[29] It is perhaps for this reason that Marxism found a particularly sympathetic reception in Russia, where intellectuals had already been busily developing the implications of Joachim's "third stage."[30]

One frequently hears it said that Marx is a "religious thinker."[31] The salvageable truth behind this statement is that Marxism, like the "civil religion" schemes of Rousseau or Comte, draws on an external shell of approaches and images traditionally connected with religion, especially prophetic and apocalyptic religion. Riemer, who advocates a "prophetic" approach to politics, finds so many prophetic elements in Marxism that it is difficult for him to associate Marxism with "non-prophetic" models of political theory (i.e., utopian or Machiavellian models).[32]   Voegelin portrays Marx as an "activist mystic" whose prophecy was originally about revolution, but who, after the failure of initial communist revolutionary efforts, adopted the compromise position of preparation-for-revolution;[33] and Lenin, as the high priest taking up where Marx had left off, can be characterized as developing a new secularist "two swords" (Toilers-plus-Vanguard) theory to implement a "dictatorship of the proletariat," following the pattern of medieval pontiffs working out the logistics of the *sacrum imperium*.[34]

---

[28]*Wall Street Journal*, Friday, July 5, 1985.

[29]Jürgen Moltmann, *The Trinity and the Kingdom*, p. 206.

[30]Karl Löwith, *The Meaning of History*, p. 210.

[31]See e.g. Bruce Mazlish, *The Meaning of Karl Marx*, pp. 5-6.

[32]Neal Riemer, *Karl Marx and Prophetic Politics*.

[33]Eric Voegelin, *From Enlightenment to Revolution*, Ch. 10.

[34]Cf. Barry Cooper, *The Political Theory of Eric Voegelin*, p. 69.

National Socialism, aiming to set up its own version of a kingdom of God based not on the international unity of the proletariat, but on the overriding claim of a nation of beings especially chosen by Nature to rule the world, lacked the sort of sophisticated and elaborate philosophical foundations that Marxism boasted, although, if Heinrich Heine's vision is correct, political forces of incredible brutality were necessitated in Germany simply because of the mentality induced by the revolutionary anti-realist philosophies of Kant, Fichte, and the "nature philosophers."[35]   But Nazi ideologist Alfred Rosenberg—like Giovanni Gentile who had elaborated for Italy the philosophy of fascism overcoming the twin evils of capitalism and Bolshevism—tried, in collaboration with Hitler, to overcome the lack of a coherent philosophy by painting visions of a new secular Zion established in Germany by a master race which would bring order and the light of civilization to a world vacillating aimlessly between democracy and communism:

> A new peace shall make Germany mistress of the globe, a peace not hanging on the palm fronds of pacifist womenfolk but established by the victorious sword of a master race that takes over the world in the service of a higher Kultur.[36]

In Nazism, a whole set of variant secular substitutions was made—the Swastika for the Cross, the *Herrenvolk* for God's elect, *Lebensraum* for Canaan or unredeemed pagan territories, the "final solution" for the "ban," the "Fortress Europa" for Shiloh or Zion, the nation-as-organism for the "mystical body of Christ," and the "thousand-year Reich" for the millennium, which was to be "inaugurated by a *Dux* or a *Führer* who was acclaimed as a savior and greeted by millions with *Heil!*"[37]

Hans Küng points out that one important and indispensable factor in the ascendancy of National Socialism was the cooperation and even complicity of Christians, in spite of the express antipathy of Hitler and the Nazis in general towards everything religious:

---

[35]*Heines Werke*, Vol. 9, pp. 274.   See also the epigraph to this chapter.

[36]Joint prediction of Rosenberg and Hitler, cited by Peter Viereck, *Metapolitics*, p. 214.

[37]Karl Löwith, *The Meaning of History*, p. 159.

Protestant "German Christians" saw in Nazism something like a revelation, and in the Führer a new Luther—or even Christ—linking Christianity and Germanness. Prominent representatives of standard Catholic theology such as the dogmatic theologian Michael Schmans or the church historian Joseph Lortz, for their part, found that National Socialism was striving for on a natural plane what Christianity strove for on a supernatural plane (order, unity, authority, one empire, one "leader").[38]

The fact that Christians felt comfortable and even enthusiastic about a system overtly alien to Christianity may be at least partially explained by all the external accoutrements imported from the Judaeo-Christian tradition for the construction of this secular-nationalistic Kingdom. But the full explanation remains to be given—perhaps when (and if) the "speculative" philosophy of history comes back into vogue.

---

[38]*Theology for the Third Millennium*, p. 189.

XVII. Secularization—a Boon to Mankind?

With the progress of science and technology, man has stopped believing in magic powers, in spirits, and demons; he has lost his sense of prophecy and, above all, his sense of the sacred. Reality has become dreary, flat and utilitarian, leaving a great void in the souls of men which they seek to fill by furious activity and through various devices and substitutes.... Mysticism becomes mystification, community becomes communitarianism, and life is reduced to a series of unrelated experiences. Academicians and intellectuals are begged for a message, although by the very nature of things they are entrenched each in his own specialty. —Julien Freund, *The Sociology of Max Weber*

This is the age of the secular city. Through supersonic travel and instantaneous communications its ethos is spreading into every corner of the globe. The world looks less and less to religious rules and rituals for its morality or its meanings. For some, religion provides a hobby, for others a mark of national or ethnic identification, for still others an esthetic delight. For fewer and fewer does it provide an inclusive and commanding system of personal and cosmic values and explanations. —Harvey Cox, *The Secular City*

Secularization is a very doubtful operation: the secular questions become "theologized," "mythologized" and absolute. Political ideology is the *avant garde* of an absolute future; the field of political action becomes an eschatological battlefield, and finally the political opponent can and does become the apocalyptic power of evil and is understood and treated as such. —Ian Lochman, *Encountering Marx*

TURNER: I, for one, don't see secularization as a tragedy. In the history of the Western world, so much mischief has been done in the name of God and religion that an "alternative approach" was bound to be tried, sooner or later.

137

CRANSTON: You wouldn't want to compare the mischief perpetrated in God's name with the mischief done in behalf of the Third Reich or the Third International, would you?

TURNER: I'm not so sure. If religious power-brokers of the past had had access to some of the weapons of mass destruction that the twentieth century has produced, we might not be here discussing the matter. Can you imagine the scenarios that would have resulted if the Crusaders under Pope Innocent III or the Anabaptist revolutionaries under Thomas Münzer had been in possession of that presidential brief case with the "nuclear button"? I suspect that no great degree of self-control would have been manifested.

CRANSTON: If you cited Ghengis Khan or Nero as your examples, you might have a stronger argument. But in any case, the telltale factor is not religion or the absence of it, but the dynamics of power mixed with appreciable degrees of madness. There is no tried-and-true defense against insanity.

TURNER: My point is that the Christian religion doesn't seem to mollify and humanize the drive for power, or even give a boost to the mental health of those in power. And a charismatic but loony leader who spouts off commands in the name of God is too much of a burden for any world which aspires to rationality.

CRANSTON: But religion rightly understood—and separated from political power—does reduce the probability of such an event. And this *separation of domains* is precisely the boon we moderns have derived from secularization.

TURNER: I thought you saw secularization as a step backward.

CRANSTON: Yes and No. I would want to differentiate the reductionistic secularization of, e.g. Voltaire, Feuerbach, and Marx from the moderate secularization of, e.g. Kant or Hegel. The former group are religious devotees of the replacement of religion; the latter have simply taken positions leading up to separate but complementary domains. Thus Kant, advocating the establishment of a rational kingdom of morality, takes care to leave room for faith and religion as a distinct sphere complementary to the rational sphere; and Hegel, while emphasizing *Sittlichkeit* and constitutionalism as the natural expressions of the Christian spirit, nevertheless insists that Christianity is a *sine qua non* if there are ever to be such expressions.

TURNER: I don't think Löwith or Voegelin would agree with your categorization of Hegel as a "moderate" secularizer.

CRANSTON: Löwith pinpoints Hegel as being the historical source of much of the secularization that has taken place in the nineteenth and twentieth centuries, but he explicitly recognizes that Hegel's position is "neither sacred nor profane";[39] he characterizes it as a "Realized transcendence"—something similar to the "realized eschatology" of some theologians.[40]   Just as those theologians maintain that the kingdom of God was realized with the coming of Jesus, Hegel held that the "beyond" of Absolute Spirit has finally been assimilated in the coming-to-self-consciousness of the modern world—a world wherein philosophy is entrusted with the task of putting the truths of Christianity into conceptual form, justifying Providence, and maintaining the flame of eschatology in everyday life and politics. It's a very complex and nuanced kind of "secularization" that many have tried to oversimplify. It's little wonder that Hegel has become the Promethean model of atheism to some, and a Buddhist-style mystic to others who picked up on other parts of his message. But he is neither.

TURNER: So you are advocating the nuanced ambivalence of a "realized transcendence"?

CRANSTON: No. I am no Hegelian on this issue. Hegel himself didn't go far enough. In most other areas in his philosophical system, he advocates a paradoxical state of unity-in-distinction, sometimes even going to the trouble of using the formula, "identity of identity and difference."[41]   But his interpretation of the relationship between religion and secular life seems to be more in terms of a synthetic unity, rather than the more complex unity-in-distinction. No doubt this was due to his concern for differentiating the presumably more harmonious Protestant approach from

---

[39]*The Meaning of History*, pp. 58-9.
[40]See above, p. 62.
[41]Hegel, *Werke* 2:96.

what he perceived to be endemic conflict between the Catholic Church and the state for political power. A more consistently Hegelian model would seem to me to be one which combined cooperation with constructive competition, separation with coordination. Nevertheless, he was clearly not a card-carrying member of the reductionist secularization camp.

TURNER: Your defense of "moderate" secularization is reminiscent of Harvey Cox's *Secular City*—a celebration of the coming-to-maturity of religion in modern secular expressions, without any of the hostility to traditional religion characteristic of the "reductive" type of secularization.

CRANSTON: Not quite. Cox's celebration of the "secular city" was based on the relaxation of the non-pluralistic, oppressive domination of religion over peoples' lives. But the secularization of the 60s which he was trying to interpret was taken to extremes in the "death of God" movement, spearheaded by theologians who had great difficulty explaining how they differed from atheists purely and simply. But such movements lost steam, religion showed a great resurgence in the 70s, and Cox reversed himself,[42] acknowledging that he had failed to notice the dawn of a "post-modern" era in religion and theology. And Cox is not alone in backing out of the secularization corner. Even Marxists have reversed themselves. Initially there were just a few lone voices like the maverick Marxist student of the Bible, Ernst Bloch, and other revisionist Marxists like Sean Sayers and the American Michael Harrington, who bemoaned the lack of "transcendence" in Marxism, without quite wanting to return to the religious brand of transcendence. Now there is a massive return to religion in areas of the world that used to be considered strongholds of atheistic Marxism.

TURNER: Do I detect a "return to old-time religion" thesis here?

CRANSTON: No. Things have changed. What's important now is to let religion be religion, secularly involved without claiming political power in name of religion. And let the secular sphere be secular and humanistic, in constructive competition with religion for the

---

[42]See *Religion in the Secular City*, p. 19-20.

benefit of humanity, without trying to reduce religion to secularity or exert power over religion in the name of the state.

TURNER: This sounds to me like a description of what liberal democracy and liberal-democratic socialism, as two branches of the sort of "moderate" secularity you favor, are already doing.

CRANSTON: This, perhaps more than economic and political factors, or a "Hegelian" "end of history," or the "triumph of capitalism," explains the success of liberal democracy and democratic socialism. They have given due attention to human nature, with its ineradicable religious instincts, as well as its mixture of selfishness and altruism.

TURNER: Also a certain element of luck! It has been quite fortunate for us that the fatal worldwide economic crises of capitalism predicted by Marx, as well as the Soviet nuclear first-strike predicted by the "cold warriors," never reared their ugly heads. Or would you call that "Providence"? A reward divinely bestowed on the Christian "West" for tolerating religion and encouraging religious pluralism?

CRANSTON: To take a position on "luck vs. providence" is to take a side—secularization vs. religion. I think it would be more accurate to say that the success is due to a combination of luck or Providence with the fact that these liberal systems have taken over in the secular sphere some of the main values of the Christian tradition—equality of all men, value of the person, freedom of conscience, etc.

TURNER: Considering the continuance of racism, sexism, ethnocentrism, nationalism and religious bigotry in these systems, I would suggest your apologetic for Western democracy is premature.

CRANSTON: Possibly. I was merely observing that the openness to religion and religious values, combined with flexibility and the possibility of change, are plus-factors. In practice they do involve some reductive secularization, and only approximate to the moderate secularization which I would defend.

TURNER: You have taken Marxism as the example of reductive secularization in political theory. Do you discern any major models for non-reductionistic, "moderate" secularization in political theory?

CRANSTON: I think a good contemporary example is Neal Riemer's theory of "prophetic politics."[43] Riemer sees "liberal democratic" politics as an important compromise between pragmatic "Machiavellian" politics and impractical "utopian" politics, but deficient because of its provincialism and utilitarian social consciousness. As the next step beyond liberal democratic theory he proposes prophetic politics, which combines universalism (commitment to peace, freedom, justice, love, truth and prosperity for all), with a commitment to the least free, and a strategic criticism of the deficiency of governments in implementing such values. He openly recognizes that this would be a secular continuation of a tradition that begins with the Old Testament prophets, but suggests that we take over this tradition in the purely secular sphere and make it our own. This is secularization become self-conscious—realizing its debt to religion, but reviving the tradition of prophecy in an autonomous, "secular" fashion independent of any religious commitments.

TURNER: Who can disagree with Riemer's ideals—universal compassion, liberation of the oppressed, etc.? But is it a model for politics? I think not. It seems overly platitudinous to me. Everyone will nod in assent: "those are great ideas." But they are not likely to inspire mobilization.

CRANSTON: Admittedly, Riemer's theory is not highly elaborated like Marxism. But he is doing what Marx did *sans* reductionism. It's a good start.

TURNER: Riemer seems to have his problems differentiating the new approach he advocates from the approach of Marxism.

CRANSTON: But haven't we encountered a similar difficulty ourselves: that Marxism and other such systems have derived their broad appeal from being "wolves in sheep's clothing," so to

---

[43]Neal Riemer, *The Future of the Democratic Revolution*, Part III.

speak—sporting the regalia of religion without any of the inner content? Riemer's difficulty runs parallel to our own.

TURNER: I think he is simply inconsistent, characterizing Marxism pejoratively as "utopian" in *The Future of the Democratic Revolution*, and then agonizing over whether Marxism is truly a utopian theory, or actually a major step in the prophetic direction, in his follow-up book, *Karl Marx and Prophetic Politics*.

CRANSTON: Marx himself seems to have purposely tried to create a smoke screen in that respect, coming out so strongly against "utopian" socialists, whereas he was the most utopian of all—thoroughly unrealistic about human nature, thoroughly romantic about the para-celestial communistic society that was coming.

TURNER: But without that "utopian" element, would anyone have *listened* to him? You can't mobilize a third of the world with realistic, down-to-earth calculations of probabilities for the social engineering of polymorphously motivated, fallible man.

CRANSTON: I think you have put your finger on a major "occupational hazard" for those who would like to accomplish some of the objectives traditionally pursued by religion, but without the religious prerequisites for motivation.

TURNER: If the religious motivation were more unequivocally focused on justice and equality, and were clearer and more accessible to a broad spectrum of humanity, perhaps Marx and the "atheistic humanists" wouldn't need to go to such trouble to compensate for perceived deficiencies in the "real thing."

XVIII. Religious Experience, Chosenness, and Political Expression

I find it hard to believe that principles can exist which make no difference in facts. But all facts are particular facts, and the whole interest of the question of God's existence seems to me to lie in the consequences for particulars which that existence may be expected to entail. That no concrete particular of experience should alter its complexion in consequence of a God being there seems to me an incredible proposition.... The appearance is that in ["prayerful communion"] something ideal, which in one sense is part of ourselves and in another sense is not ourselves, actually exerts an influence, raises our centre of personal energy, and produces regenerative effects unattainable in other ways. —William James, *The Varieties of Religious Experience*

Everyone's true happiness and blessedness consists solely in the enjoyment of good, not in priding himself that he alone is enjoying that good to the exclusion of others.... Surely [the Hebrews] would have been no less blessed if God had called all men equally to salvation, nor would God have been less close to them for being equally close to others.... [They believed] that their kingdom was God's kingdom and that they alone were God's children, while the other nations were God's enemies for whom they therefore felt an implacable hatred. —Baruch Spinoza, *Tractatus Theologico-Politicus*

[The Jews] survived 2,000 years of discrimination, lack of equality and persecution not because of their power but because of their loyalty to their ideals and their indestructible faith in a better future, in being "the chosen people...." —Nahum Goldmann, "Zionist Ideology and the Reality of Israel"

The cult of unity on the political level is only an idolatrous *ersatz* for the genuine religion of unity on the personal and spiritual levels. —Aldous Huxley, *The Perennial Philosophy*

It is possible that there is some dovetailing between "religious experiences" and the psychological state that Freud dubbed the "oceanic experience" and which other psychologists have referred to as "peak experiences"—sudden feelings of elation and fulfillment that seem to come unbidden. At the outer fringes of psychopathology, such feelings may form part of psychotic syndromes such as the manic phase of manic-depressive psychosis. But non-psychotic and probably healthy religious experiences, although ordinarily short-lived and often superficial, also seem to be common among the general populace, and particularly in evangelical denominations such as Pentecostalism, which feature highly emotional communally-encouraged expressions of religious devotion.

"Religious experience" is also used by some writers, e.g. William James, as more or less synonymous with "mystical experience," which generally connotes something more profound, less on the periphery of emotions and psychic reactions, and sometimes so long-lasting that it becomes a habitual state. It is this experience that the philosopher Ludwig Wittgenstein refers to at the end of his *Tractatus Logico-Philosophicus* as "the mystical"—a para-cognitive state which is essentially so ineffable that it would be nonsensical (especially for an analytically-oriented philosopher) to try to put it into words and concepts.

Mystical experience seems to be characterized primarily and initially by a sense of extraordinary unity and unification. William James, on the basis of his empirical examination of reports and descriptions of religious experience, gives us the following summary:

> Religious rapture, moral enthusiasm, ontological wonder, cosmic emotion, are all unifying states of mind, in which the sand and grit of the selfhood incline to disappear, and tenderness to rule. The best thing is to describe the condition integrally as a characteristic affection to which our nature is liable, a region in which we find ourselves at home, a sea in which we swim; but not to pretend to explain its parts by deriving them too cleverly from one another.[1]

W. T. Stace, concurring with James on the sense of unity,[2] goes on to say that the experience of unity is more precisely an experience of the unity of the self, which is extrapolated into an ultimate universal and cosmic unity:

---

[1]William James, *The Varieties of Religious Experience*, p. 221.
[2]W.T. Stace, *The Teaching of the Mystics*, p. 21.

> In all cultures, with the possible exception of Buddhism, this
> undifferentiated unity is interpreted as the unity of the self.
> And this unity of the individual ego is further interpreted as
> being either identical with, or at least as having reached
> 'union' (in some sense) with, the Universal Spirit.... The
> fully developed mystical consciousness involves the disappear-
> ance of *all* distinctions, including that between subject and
> object, between the individual self and the Universal Self....[3]

Stace underlines the fact that this experience, in contrast with
most normal experience, is not the experience of any discernible *object*.[4]
Possibly the closest psychic analogies would be states of extreme anxiety
in which the anxious person cannot pinpoint any specific object of fear
or concern, or a state of extreme happiness that cannot be related to any
specific cause. Eric Voegelin relates such experiences to the condition
of *metaxy*, an in-between state which puts consciousness into continuity
with a transcendent dimension, and is essentially non-object-oriented.[5]

But, explains Rudolph Otto, the fact that there is no "object" in
the usual sense in religious-mystical experience does not imply that the
experiencer is locked into him/herself:

> A characteristic common to all types of mysticism is the
> *Identification*, in different degrees of completeness, of the
> personal self with the transcendent Reality.... "Identification"
> alone, however, is not enough for mysticism; it must be
> Identification with the Something that is at once absolutely
> supreme in power and reality and wholly non-rational.[6]

In sum, the experience in question characteristically involves a
sense of absolute fulfillment and unification, coming into play suddenly
and quasi-instinctively; and which in its most intense manifestations
seems to put the subject in contact with, or even make the subject
identical with, a transcendent, absolute Subject. At its deeper intensities
it is overwhelming and unforgettable, and, epistemologically, a matter of
absolute certitude—but still a revelation so mysterious that its expression
cannot even be approximated in conventional language. And just as in
ordinary perception, while there can be no doubt about the actual

---

[3]Ibid., pp. 238-9.

[4]Ibid., p. 22.

[5]See James Rhodes, "Philosophy, Revelation, and Political Theory."

[6]Rudolf Otto, *The Idea of the Holy*, p. 22.

experience of perception, falsity can enter in when the perceiver tries to relate the perception to specific objects or features of objects—so also in mystical experience the initial revelatory certainty of enlightenment *may begin to dim* when the mystic inevitably connects the experience with the symbols most meaningful in his/her religious/cultural horizons.

Diverse interpretations and diverse religious symbolizations seem to result, according to Stace, just at that point where the mystic goes beyond the immediate factual certainty of the experience to interpretations involving a great degree of relativity:

> Every religion can appropriate [this originary undifferentiated unity] and interpret it in terms of its own dogmas. Thus Eckhart interprets it in terms of the doctrine of the Trinity, Plotinus as the One, Buddhism as Nirvana.[7]

Voegelin hypothesizes that the experience of *metaxis* (irruption of the divine into the human order) is common to great philosophers, prophets, founders of religions, and is a major source for them of inspiration, insight or motivation.[8] If this is true, it would seem to follow that the Judaeo-Christian notion of the *kingdom of God* could be best characterized as the unique way that religious founders and prophets in the mainstream Western tradition have interpreted an experience that is generically comparable to, or even identical with, experiences that led in other cultures to the founding of other religions in which other themes were pivotal. Thus, paralleling the development of the Western religions, the great Indian mystics interpreted their yogic experiences in terms of traditional Indian deities, sometimes even concretized in visions connected with the experiences; and the Buddha symbolized his experience in the rich constellation of images that were already accessible in his milieu. This approach to interpretation of the formation of religions, of course, relativizes the variety of symbolizations in the religions of the world, and does nothing to account for a bona fide *incarnation*. But it also absolutizes the source experience from which many religious revelations are hypothesized to emanate, and underlines the possibility and importance of properly interpreting prophetic inspirations: "Prophets can always control their prophetic spirits," St. Paul assures us.[9]

---

[7]W.T. Stace, *The Teaching of the Mystics*, p. 239.
[8]See James Rhodes, "Voegelin and Christian Faith."
[9]1 Cor. 14:32.

If indeed there is some room for interpretation on the part of the mystic or the religious founder who has had the originary experience, one avenue of interpretation would seem to be in the direction of a sense of special election, or *chosenness*. The experience, after all, comes as a gift, unattainable by normal psychic efforts; and the experiencer is lifted up for a time above his ordinary consciousness and the ordinary consciousness that others must have. What is to keep him from concluding that he has been especially selected out by Yahweh, or Brahmin, or even the great void of Nothingness in which the world is thought to hover, for special favors and special prerogatives? What is to keep him from concluding that he is God's favorite, a chosen one, perhaps singled out for some special emissary role? And if the experience were to be shared by a group—e.g. by the Israelites in the desert when they were motivated to make their special covenant with God, or by the early Christians at Pentecost when they were apparently overtaken by the Holy Spirit and began to "speak in tongues"—why should not that group come to the analogous logical conclusion that they were in some special way chosen by God, in preference to all the other groups of people in the human race?

This self-interpretation in terms of chosenness, no doubt common to Moses and David and Jesus and Buddha and Mohammed, as well as Cotton Mather and Joseph Smith, and early Franciscan conventuals and the Puritans and the Amish in America, not to mention contemporary Israeli Zionists, is itself susceptible to multiple and varied extensions and sub-interpretations. There is a paradoxical kind of chosenness, no doubt elicited by a powerful experience, which is oriented to *self-effacement* and dissolution—such that one is singled out to be freed from individuality and isolated selfhood, and be one with Nirvana like Buddha, or be dissolved so that "only Christ lives" in the self like St. Paul, or like Meister Eckhardt to be so unified with the deity that the distinction between deity and self is completely abrogated. There is also a *mission-oriented* feeling of chosenness, which constituted the theme of much of the prophetic literature of the Old Testament—a universalist potentiation and extension of God's concern not just for the Israelites, but also for Niniveh[10], for the Ethiopians and Philistines,[11] for Egypt and Assyria[12] and Moab[13] and all nations.[14] It is in this prophetic context that

---

[10]See the book of Jonas, passim.

[11]Amos 9:7.

[12]Isaiah 19:25.

[13]Jerem. 48:31.

the particularism of the Yahwist religion is seen to be tied in with, and complementary to, universalism, although still falling short of the unqualified universalist ideals of Christianity.[15]

But there is also an *exclusivist* chosenness, extrapolating what seems to be a special concern and providence of God into preferential and discriminatory treatment for particular individuals or particular groups—leading to separatism, devaluation of outsiders, and hatreds with genocidal potential. This is the interpretation of chosenness that led the Psalmist(s) to claim for the Israelites a kind of "territorial right of eminent domain" in the world:

> Yahweh...led his happy people forward, to joyful shouts from his chosen, and gave them the pagan's territories. Where others had toiled, they took possession, on condition that they kept his statutes and remained obedient to his laws.[16] To put them [the Israelites] in the land you dispossessed the nations, you harried the peoples to make room for them.[17]

And the path from eminent domain to world domination is also outlined:

> Yahweh brings the peoples under our dominion, he puts the nations under our feet; for us he chooses our heritage—the pride of Jacob, whom he loved.[18]

The prophet Amos draws attention to the fallaciousness of this brand of chosenness, which implies that Israel is somehow God's pet and that God has not done marvelous things for other nations like Ethiopia:

> Are you not just like Ethiopia's sons to me, sons of Israel?
> ...Did I not bring Israel up from the land of Egypt—and the Philistines from Caphtor, and the Arameans from Kir?[19]

---

[14]Malachi 2:10; Isaiah 52:10, 56:7.

[15]Dale Patrick, "The Kingdom of God in the Old Testament," pp. 76-7.

[16]Psalm 105:42-45.

[17]Psalm 44:2.

[18]Psalm 47:3-4.

[19]Amos 9:7.

The separatist and exclusivist tendencies that Amos castigates were, according to Voegelin, continued in Talmudic Judaism[20]—tendencies which were interpreted by gentiles as misanthropic (*odium generis humani*), and which involved much backsliding from the universalism of late Judaism:

> The universalist implications of the experience [of a transcendent-divine reality] were never successfully explicated within Israelite history. The spiritual meaning of the exodus from civilization was well understood but nevertheless remained inseparable from the concrete Exodus from Egypt; the Kingdom of God could never quite separate from Canaan; the great original revelation remained so overwhelmingly concrete that its spiritual renewals had to assume the literary form of additions to the Instructions; and the word of God to mankind through Israel became the sacred scripture of a particular ethnico-religious community.[21]

Thus, Voegelin concludes, Yahwism became a major obstacle to the universalism extolled by the prophets.[22]

One might reasonably expect that Christianity, which characterized itself as the "faithful remnant"—the true Israelites signalized not by tribal or ethnic heritage but by faith—would be able to avoid the pitfalls of extreme separatism, exclusivism and elite superiority/dominance with relationship to outsiders. But under Catholicism, such tendencies evolved into the paradoxical extreme of an officially "universal" church considering itself separated out from most of the world for special privileges and protection from God, and even having the exclusive access to eternal salvation. The fact that the majority of people in the world who did not belong to the Church could not be saved was spelled out in the famous formula of the Fourth Lateran Council (1215) —"Outside the Church there is no salvation"—and, in case there were any doubt as to the final destiny of those outside the Church, the ecumenical council of Florence in 1442 went on to decree that

> The holy Roman Church ... firmly believes, confesses, and proclaims that no one outside the Catholic Church, neither heathen nor Jew nor unbeliever nor schismatic will have a

---

[20]Eric Voegelin, *Order and History* I, p. 144.

[21]Ibid., p. 164.

[22]Ibid., p. 216.

> share in eternal life, but rather is condemned to the eternal fire
> prepared for the devil and his angels, unless he joins [the
> Catholic Church] before his death.[23]

Until the mid-sixties and Vatican II, when this position was defused, many sincere Catholic theologians, convinced that it was wrong to take the catholicity out of Catholicism, expended considerable and commendable effort in showing how someone outside the Church could still belong to the "soul" of the Church or be excused from his non-membership because of "invincible" ignorance. But should such effort really have been necessary in a "universal" religion?

Non-Catholic denominations, not to be outdone by the Catholics, also developed exclusivist interpretations of chosenness. Some major contenders to chosenness in recent centuries have been the Puritans, under whose influence early American colonists began to consider themselves the true Israelites fleeing from Babylon (the Old World) to the New Canaan (America) by means of a mass baptism (the crossing of the Atlantic), in order to establish God's kingdom on earth, a New Zion.[24] In the nineteenth century the Mormons in America, claiming to be descendants of the "lost tribes of Israel," established a revised version of Zion in which salvation was restricted to an extremely minuscule group of people living on the face of the earth. A Calvinist version of chosenness was propagated in South Africa by Afrikaaners, whose trek inward from Cape Colony in 1837, resulting in the killing of thousands of natives along the way, was likened to the flight of Israel from Egypt to the Promised Land (in 1934 extremist Afrikaaners declared their "purified National Party" to be "God's chosen people").

Depending on which direction the self-consciousness of a "chosen" group takes, the expressions of chosenness in the world will be sharply divergent: On the one hand, the sense of being divinely empowered and protected can confer a consciousness of freedom from the cosmic cycles of nature which rule the destinies of all beings; and the sense of being directed by a divine spirit and law may carry with it a consciousness of freedom from human authorities, and especially from self-described "divine" nations and monarchs. In short, it may impart that spark of spiritual freedom that is the *sine qua non* for obtaining and perpetuating the "open society" that Karl Popper deems essential for the perpetuation of freedom of thought and speech and action, or for

---

[23]Cited by Hans Küng, *Theology for the Third Millennium*, p. 231.
[24]See Sacvan Bercovitch, *The Puritan Origins of the American Self.*

supplying that orientation to "transcendence" that Eric Voegelin considers to be necessary for proper orientation towards a "universal" (not provincial, not nationalistic, not "ecumenical"-totalitarian) mankind. A direct, "vertical" conscientious relationship with, and answerability to, God alone, is implied in one's "chosen" status, and this is necessarily coupled with a strong conviction of one's worth as an individual. Complementary and corresponding to this "vertical" relationship is a "horizontal" coordination with those who are similarly graced (which in a pluralistic approach may include other groups besides one's own), and a fraternal concern for all those outside the "chosen" groups whose well-being and enlightenment is taken on by the "chosen" as a mission connected with their own prerogatives.

In further extensions, the same sense of chosenness, interpreted as a constellation of privileges and a base of power, can lead to the phenomenon that Henri Bergson calls "crystallization"—the "crystallization, brought about by a scientific process of cooling, of what mysticism had poured, while hot, into the soul of men."[25] In other words, just as Jacob was singled out for a vision of the "kingdom of God" in a dream, and subsequently vowed to build a temple commemorating the sacred site on which this revelation had been received[26]—the group bound together by mystical commitment will very likely feel impelled to enshrine the experiences that brought them together in organized, institutionalized religions and/or political traditions. This same process may also lead to the formation of ideal societies—religious communities dedicated to the systematic pursuit of a higher type of perfection, such as the Benedictines or the Mennonites.

This process of crystallization may be conjoined with what Eric Voegelin calls *metastasis*, an attempted complete-overhaul in the constitution of being itself, to make it conform to a prophetic vision.[27] In its more positive and beneficial manifestations, *metastasis* resulted in Second Isaiah's portrayal of a peaceful world centered around a reconstituted Israel. But carried to an extreme it led to utopian visions of men led completely by the spirit of God in a paradisiacal new earth, and/or of a completely unified world order (what Voegelin calls "ecumenical" unity) under the aegis of God himself.

It seems a long way from the highly subjective kinds of experiences that seem to be entailed in mysticism to the socio-political

---

[25]Henri Bergson, *The Two Sources of Morality and Religion*, p. 227.
[26]See Genesis 28:10-22; Wisdom 10:9-10.
[27]Eric Voegelin, *Order and History* I, p. 452.

sphere; and it may be possible that for some mystics without the charisma of leadership or the talent for rhetoric the experience may remain merely interior and private. But we cannot bank on this. The fact that the experience can be translated into objectivity in counterproductive and destructive ways has led some to opt for the construction of a humanistic world, free of the possible dangers attendant upon religion. This would be quite an ambitious undertaking, no doubt comparable to some of the utopian or "ecumenical" ventures undertaken at times in the name of religion; but with very little hope of success, since it would require the eradication of religious experience itself, which seems to be at least a constant in human nature, if not something on the level of an instinct, as some have suggested.

However, it might be worthwhile to contemplate what might result if such calls for the abolition of religion met with success. Would it result in the world envisaged by Dmitri in Dostoevski's *The Brothers Karamozov*, in which people, no longer restrained by religious inhibitions, would feel free to do whatever they liked, as long as they could get away with it? Updating Dostoevski, Glenn Tinder suggests in a recent article that

> We cannot give up the Christian God—and go on as before. We must give up Christian morality too. If the God-man is nothing more than an illusion, the same thing is true of the idea that every individual possesses incalculable worth.[28]

Tinder is also in effect reopening the question raised by Hegel: if a virtuous citizenry is the backbone of "republican" government, is not religion a necessary, although not a sufficient, foundation for the virtuous citizenry? Can modern democracies maintain their commitments to equality without the belief that each person is created in the image of God? Can governments find other more efficient means of inculcating a sense of fraternity and prevent society and the marketplace from becoming a manifestation of "survival of the fittest," in the absence of any belief in the fatherhood of God giving rise to the brotherhood of men? Can the belief in individual liberty survive in an atmosphere in which there prevails a necessary and exclusive subjection to, and conditioning by, a variety of environmental and hereditary causes? Will there be any institutionalized, strategic check on the excesses of power-

---

[28]Glenn Tinder, "Can We be Good Without God?" *Atlantic Monthly*, De. 1989, p. 80.

appropriation to which governments are prone, to take the place of the moral checks that used to come from religions? And are we willing to engage in some wholesale "controlled scientific experiment" with atheism and irreligion, to see whether the socio-political situation of most citizens would improve or deteriorate?

XIX. Does Democracy need Redefinition?

Of the three [democratic values, liberty, equality and fraternity], it is liberty that is the dearest, whose absence is most painful, whose limitation is most quickly noted. —Carl Cohen, *Democracy*

It is evident that all forms of the state have democracy for their truth, and for that reason are false to the extent that they are not democracy. —Karl Marx, *Critique of Hegel's Philosophy of Right*

Democracy in [the] broader sense has always contained an ideal of human equality, not just equality of opportunity to climb a class ladder, but such an equality as could only be fully realized in a society where no class was able to dominate or live at the expense of others. —C. B. Macpherson, *The Real World of Democracy*

The democratic method is that institutional arrangement for arriving at political decisions in which individuals (i.e. the elite, and potential representatives of the people) acquire the power to decide by means of a competitive struggle for the people's vote. —Joseph Schumpeter, *Capitalism, Socialism and Democracy*

[Democracy is] the continuous effort of the citizens through the medium of government to maintain society in a state of limited equilibrium between extremes of chaos and tyranny. —M. ten Hoor, *Freedom Limited*

CRANSTON: I think we are agreed that religious commitment to the Kingdom can have portentous implications for politics, for good or for ill. If this is true, we should consider the specific implications of the idea of the Kingdom for democracy. But this is more easily said than done. Democracy is not at all a clear-

157

cut concept. Some define it in terms of liberty, others in terms of equality, institutionalized competition for votes, etc.

TURNER: Recently I was on a committee which was concerned with bringing in some noted speakers on democratic themes. One of the committee members, a journalist, at the very outset of the meeting, commented, "for God's sake, let's not have any more of this stuff about how democracy is defined." He wanted to get lecturers who would concentrate on concrete practical problems. He was particularly concerned about the state of democracy in Mexico and other countries in which opposition political parties exist only in name, because of the tight control exercised by the party in power.

CRANSTON: That very example illustrates a "practical" problem not unrelated to problems of definition: If you define democracy in terms of multiple political parties, and if the incumbent party can always rearrange things to make a fair election practically impossible, the definition turns out to be inadequate. You have an incentive to go back to the drawing board.

TURNER: I doubt that changing the definition of democracy will help opposition parties anywhere. In any case, it may be next to impossible to get any consensus on a definition. I can't help thinking about that now-famous judge who, when asked to define what he meant by—excuse the comparison—pornography, said, "I can't define it. But I know it when I see it." It's one thing to know something, and quite another to be able to define it.

CRANSTON: I wouldn't be so pessimistic about the limits of human reason, and about the possibility of getting an agreement of the majority on a working definition, if not a 100% consensus. Like the notion of a "kingdom of God," the idea of democracy is complex. On the other hand, it is our creation; democracy didn't just descend on mankind as a revelation from on high. If we created it, we should be able to glean a fairly good idea of what it is.

TURNER: I presume that's the editorial "we" that you are referring to. What do you think it is that "we" created?

CRANSTON: Government of the people, by the people, for the people. Which is what the ancient Greeks before us also created, I believe.

TURNER: We must take into account the fact that the Greeks had a very different view of "people" than ourselves. They excluded slaves and women from political processes; and the poor were practically excluded—because of their lack of leisure for engaging in politics, because of the fact that they owned no house in Athens or the Peiraieus to facilitate their attendance at the assemblies, etc.

CRANSTON: Granted, there are some important differences between our more extensive concept of democracy and theirs. But if we concentrate on what they were trying to *avoid*, we find a notable similarity. They were intent on avoiding the possibility of tyranny, and they applied themselves to constructing constitutional bulwarks to hedge against that possibility. They had different "tyrants" in mind than we, of course; but aside from that their objectives were kindred to our own.

TURNER: If democracy is a measure devised against tyranny, it's ironic that Plato considered democracy to be the next step on the way to tyranny.[29]

CRANSTON: Yes, but he reasoned that tyranny was commonly a reaction to the extreme indirection and chaos that was associated (in his estimation) with democracy; he argued that any kind of leadership becomes a welcome relief from such extreme chaos. It is of course possible that the decentralization connected with democracy will be carried to a chaotic extreme. But this doesn't have to be the case.

TURNER: To Plato, and to elitists in general, too much democracy spells indirection and discord. But if chaos is not an essential characteristic of democracy, what is?

---

[29]*Republic* VIII, #562-4.

CRANSTON: *Decentralization* sticks in my mind as the chief salient characteristic of democracy—an equal and opposite reaction to the centralizing tendencies of political power-brokers.

TURNER: Decentralization goes back further than the Greek invention of democracy. It began the first time a monarch decided to share power with counselors or nobles. Democracy just carries this process further to the grass-roots—or what are considered at the time to be the grass-roots.

CRANSTON: It's in this context that John Bright is justified in referring to the ancient Israelite confederacy as a "democracy,"[30] although democracy hadn't officially been invented. Moses, with the help of a timely divine revelation, decided to share his authority with seventy elders,[31] and devised a system of local government under "judges."[32] The keynote was local autonomy, with occasional confederate alliances for fighting wars. The arrangement was similar to the Greek amphictyonic leagues.[33]

TURNER: The big difference between the "decentralization" of such confederacies and Athenian democracy was, of course, that the Athenians consciously chose decentralization, and endeavored to institutionalize it, when they could have chosen otherwise.

CRANSTON: To take that circumstance into account, we could say that decentralization is a genus, and both confederation and democracy are species of decentralization, the latter being characterized by greater consciousness and constitutional planning.

TURNER: Would you consider the republic as still another stage in decentralization?

CRANSTON: Yes. It seems to me to be a new and revised species of decentralization after democracy, fit for larger populations, and prudently equipped with a suitably powerful elite group to keep populism from degenerating into tyranny.

---

[30]*The Kingdom of God*, p. 31.
[31]Numbers 11:14ff.
[32]Deut. 16:18.
[33]See above, p. 29.

TURNER: And lest this more moderate, large-scale species of decentralization be carried too far, empire was very soon reintroduced and carried the day in the middle ages.

CRANSTON: The feudal system provided a timely counterpoint to the centralizing propensities of empire. But it seems to me that the real turning point out of the grinding mechanisms of centralization in the middle ages was Joachim of Fiore's "stage of the Holy Spirit."[34] This was not just abstract theory; certain pathfinding groups of followers actually tried to put his theory into practice.

TURNER: But this is not exactly a species of political decentralization.

CRANSTON: The distinction of "political" and "religious" in the middle ages is more of a mental distinction than a real distinction. In the context of highly centralized ecclesiastical/political control, Joachim preached the advent of direct rule by the Holy Spirit. No more obeisance to hierarchies and lords. No more mediators. Even his scheme of trinitarian decentralization—replacement of the law of the Father and the Son with the indwelling inspiration of the Holy Spirit—had political implications. The Law of the Father and the Son was, after all, promulgated and administered to a great extent by both religious and political authorities.

TURNER: If you include Joachim as a milestone in decentralizing tendencies in the context of combined church-state hegemony, you would also have to include Martin Luther, who seemed to define once and for all for many Christians what freedom from hierarchies and direct guidance by the Holy Spirit involved.

CRANSTON: Yes. There is, of course, the problem that Luther's politics were arch-conservative. But the principles that he set in motion in the ecclesiastical realm did seem, in spite of his politics, to carry over logically into the political realm, as Hegel observed.[35]

---

[34]See p. 90 above.
[35]See above, p. 114.

TURNER: Yet while Hegel makes Protestantism the basis for a "free society," he is no champion of democracy. Hegel seems to be on a different wave-length than we are with regard to the term, "democracy."

CRANSTON: As were many others in the Enlightenment and post-Enlightenment eras—including Rousseau, Jefferson, and Madison. They were using the term in the strict sense, with Athens as the prototype. And like Plato[36] who in his later work opted for a political mixture of monarchy and democracy, and Aristotle[37] who recommended a combination of oligarchy and democracy, the American founding fathers specifically favored a "mixed government," which they called a "democratic republic."

TURNER: That expression seems to introduce even further terminological confusion. The idea of a republic as conceived by Polybius[38] was supposed to be a judicious *mixture* of the best of monarchy, aristocracy and democracy. So a "democratic republic" would be a mixture of a mixture and something contained in the mixture!

CRANSTON: They were closer to the usage of Montesquieu than Polybius. Montesquieu defines republics as governments in which power is invested in the people, but divides republics up into "democratic" and "aristocratic." They also adopted Montesquieu's idea of a clear separation of executive, legislative and judicial powers. The result is what we now call "representative democracy"—"democracy," for short.

TURNER: And so, when we use the term "democracy" nowadays, what we really *mean* is "mixed government"—a sort of middle-of-the-road government trying to straddle the fence in various ways between extreme the-people-be-damned centralization and the unmanageable chaos and anarchy that would ensue if the masses actually took political matters into their own hands.

---

[36]*Laws* VI, #757.
[37]*Politics* II,6;IV, 11-12.
[38]*Histories* III, 6.

CRANSTON: And the term "republican," as applied to governments (not political parties), has also in the meantime become functionally synonymous with "democratic."

TURNER: But the American "republican" or "democratic" system differs from other similar systems in view of the additional federative principle.

CRANSTON: The creation of a "federal" republic by the founding fathers is of a piece with their general gravitation towards "mixed government." It was meant to counterbalance the extreme decentralization of the former confederation of the colonies. And it seems to me that the development of the Federal Republic of Germany after World War II was comparable to this, insofar as it was a move to counterbalance the traditional extreme decentralization of the various *Lände* that make up Germany.

TURNER: It is interesting that "democratization" in contemporary usage has come to mean almost exclusively the decentralization of erstwhile Marxist regimes.

CRANSTON: Which is their way of creating their own version of "mixed government."

TURNER: If we consider the evolution of democracy and democratization since the time of the Athenian experiment, it seems that a major problem all along has been bigness—maintaining the ideals of decentralization for larger and more diverse populations. Both Machiavelli in his *Discourses* and Montesquieu in his *Spirit of the Laws* thought modern states to be caught up in a dilemma between the endemic weakness and security problems of a small republic, and the tendencies to factional disintegration in larger republics. A few years later, David Hume in his *Idea of the Perfect Commonwealth* championed the idea that a large republic, well constructed, would be able to avoid such disintegrative tendencies. Some American founders, reflecting such political theories and drawing on their own experience with the divisiveness attending their erstwhile Articles of Confederation, went to great lengths to stave off the possibility of future disintegration by a combination of popular sovereignty with strong national federalism.

CRANSTON: Madison and Hamilton, it is true, were sanguine about bigness, and the type of diversity that could keep petty factionalism at bay in a large republic. But the architecture they devised for bringing about unity-in-diversity often seems to be inadequate for the accomplishment of its designs. Extremely heterogeneous racial, ethnic and religious mixtures with strong inner cohesiveness and limited interaction outside the group constantly appear on the horizon, and are a challenge to any large democratic republic. It's much easier to keep it smoothly functioning with a more homogeneous population. Hence the highly restrictive immigration laws in many countries.

TURNER: On the other hand, isn't pluralism almost an essential characteristic of *modern* democracy? Could we, for instance, have a democracy for just one ethnic, religious or racial group and exclude all others?

CRANSTON: This of course approximates the situation in Israel today. Although Arabs in Israel can become citizens, only Jews are able to be Israeli nationals. Major privileges, administered by the World Zionist Organization/Jewish Agency (Status) Law, are allotted only to Jewish Nationals. The ethnic, and to a great extent religious, homogeneity of Israeli nationals is a strategic check to the disintegration and disorder that could have been attendant on the massive immigration of non-Jews.

TURNER: Statutory homogeneity of that sort seems *prima facie* to be an elitism contradictory to the pluralistic spirit of democracy.

CRANSTON: There is no democratic rule book with the guidelines for pluralism. Theoretically, you could have a democracy just for Catholics, or just for blacks (Jefferson once suggested setting up a separate state just for emancipated slaves), or just for Palestinians (if e.g. some portion of the Middle East were set aside to build a Palestinian state). The Jews could also claim with some credibility that there is so much diversity among them that there is no danger of their becoming a completely homogeneous society.

TURNER: But I think you and I and most people would be unreceptive to the idea of an exclusively Catholic, or black, or expatriate Italian democracy. Are we making an exception with regard to the Jews, and possibly also the Palestinians?

CRANSTON: I think the misgivings I detect in your question are analogous to those I have about "chosenness," which can easily degenerate into exclusiveness combined with a sense of superiority over others. This is a development that has explosive potential, whether in religion or in politics.

TURNER: By "explosive potential" you mean, for example, a situation where the Israelis began to consider themselves not just separate and equal, but a superior species of humanity—something on the order of Hitler's "Master Race." But it is almost inconceivable that survivors of the Holocaust could take on such fascist characteristics.

CRANSTON: I find it unimaginable.

TURNER: But there is an additional problem that has to do with consistency: If there is, as you say, no "rule book" dictating guidelines for pluralism, how can we consistently make a distinction between the exclusion of non-Jews from the full rights accorded to Jewish nationals in Israel and the exclusion of non-whites from the rights accorded to whites in South Africa? Why should not the white South Africans have an analogous right to set up a democracy (republic) for whites only? Why do we associate apartheid necessarily with prejudice and discrimination, rather than a "separate but equal" setup?

CRANSTON: I think that the major difference in the two cases is that the United Nations Organization set up the state of Israel to solve a major world problem of resettlement. It was done in the interests of world order and world peace by the only representative body of the nations of the world. But no such act of the world community was involved with the Boer settlements in South Africa.

TURNER: The U.N. didn't cede the West Bank and Gaza to the Israelis.

CRANSTON: It seems to me that Israel's appropriation of these territories was a direct result of the U.N.'s abdication of its duties of providing security for Israel after setting up the political apparatus. So the Israelis in the security vacuum felt it necessary to take matters into their own hands.

TURNER: So we need a U.N. security force on the borders of Israel in perpetuum to keep the two sides apart? You seem to have a different and much more cohesive U.N. in mind than I do.

CRANSTON: Possibly the U.N. made a mistake in the way they handled the Jewish resettlement problem. But they would also be the logical choice to remedy the mistake.

TURNER: Paradoxically, it seems to me that the greatest security for Israel would be in assimilation. Some early Zionists had suggested that Jews and Palestinians should live and interact in Israel as equals. If their advice had been followed, would resentment have built up to the present heights?

CRANSTON: Would "assimilation" be possible with security, and without losing their religious identity?

TURNER: Jews lived in Muslim-controlled lands for centuries, and fared generally quite well—much better than they did in Christian lands. The great pogroms and persecutions were at Christian hands. In regard to the religious-identity concern, varying degrees of assimilation are conceivable. Assimilation doesn't necessarily entail intermarriage, compromise on dietary laws, etc.

CRANSTON: The Jews who inhabited Israel were mostly from Europe, and came with very different experiences regarding tolerance, or the lack of it. They were also very distinct culturally because of the same European background. And they were met with hostility, when they expected the Palestinian inhabitants to welcome them. They could have assimilated, and possibly should still do so. In any case, that is one "buck" that doesn't stop at the U.N.

TURNER: There is one "buck" that does stop at the U.N.: namely, that an international organization with the assent of its democratic membership should have set up a national entity which would almost certainly encounter insuperable problems in maintaining democratic structures.

CRANSTON: That was paradoxical, but no doubt unavoidable, given the historical situation at the end of World War II.

TURNER: There are many watershed events in history that lead to speculative questions as to whether they were avoidable or not. And this is certainly such an event. But it is euphemistic to call it "paradoxical." It was no paradox, but a contradiction—a contradiction which still has to be resolved.

XX. The Dialectics of Democracy

Two great divisions ... have always existed in free communities.   The deeper we penetrate into the inmost thought of
[political] parties the more do we perceive that the object of
the one is to limit, and that of the other to extend, the authority
of the people.... Aristocratic or democratic passions may easily
be detected at the bottom of all parties.... —Alexis de Tocqueville, *Democracy in America*

What is at the heart of the difference between [the constrained and unconstrained visions of human nature] is the
question as to whether human capabilities or potential permit
social decisions to be made collectively through the articulated
rationality of surrogates, so as to produce the specific social
results desired....   Pending the ultimate achievement of an
unconstrained society, the locus of discretion in the unconstrained vision is the surrogate decision-maker (individual or
institutional), choosing a collective optimum.... By contrast, in
the constrained vision, the loci of discretion are virtually as
numerous as the population.... The unconstrained vision is
clearly at home on the political left..., but the constrained
vision, while opposed to such philosophies, is also incompati-
ble with the atomism of thoroughgoing libertarians.   In the
constrained vision, the individual is allowed great freedom
precisely in order to serve *social* ends—which may be no part
of the individual's purposes. —Thomas Sowell, *A Conflict of
Visions*

"Dialectics" (*dialectica*) in ancient and medieval philosophy
generally had the connotation of a systematic logical analysis of opposite
opinions, often for the purpose of mediating between them. In modern
German philosophy, under the influence of Hegel and other German
idealists, the term "dialectic" came to mean a progression to various
stages of equipoise and paradoxical coordination between opposites.
Whether this dialectic took place between opposite *ideas* or opposite parts
or aspects of *reality* is still a matter of dispute.

Karl Marx, bypassing questions about real vs. logical dialectic, took over Hegel's dialectical "method" for the purpose of conducting a scientific analysis of the progressions of class conflicts in the world, and Marx's collaborator, Friedrich Engels, out-Marxing Marx, even applied the dialectic to evolutionary progressions taking place in the physical, chemical and biological world. Engels' lead was followed until recently by many Soviet "diamat" theoreticians, who applied "dialectical" analysis to the physical and social sciences as well as to history and politics; and some Western Marxist-oriented scientists have offered an apologetic for this general approach to scientific analysis.[1] Some non-Marxist attempts to produce dialectical-scientific systematizations have also been made.[2]

I have argued elsewhere that claims about dialectic in the *world* have rested on a shaky foundation.[3]   There does not seem to be any evidence of necessary and predictable "dialectical" progressions in the natural or social world.   But this is not to say that real and social oppositions are not to be found between proponents of "dialectically opposite" *ideas*.   If modern democracy, as was argued above,[4] is essentially an attempted mixture of what is best in classical forms of government, and if the "mixture" in question is a mixture of opposite ideas which have continuously and predictably come to the fore in governments from time immemorial, then the makings of a "dialectic of democracy" are at hand. Although we may not reasonably hope to come up with any astute analysis in "diamat" style of the necessary progressions of democratic oppositions leading to some final state of democratic homeostasis, we should not encounter any insuperable hurdle in identifying some of the primary opposed ideas that democracy is committed to mediating.

---

[1]See e.g. Richard Levins and Richard Lewontin, *The Dialectical Biologist* (Cambridge: Harvard University Press, 1985), and other works by these authors.

[2]See e.g. Stéphane Lupasco, *Les trois Matières* (Strasbourg: Éditions Coherence, 1982) and Errol E. Harris, *Formal, Transcendental and Dialectical Thinking* (Albany: State University of New York Press, 1987), Part III.

[3]See Howard P. Kainz, *Paradox, Dialectic and System: a Contemporary Reconstruction of the Hegelian Problematic* (University Park, Pa.: Pennsylvania State University Press, 1988), pp. 70ff.

[4]See p. 162.

As has been observed,[5] the origin of democracy seems to have been an attempt to check the centralizing tendencies of autocratic and tyrannical governments; but when democracy's decentralizing propensities went too far, or were perceived as having the potential for inducing states of anarchy and chaos, centralizing checks on this originally decentralizing "check" were devised. Modern democracies, as a result, are various strategies devised by various peoples with specific needs and traditions for maintaining unity through direction by a central leadership while also granting sufficient autonomy to local and intermediate segments of the polity, and, in the final analysis, even to the individual citizen. Thus the main dynamic and dialectic in democracy consists in the *Restriction vs. Expansion of the Power of the People*—the current and counter-current described at the outset of this chapter by Toqueville as a division between "aristocratic" and "democratic" passions. This division was discernible even in ancient Athenian democracy, which divided up into a "democratic club" and an "oligarchic club". Both democratic and aristocratic/oligarchic "passions" are based on a fundamental insight into human nature. (We omit from consideration here complications resulting from deceit, such as the potential tyrant who deceives the people regarding his devotion to democracy in order to get into power.) The democratic "passion" is based on an insight into the fundamental competency and/or trustworthiness of the average man, the aristocratic on the diametrically opposite insight into the incompetency and/or untrustworthiness of the average man. We might go further and comment, like Nicholas Pastore in his study of social attitudes of scientists,[6] that a basic optimism about human nature seems to correlate with liberalism and the pessimistic view seems to correlate with conservatism. But even where no deceit is involved, some qualifications have to be made because of the disparate meanings attached to terms and the disparate subjective intentions of individuals:

> *"Restriction vs. expansion of the power of the people"*:
> First of all it is important to know just how inclusive the term "people" is meant to be. The Athenian "democratic club" was interested in extending the authority of "the people"; but not even these proto-liberals contemplated including women and

---

[5]See above pp. 160ff.

[6]Nicholas Pastore, *The Nature-Nurture Controversy* (NY: King's Crown Press, 1949).

slaves in their reckoning; and the more democratically oriented among the American founding fathers had similar reservations.

Even if "the people" is defined in the broadest possible way, to include all mentally competent adults in the polity, one would want to know something about the type of "sovereignty" to be entrusted to them. Would this be a sovereignty over their own lives as individuals, perhaps the power to get government "off their backs" or even the power to get rid of government altogether? Or would it be sovereignty as a society, controlling matters through collective participation in political processes? In the former case, we could be encountering anything from a libertarian to an oligarch or anarchist in democrat's clothing.

Even if "a broad-based sovereignty of the people through political processes is meant," one would still want to know something about the nature of the "political processes" contemplated. More specifically, one would want to know whether maximally direct control, depending on the size of the citizenry, is preferred, or maximally indirect control through representatives. In the latter case again, the sincerity of one's "democratic passion" may be open to question.

Finally, even among those who believe in a maximally direct political control of the people in general, a subtle distinction may exist between those who believe these people are actually competent and trustworthy to exercise this control, and those who lean only towards a belief in potential competency and trustworthiness. In the former case, the democratic "solution" that suggests itself is to simply remove the obstacles that now prevent these competent average citizens from attaining the sovereignty they are entitled to. In the latter case, however, the implication is that elite and possibly charismatic leadership is required to raise their state of competency from potentiality to actuality; and possibly also a rather protracted interim subjection to this leadership may be contemplated, involving suitable "testing" procedures to make sure that the potentialities have really been activated after all. In other words, doubts about the real or actual competency of the average person easily translate into the non-democratic species of political "passion," and even into overt totalitarian measures, as happened when François Babeuf tried by propaganda and forcible elimination of opposition to raise the consciousness of the average eighteenth century Frenchman to an appreciation of the merits of the Revolution.[7]

Similar but converse qualifications would have to be made with regard to those propelled by the "aristocratic passion." For example, are the "aristocrats" exclusive or inclusive in their interpretation of the "people"? In other words, do they want to restrict the power of the people in general (including *themselves*), or just certain classes? Do they doubt the actual competency of the people, as thus defined, or only the potential competency? Doubts concerning *potential* competency may be based on purely environmental factors, in which case the doubters could be "closet democrats," using aristocratic or oligarchic status to create environmental conditions which would make self-activation of citizen-potential finally possible. And whether competency is understood as actual or potential, the thoroughgoing advocate of aristocratic excellence may, in a self-depreciating manner, extend his doubts about competency even to him/herself, advocating a filtering process in which tradition or moral standards or family solidarity will tend to bring the best to the top in spite of any twisted intentions on the part of aristocrats or democrats. This conceivable and consistent, but rather unlikely, scenario is suggested by Thomas Sowell in his apologetic for the "constrained vision," in which a modest and unassuming conservative, trusting like Adam Smith in an "invisible hand," will submit his/her own and others' necessarily questionable actions to a filtering process which will distill what is most conducive to the common good out of them.

Corollary or subsidiary to this fundamental dialectic of extension vs. restriction of the power of the people are a variety of other more obvious and better known dialectical relationships:

> *Liberalism vs. conservatism*: The classical liberalism of John Stuart Mill combined a committment to individual autonomy and the privacy of moral choice with an equally strong committment to the extension of the power of the people in the face of establishments and traditions. The fact that these two committments are often difficult to coordinate is illustrated in the evolution of the term, "liberalism." In the early twentieth century,

---

[7]See J. L. Talmon, *The Origins of Totalitarian Democracy*, Ch. 4.

it connoted something akin to what "libertarianism" connotes today, with the distinct emphasis on individual autonomy; in the American New Deal liberalism of the 30s and the 40s the focus was on governmental intervention to empower the people; the present version of liberalism, which emphasizes pluralism and egalitarianism and freedom of moral choice, but wants to avoid bureaucracy and over-legislation, is showing signs of stress in harmonizing the elements of the classical ideal.[8] Conservatives have often taken their cues from the vicissitudes of emphasis among liberals -- counterbalancing individual autonomy with committment to family and community, private moral choice with public tradition and mores, the power of the people with national identity and pride in charismatic leadership. Conservativism, true to its name, has evolved more slowly than liberalism, although its continuing emphasis on tradition to counterbalance the variables of individuality has taken a recent swing towards greater emphasis on religion and capitalistic patterns of life.

"Left-"leaning liberals who believe, like Rousseau or Marx, that the natural innocence or altruism and creativity of man has been stifled by political and/or economic perversions, will tend to place great emphasis on the power of a society to better itself by simply changing the political and/or economic environment to which the average man is subject; a complete transformation of man may be projected as the scientifically predictable result. "Right-"leaning conservatives like Hobbes and Burke, impelled by a more pessimistic view of human nature, tend to be diffident about the possibility of producing human amelioration by socio-political reforms or revolutions, and emphasize the necessity for gifted individuals to work within existing structures to excel and achieve.

Elitism vs. Populism: In our era, "expansion of the power of the people" may conjure up images of mass German support for Hitler or the "Green Book" people's democracy of Omar Khaddaffi or revolutionary

---

[8]See H. Kainz, *Democracy East and West*, p. 137.

Islamic fervor sweeping the Ayatollah Khomeini into unquestioned dictatorial sovereignty—rather than, for example, the more moderate appeals to "people power" in U.S. by the Progressive Party of Senator La Follette or the Socialist Party of Norman Thomas. As Talmon observes, we seem to have come to the conclusion that through the postulation of unanimity and "through a constant appeal to the people as a whole, not just to a small representative body," dictatorship almost inevitably arises.[9]

The complexity of modern civilization is another factor contributing to the distrust of populism. In this age of specialization, the main question may be, "How do we keep the people from making a shambles of political order or even supporting a mindless dictatorship?" rather than "How do we restore rightful power to the grass-roots citizen?" Certainly it would be impossible to entrust the control of nuclear energy, or national macro-economics, or the computer programs of Defense Department computers, even to highly educated but non-specialized persons. So we have become dependent on an elite group of industrialists, politicians, scientists, economists and military strategists who make and administer policy in the name of all. Thus, as MacIntyre notes, it is not surprising that recent Western political study seems to underline the indispensability of elites in modern democracy, although this tendency is *prima facie* in contradiction with the liberal democratic ideal of broad participation.[10]

But the maintenance of broad popular participation in some form is of the essence even in large Western industrial democracies. If, for example, we arrived at a political pattern in which only 10% of especially interested voters typically went to the polls to elect the handful of specialists who would make vital decisions about their life and who would appoint other specialists to make some of these decisions, we might be at the cutoff point where what democracy remained was

---

[9] J.L.Talmon, *The Origins of Totalitarian Democracy*, p. 48.
[10] Alastair MacIntyre, "Recent Political Thought," p. 185.

only a democracy in name. This extreme example may at least demonstrate that a wholesale willingness to relegate government to specialists would be a complete departure from the spirit of democracy, although some mechanics of democracy like free elections might still be in place.

Libertarian Democracy vs. Social Democracy: In 1906 Werner Sombart, a professor in Germany, published a book entitled, *Why is there no Socialism in the United States?*[11] His thorough but not always self-consistent account of the failure of socialism to "catch on" in the U. S. surveys such factors as the especially favorable conditions for capitalism in the U.S., the strength of the American two-party system, upward mobility in the U.S., and the possibilities of freedom symbolized by the Western Frontier. He ends up with a hunch rather than a conclusion derived from preceding arguments:

> All the factors that till now have prevented the development of Socialism in the United States are about to disappear or to be converted into their opposite, with the result that in the next generation Socialism in America will very probably experience the greatest possible expansion of its appeal.[12]

Sombart was better at his sociological analysis of the past than at his prognostications for the future. Socialism in the U.S., whether of the democratic European variety or the Marxist type, has elicited just as lukewarm a reception since Sombart's perceptive book as before it, with the exception of some minor surges of interest at the time of the Great Depression and during the Vietnam war years. Americans tend characteristically to look upon socialism as an unnatural and foreign movement. At least this is the overt attitude, derived

---

[11]Translation of *Warum gibt es in den Vereinigten Staaten keinen Sozialismus?* by Patricia M. Hocking and C.T. Husbands (NY: Macmillan, 1976).

[12]Ibid., p. 119. Italics omitted.

from a rather consistent libertarian orientation, resistant to any signs of social regimentation and stifling bureaucratization. But covertly and unofficially, in testimony to the thrust of democracy towards broader participation in benefits, more than a little "socialization" of a rather eclectic type has taken place: Minimal retirement funding and death benefits through the social security system, temporary unemployment benefits, piecemeal aid for the indigent, partial medical services for certain specified groups and pathologies, and even occasional stabs at government ownership of industry in times of crisis (e.g. the takeover of the railways by Amtrak and the more recent interim government executorship of Savings and Loans assets).

Thus liberals of the social-democratic spirit in the U.S., carefully avoiding explicit or implicit association with socialism proper, have been able to accomplish under democratic auspices and in the form of a "social net" much of what has been accomplished in European democracies in a more systematic fashion, and not infrequently through a socialist or social democratic political party. The contrasts of America and Europe in this respect are remarkable. For example, the provisional constitution (*Grundgesetz*) of the Federal Republic of Germany, in effect since the end of World War II, specifies that Germany is to be a social welfare state, and includes recognition of the equal rights of men and women and provisions for the equal care of legitimate and illegitimate children; and delegates to the legislative and judicial branches the task of concretizing governmental protection of the socially weaker, and the right to work, to education, to housing, etc.

Liberty vs. Equality: In judgements that are made concerning relative liberty or relative equality, the political perspective of the judger is of the utmost importance. Alexis de Toqueville, from the perspective of a French Aristocratic student of American mores worried about collective mediocrity and the "tyranny of the majority" in democracies, discerns the orientation towards equality as the keynote of the American political disposition:

The more I advanced in the study of American society, the more I perceived that ... equality of condition is the fundamental fact from which all others seem to be derived, and the central point at which all my observations constantly terminated.[13]

But Hannah Arendt, judging from a traditional liberal perspective at a time when New Deal liberalism still prevailed, concludes that the key to the success of the American Revolution, in contrast to the French Revolution, was that it was inspired by the desire for liberty rather than by a "quest for bread" that mobilizes hordes of suffering individuals into one body driven by one will[14]:

The direction of the American Revolution remained committed to the foundation of freedom and the establishment of lasting institutions, and to those who acted in this direction nothing was permitted that would have been outside the range of civil law. The direction of the French Revolution was deflected almost from its beginning from this course of foundation through the immediacy of suffering; it was determined by the exigencies of liberation not from tyranny but from necessity, and it was actuated by the limitless immensity of both the people's misery and the pity this misery inspired.... When the predicament of mass poverty had put itself into the road of the Revolution that had started with the strictly political rebellion of the Third Estate ... the men of the Revolution were no longer concerned ... with equality in the sense that everybody should be equally entitled to his legal personality.... The Reign of Terror ... equalized because it

---

[13]Alexis de Toqueville, *Democracy in America*, p. 26.
[14]Hannah Arendt, *On/Revolution*, p. 89.

left all inhabitants equally without the pro-
tecting mask of a legal personality.[15]

Proponents of both liberty and equality are beset
by often unanticipated complexities, once they move to
put their initial insights into practice. The libertarians
must decide whether to set their objectives on the
attainment of freedom in the negative sense—i.e.,
freedom from external obstacles to doing what one
wants or considers to be obligatory; or on the attainment
of freedom in a positive sense—i.e., the maximal
fulfillment of one's inner potentialities. The former
objective could be attained to some extent by judicious
legislation and appropriate legal procedures; the attainment of the latter would require endless prudential
environmental adjustment, lest the libertarian find
himself in the ridiculous position of, for example, telling
the economically deprived or abused or handicapped
child that they are just as free as anyone else to fulfill
their potential. The choices for egalitarians are not any
easier to make. They must decide whether to aim at
formal equality under the law, which is one of the great
progressive accomplishments of democratic systems; or
to aspire further to an economic equalization which will
help to compensate for some of the major unavoidable
inequalities of condition that result from circumstances
beyond one's control. It is with regard to the latter
objective that an egalitarian theorist such as Green
concludes that equality is for all practical purposes
unattainable under the informal class structures and
"caste" system of capitalism.[16]

It should be noted that it is at the point where
maximal standards for both liberty and equality are
advocated that the two values begin to converge. The
libertarian who wants to procure maximum liberty for
all, regardless of disadvantageous circumstances, is not
easily distinguishable from the egalitarian who insists on

---

[15]Hannah Arendt, *On Revolution*, p. 87.

[16]Philip Green, *Retrieving Democracy: In Search of Civic Equality*,
Ch. 2.

removing or minimizing the major inequalities resulting from an individual's membership in a particular economic/social class.

In spite of this apparent convergence of aspirations, Gregory Vlastos concludes that the liberty/equality dialectic is unresolvable, since unequal distribution of resources would be required to equalize benefits in cases of unequal need.[17]   Carol Gould, on the other hand, considers Vlastos' conclusion over-hasty, and concludes that liberty can be reconciled with equality if there is agreement to the principle of equal rights of all citizens to the conditions of self-development (conditions which may be unequal).[18]

Gould and others who project a final solution of the liberty vs. equality dialectic are overoptimistic. This dialectic, like the others cited, is in the final analysis irresolvable. But this is an essential characteristic of, rather than a defect in, democracy. Even if a highly sophisticated social engineering apparatus could resolve all the conflicts in an expeditious and semi-automatic fashion, this would not be desirable in a democracy. For the essence of a democracy is the constant dialogue/debate taking place between proponents of the dialectically opposed ideals —liberty vs. equality, conservativism vs. liberalism, etc. Optimally this dialogue/debate should be perpetuated by two political parties championing the alternative positions, or multiple parties advocating various aspects of the contrary positions. But of course, political-party ideals and platforms do not always follow along neatly on one side or the other of the opposed positions. For example, one could not generalize that in the U.S. members of the Republican party are conservative and libertarian while Democrats are liberal and egalitarian; and the evolution of viewpoints in both parties has been so radical in the last century that any assessment of future trends in the parties would be hazardous.[19]

Granted that dialectic in democracy is inevitable and irresolvable, the main challenge of modern democracy is to prevent dialectic from becoming dichotomy, constructive tension from becoming sterile conflict.

---

[17]Gregory Vlastos, "Justice and Equality," in Richard Brandt, ed., *Social Justice, pp. 40-3.*

[18]*Rethinking Democracy*, (Cambridge: Cambridge University Press, 1988).

[19]See H. Kainz, *Democracy East and West*, pp. 75-6.

How this dynamic can be attained and maintained may be clarified by a psychological analogy—a variation on Plato's methodological device in the *Republic*:[20]

If we can make a meaningful distinction between the "potential" and "actual" self, or between the "ideal" and "real" self, or, to use more behaviorally-oriented terminology, between the "level of aspiration" and the "level of attainment"—it is obvious, on the one hand, that too great a disparity between ideal and real would be immobilizing, while, on the other, little or no disparity would lead to an absence of dynamism altogether. For example, if one with only moderate mathematical ability sticks stubbornly to a personal ideal of becoming a nuclear scientist, psychological stagnation would result; but if one's main aspiration in life is simply to get up every morning and have a cup of coffee, attainment of the higher reaches of psychological maturity might be in serious doubt. What seems to be requisite for maximum, healthy psychological progress is a moderate tension between one's real, empirical self and the self that one wants to become—a tension that is optimally never overcome, and helps the individual avoid both smugness and neurotic dissatisfaction with self, during his or her lifetime.

So too in democracy. The conflicts between the conservatives and liberals, libertarians and egalitarians, can reach such extreme impasses that government is immobilized; or such pragmatic compromises that all constructive democratic dynamic falls by the wayside. A political party championing one of a pair of opposed values may envision a perfect political situation emerging, if only the values which this party champions could be victorious. But if the victory of one meant the defeat of the other, rather than just a temporary ascendancy, the victory would be a pyrrhic victory, at least for democracy.

---

[20]See above, p. 105; and H. Kainz, *Democracy East and West*, pp. 127-8.

XXI. Democracy and the Kingdom of God

The Israel of the early days in Palestine was not at all a nation as we would understand the term. On the contrary, she was a tribal league, a loose confederation of clans united to one another about the worship of God.... Society exhibited no class distinction, no wide rift between rich and poor, ruler and subject, but that rather complete democracy characteristic of nomadic life. —John Bright, *The Kingdom of God*

The Kingdom ideal contains the revolutionary force of Christianity. When this ideal faded out of the systematic thought of the Church, it became a conservative social influence and increased the weight of the other stationary forces in society. If the Kingdom of God had remained part of the theological and Christian consciousness, the Church could not, down to our times, have been salaried by autocratic class governments to keep the democratic and economic impulses of the people under check.... Reversely, the movements for democracy and social justice were left without a religious backing for lack of the Kingdom idea. —Walter Rauschenbusch, *A Theology for the Social Gospel*

This symbol [of the kingdom of God] utilizing kingship metaphors is no longer appropriate for bridging faith and public life. In the revolutions of our time kingdom metaphors have lost their savor. They no longer can nourish us in a post-monarchical life, whether politically or religiously. In the decline of kingship images we gain new appreciation of the covenantal and conciliar themes embedded in the symbol of a Federal Republic. The clarification of the meaning of this symbol can have enormous impact not only on Christian faith and worship but on public life as well. —William Johnson Everett, *God's Federal Republic*

William Johnson Everett presents would-be democratic Christians with an interesting and timely challenge: Isn't the whole idea of a "kingdom," which is pivotal in the Christian faith, so overladen with historical images of centralization and limitation of people-power, that it is in the final analysis inimical to the development of the democratic ideal? Can a Christian whose guiding motivation is to bring about the absolute rule of God over all be committed in even a moderate, "republican" degree, to constant consultation with, and input of, the will of the people, so that the people can in fact rule themselves? Did not the idea of a "City of God" lead in Catholicism to a transformation of the biblical idea of covenant into hierarchy and Empire?[1] And did not the Protestants in their turn reinterpret the communal *covenant* under God's kingship in terms of a detached, legal, social "contract" between individuals?[2]

Hegel, as we have seen,[3] would want to add that, since the kingdom of God became arrested and fossilized as an *ecclesiastical* kingdom in Catholicism, Catholicism is ipso facto alien to modern concepts of free society. But Auguste Comte, countering Hegel's bias towards Protestantism, would certainly want to point out in addition that the traditional Protestant admiration for the Israelite theocracy, and for the Zion-inspired identification of religious commitment and political power, has had its own share in producing some of the obscene collusions of Christianity and politics in history[4]—shockwaves from which the world is still recoiling.

If we were to take such criticisms seriously, we might have to conclude that either Catholics or Protestants, or both, must make a choice between democracy and the kingdom of God; that to be dedicated to democracy *and* the kingdom of God is out of the question. Or, if we were in a more "mediating" frame of mind, we might conclude that either democracy or the Kingdom would have to be relativized, subordinated to its rival; or else radically revised in concept—which is Everett's proposal.

But Everett may be over-hasty in dismissing the "kingdom" symbol as no longer relevant and viable. As has already been noted,[5] the original idea of the kingdom of God was anything but autocratic. Even if the Old-Testament "guilty conscience" about monarchy is an

---

[1]William Johnson Everett, *God's Federal Republic*, pp. 107-110.

[2]Ibid., p. 115.

[3]See p. 114 above. Since the present chapter will be drawing together many points from preceding chapters, the reader should steel him/herself for a multiplicity of cross-references.

[4]See Auguste Comte, *The Positive Philosophy*, pp. 285-6.

[5]See p. 29 above.

attitude impressed upon forebears by later generations of Israelite or Jewish redactors who had seen all the disasters attendant upon perpetuating the Davidic monarchy,[6] it does seem that the early confederacy was de facto set up to obviate autocracy, and even constituted, as Bright comments above, a species of democracy.

Making an even stronger statement than Bright are Ben-Asher and Dimant[7] who suggest that the idea of democracy could be traced back with justice to Hebrew origins. The evidence is impressive. In the Mosaic code and prophetic books are numerous features that we associate with modern Western democracy: separation of civil authority from religious authority; a judiciary (the priesthood) independent of the "judges" (*Shoftim*),[8] who functioned as executive leaders and commanders-in-chief, and were elected by each of the twelve tribes; a loose central government under a legislative body (later the *Sanhedrin*, composed of Pharisees and Sadducees) and the "popular assemblies," which could be summoned to deliberation by the *Shoftim*; and even the election of kings[9]. This highly decentralized political structure was buttressed by what we might consider to be extraordinarily enlightened laws for that era: stipulations for equality before the law,[10] of rich and poor, Hebrews and foreigners, and even of kings and people[11]; prohibition against punishment of individuals because of crimes of their ancestors[12]; guarantees against unlawful entering of one's house[13]; punishments stipulated for killing of slaves and servants; and standards set for the fair treatment of foreigners.[14]

If such structures and legal procedures represent in even a rough way the initial Hebrew interpretation of what the "kingdom of God" was all about, we have a *prima facie* indication that the idea of the Kingdom

---

[6]See above, pp. 16, 30, 16, 30.

[7]Naomi Ben-Asher, *Democracy's Hebrew Roots*, Ch. 1; Max Dimant, *Jews, God, and History*, p. 41.

[8]See p. 29 above.

[9]See e.g. 2 Sam. 5:1-5.

[10]Exodus 23:1-8; Deut. 16:18-20; Lev. 24:22, 19:34.

[11]Deut. 17:14-20; 2 Sam. 12:1-9; 1 Kings 21:19. See also Eric Voegelin, *Order and History*, I, p. 370.

[12]Deut. 24:16; Ezek. 18:1-20.

[13]Deut. 24:10-11.

[14]Lev. 19:33-34; Exod. 22:20, 23:9; Deut. 1:16, 5:14, 10:19; Jerem. 7:5-6; Ezek. 37:1-14.

may not only be compatible with democracy, but a definite step in the direction of democracy. As has already been indicated,[15] the idea of "God as *sole* king," in devaluing subjection to any human authority, seems to place a value on democratic institutions. Everett, in the apprehensions running through his book concerning the Christian "kingship" symbols, seems to be implicitly, and unnecessarily, holding the pseudo-theocratic[16] Davidic monarchy rather than the early confederacy as the epitome of, and paradigm for, the Kingdom, and thus to be continuing in a line of interpretation common to early Christians, Jews, and modern conservative Protestants.

As was mentioned above,[17] there are indications that many of the things we associate with modern democracy can be traced much more surely to Christianity than to ancient Greece. In early Christianity, as in early Yahwism, an affinity with major democratic principles can be discerned. The commitment of early Christians to the principle of human equality was manifested in the extremely decentralized species of communism which is described in the *Acts of the Apostles*; and ecclesiastical democracy was manifested in the common election of bishops and deacons.[18] Pagels notes that the Biblical concept of equality, based on man's creation as the "image of God," is common to early Christians in the Roman Empire and to American Revolutionaries subscribing in the Declaration of Independence to the "self-evident truth" that "all men are created equal."[19] Gascoigne finds Hegel's constant emphasis upon the Christian derivation of the idea of a modern free state suggestive. Downplaying Hegel's monarchical predilections,[20] he suggests that, after we make certain allowances for the sharp differences between Hegel's vantage point and ours, "a Christian understanding of history which would learn from Hegel can accept his derivation of the *Declaration des droits de l'homme et du citoyen* from the Biblical understanding of man"[21].

In spite of the apparently multiple contributions of Christianity to democracy, the aristocratic structures and predispositions of the

---

[15]See above, p. 12.

[16]See p. 31 above.

[17]See above, p. 127.

[18]See Hans Küng, *The Church*, p. 409.

[19]*Adam, Eve, and the Serpent*, p. 55.

[20]See p. 120 above.

[21]Robert Gascoigne, *Religion, Rationality and Community*, p. 269.

institutional Church were, as Everett observes,[22] a movement away from the fraternal/democratic spirit of "covenant," counterbalanced by occasional thrusts towards democratization—for example, the many attempts to inaugurate Joachim of Fiore's "Stage of the Holy Spirit,"[23] the conciliar movement of the fifteenth century, and Protestantism itself. But Everett's solution for remedying this loss—namely, a more socialized federalism inspired by Biblical covenant, less of the "quid pro quo" barter-arrangements of pragmatic democracy, more republican "publicity" (consciousness of the common "weal" to counterbalance the primacy of the individual[24])—seem in the last analysis too cerebral. It is as if someone were asking Christians, by intense mental application, to convert their habitual commitment to the Kingdom into a corresponding commitment to "God's Federal Republic." This proposal is also tainted with chauvinism, since a characteristically American ideal of federal constitutional government is, for all practical purposes, being extrapolated into the universal ideal to be promulgated with the help of Christianity.

But most importantly—the radical re-symbolization recommended by Everett is not *necessary*. There is not *necessarily* any compromise to democratic principles from a Christianity which holds that God, rather than any human being, is king. If, for example, one thought, as did many ancient Christians in electing their bishops, that "the voice of the people is the voice of God" (*vox populi vox Dei*), the belief in the Kingdom approximates the populist extreme of democracy. It may happen, of course, that various human intermediaries or a single intermediary is designated as "God's representative on earth." In such cases, compromises to democracy can result, depending on just how absolute the power of the representative or representatives is construed. *But compromises to the democratic-republican ideal can just as easily develop in "God's Federal Republic," if, as we may safely surmise, it is to be administered by any human intermediaries or representatives.* This is just to say that no religious symbolism or formula could *guarantee* liberation from nondemocratic interpretations.

"The jury is still out" regarding any final evaluation of the historical effects of the idea of the Kingdom on the development of democracy. Because of prejudice and the exigencies of the diaspora,

---

[22]*God's Federal Republic*, Ch. 4.

[23]See above, p. 90,

[24]This is the sense in which Immanuel Kant uses the term, e.g. in *Perpetual Peace*.

Jews have until recent decades been largely deprived of occupying major political offices and exerting any direct effect on the development of democracy, although Jewish philosophers like Maimonides and Spinoza have had an impact on democratic theory. In the twentieth century, as was discussed above,[25] the establishment of Israel by the International community has created new and unique problems regarding the possibility of an explicitly non-pluralistic democracy. But the old and common problems we encounter in history have to do with Christianity. Christianity, either overtly or in hidden, "secular" ways, has permeated Western civilization, in which the modern surge towards democracy has also taken place. An evaluation of the compatibility of the partners in this long-standing "marriage" leads us into two sub-questions: 1) Is the Christian "kingdom of God" conducive to democracy? And 2) conversely, is democracy conducive to Christianity?

1) Löwith's judgement regarding the *conduciveness of Christianity to democracy* is negative and harsh:

> A "Holy Roman Empire" is a contradiction in terms. A Protestant will have no difficulty in agreeing with this statement, though he will hesitate to admit that it implies in principle also the theological impossibility of a "Christian democracy" and of a Christian civilization and history.[26]

Löwith's rationale for this sharp dissociation of Christianity and democracy, however, is not based on a judgement that Christianity is undemocratic, or democracy un-Christian. Rather, he is reiterating the same view that we have found among many theologians[27]—namely, that the Christian mystery of the kingdom of God is so far out-of-reach of ordinary human endeavor that the juxtaposition of this transcendent mystery with some political order excogitated by human reason is absurd. But as we have seen,[28] Augustine, who also held to the ultimate transcendence of the Kingdom, maintained that no true republic is conceivable without a Christian basis; and this position, with due regard to the differing degree and type of decentralization entailed by Ciceronian republicanism, could conceivably carry over to democracy. It does carry

---

[25]See p. 164.
[26]Carl Löwith, *Meaning in History*, p. 190.
[27]See pp. 63, 64, 94, 117, above.
[28]P. 87 above.

over, according to Benjamin Rush, who in his 1786 essay, "Thoughts upon the Mode of Education Proper in a Republic," resuscitates the idea of a "Christian Republic" with a non-sectarian Protestant emphasis, insisting that "A Christian cannot fail of being a republican." These sentiments are seconded in contemporary Protestant thought by Niebuhr, who considers the idea of the direct rule of God in Protestantism not only compatible with, but the implicit presupposition of, modern democracy.[29] Niebuhr is here touching on a major "sore point" in Protestant theology. According to Lakeland the privatization of religion and the complete separation of faith and works, Kingdom and world—the sort of transcendence that Löwith seems to extol—constitute the most glaring and pernicious weaknesses in Protestantism.

We have already considered the claim that the doctrines of Christianity fuel the commitments to the ultimate worth of persons and to brotherhood under God, which seem to be central to the idea of democracy as formulated e.g. in the American Declaration of Independence. The Christian ideal of universal love is also cited as a spur to the overcoming of ethnic and religious chauvinism, and to the spirit of pluralism, in democracy. And certainly the exploration of the social ramifications of the Gospel at the outset of the 20th century by German Christian socialists and by Rauschenbusch in the U.S.A. have conditioned a renewed emphasis upon the traditional democratic value of equality. But some look to more sophisticated Christian doctrines as major instigators to enlightened modern democracy: Moltmann considers Christian emphasis on the doctrine of a triune God, beyond all remnants of simple monotheism (which inculcated hierarchical thinking[30]), to be the catalyst which overcomes the rift between the individual and society:

> If we take our bearings from the Christian doctrine of the Trinity, personalism and socialism cease to be antitheses and are seen to be derived from a common foundation. The Christian doctrine of the Trinity compels us to develop social personalism or personal socialism.[31]

Everett looks to the doctrine of the Mystical Body—the belief in Christ as a spiritual head in organic relationship with a diversity of members ruled by the same Spirit—as a similar hedge against hierarchy, and points

---

[29]H. Richard Niebuhr, *The Kingdom of God in America*, p. 24.

[30]Jürgen Moltmann, *The Trinity and the Kingdom*, p. 202.

[31]Ibid., 199.

to the fifteenth-century conciliar movement as an example of the sort of formations resulting from attempts to specifically apply this doctrine to society.[32] But on the doctrinal level, certainly one of the most fundamental ideological assets to democracy in Christianity would be the doctrine of the Incarnation—a connection made by Hegel, although he did not apply this doctrine to democracy but more generally to a "free modern state"; Hegel theorized that the religious insight into the unity-in-distinction of human and divine in the person of Christ would provide a necessary spiritual impetus to the realistic conceptualization of a unity-in-distinction in the socio-political sphere.[33]

There is no guarantee, of course, that Christian commitment to universal love and brotherhood will prevent the internecine factional struggles that can sound the death knell of democracy, or that Christian cultivation of a concept of a triune community of three persons in God will spill over into human communitarianism. But while it would be an overstatement to say that such concepts necessarily lead to democracy or democratization, it would be an understatement to conclude *merely* that there is "nothing detrimental to democracy" therein.

2) But even if Christianity is conducive to democracy, it does *not* necessarily follow that *democracy is conducive to Christianity*. It is conceivable, in other words, that while Christianity is a feather in democracy's cap, democracy is a thorn in Christianity's side, keeping it from implementing its vision of the kingdom of God. Conservative Catholic theologians, for example, when queried about the apparently anti-democratic hierarchical structures of their church, reply on occasion that the Church as founded by Christ is inherently monarchical, and even offer arguments from Scripture to demonstrate that Jesus did not intend his "flock" to be democratic in nature. And conservative Protestant theologians, looking forward to the final establishment of Zion by a "remnant" of the Jews before the end of the world, may be expected to subordinate what are generally considered to be democratic procedures and processes to this overweening goal.

But Paul Tillich, for one, is optimistic, with some qualifications, about the conduciveness of democracy to the Kingdom:

> In so far as democratization of political attitudes and institu-
> tions serves to resist the destructive implications of power, it

---

[32]William Johnson Everett, *God's Federal Republic*, p. 72.
[33]See Paul Lakeland, *The Politics of Salvation*, p. 107.

is a manifestation of the Kingdom of God in history. But it
would be completely wrong to identify democratic institutions
with the Kingdom of God in history.[34]

Tillich's rather nuanced optimism about democracy is based on what we
have described above as the "decentralizing" aspects[35] of democratic
institutions. The great and indisputable contribution of these institutions
to mankind has been to provide a check on tyrannical or autocratic
power-relations. Republicanism added to this the ability to offer a
maximum amount of participation to a maximum number of people.
Thus (and this seems to be Tillich's reasoning) if the main threat to the
kingdom of God is the "City of Man," and this "city" is governed by
"those who lord it over others"[36], then it follows that democracy, just by
dissipating the concentrations of power in the adversary's stronghold, is
performing a service for the Kingdom—although the services that it
performs are not in any way to be identified with the progress of the
Kingdom.

     Another important contribution of modern pluralistic and
polyarchic democracy to modern Christianity is institutionalized
coexistence, which enhances the voluntary nature of religious affiliation
and helps prevent those overly close religion-politics intertwinings that
in the past often paved the way for oppression and terror. Although
Christians in past centuries were not always convinced about the value
of religious tolerance and coexistence, Christians in the modern world are
generally in agreement that their religion can thrive best in an atmosphere
of religious freedom and freedom of conscience; and there is a consensus
of Christians in the industrialized West that democratic structures are
indeed more conducive than other political structures to the kingdom of
God.

     Is democracy possibly related in any stronger sense to Christiani-
ty? Is the democratization process in any way integrally, and not just
peripherally, related to a Christianization process, or to preparing the way
for the Kingdom? A couple of examples may help to bring this problem
into focus: Certain fundamentalist Protestant groups viewed the spread
of communism in the world as fulfillment of prophecies in the *Apocalypse* concerning the Antichrist and the coming of Armageddon. So in
a sense it was totalitarianism, and not democracy, that was hastening the

---

[34]Paul Tillich, *Systematic Theology* III, p. 385.
[35]P. 171.
[36]Matt. 20:25-6.

advent of the Kingdom. Now that the disbanding of communist party apparatus in the Soviet Union and other formerly communist regimes has taken place, and the aggressive expansion of Marxist-Leninist atheistic ideology, except in China, is becoming a distant memory from the "cold-war" era, will these same fundamentalists go "back to the drawing board" and revise their interpretations, and thus avoid losing credibility among their followers? Or will they view the dismantling of the former Soviet empire as having little or no impact on the diabolical, anti-Christian forces they consider to be operative?

A similar challenge is posed by a somewhat esoteric debate currently taking place in Catholicism between devotees of the 1917 revelations in Fatima, Portugal, of the Madonna, who allegedly prophesied the spread of communism and also the eventual "conversion of Russia." Many of these devotees now, including some high-ranking clergy, consider the movements towards democratization now taking place in the former Soviet blocks to be a sign that the prophecies have been fulfilled and the "conversion" is indeed taking place. But some of them (with political conservatives on their side) claim that current developments are simply a smoke-screen used to hide a new "catch them off their guard" strategy for diabolical world-domination. Human intentions being what they are, we can of course not be completely sure which of these factions is correct in their surmisal of the situation. But we can ask very pointedly: if a "totalitarian" regime like the former U.S.S.R. begins to allow and institutionalize free elections, liberates political prisoners, allows freedom of religion, restores confiscated church property, allows emigration of religious groups formerly persecuted, and encourages cultural exchanges of every kind—could the conservative Catholic or Protestant factions just alluded to hold their ground and respond, "Very well, but when are they going to be *converted*?" Those who would respond in this manner would have to have such an elevated idea of "religious transcendence" or the experience of "conversion" that none of these "democratization" phenomena would even approximate their standards. Possibly their concept of transcendence is close to Löwith's uncompromising attitude towards transcendence, already discussed.[37] Since they consider the matter to be an issue purely of faith, outside the parameters of rational discussion, argumentation with them is perhaps out of the question. On the other hand, *Christians who believe in the Fatima prophecies but disagree with this interpretation, if* ***they*** *are consistent, would have to look upon such democratization*

---

[37]See p. 188.

phenomena as signs of conversion, and are implicitly taking a stand on the issue raised above. To disagree that democratization has nothing to do with conversion is to imply that democratization is at least conducive to Christianization, or to that coming of the kingdom of God which is the goal and/or mission of Christianity.

Some would want to make an even stronger statement about an even closer intertwining of democracy with Christianity, or vice versa. Jacques Maritain, for example, held that Christianity is the indispensable source of democracy: "In its essential principle, the form and ideal of democracy is inspired by the spirit of the Gospel and cannot subsist without it"[38]; and he bemoaned "the disaster brought about in modern democracies, by the divorce between the Christian and democratic principles."[39] Concerning American democracy, John Courtney Murray observes that "the Bill of Rights was an effective instrument for the delimitation of government authority and social power, not because it was written on paper in 1789 or 1791, but because the rights it proclaims had already been engraved by history on the conscience of a people. The American Bill of Rights is not a piece of eighteenth-century rationalist theory; it is far more the product of Christian history."[40] G. K. Chesterton, with his characteristic eloquence, has also argued that democracy is essentially Christian:

> Even the machinery of voting is profoundly Christian in this practical sense—that it is an attempt to get at the opinion of those who would be too modest to offer it. It is a mystical adventure; it is specially trusting those who do not trust themselves. That enigma is strictly peculiar to Christendom.... There is something psychologically Christian about the idea of seeking for the opinion of the obscure rather than taking the obvious course of accepting the opinion of the prominent. To say that voting is particularly Christian may seem somewhat curious. To say that canvassing is Christian may seem quite crazy. But canvassing is very Christian in its primary idea. It is encouraging the humble; it is saying to the modest man, "Friend, go up higher."[41]

---

[38]Jacques Maritain, "Christianity and Democracy," p. 244.

[39]Ibid., p. 245.

[40]J. C. Murray, S.J., *We Hold These Truths: Catholic Reflections on the American Proposition*, p. 39.

[41]G. K. Chesterton, *Orthodoxy*, pp. 119-20.

One need not take the extreme position exemplified by Maritain or Chesterton to realize that a strong positive relationship between the kingdom of God and democracy would be easier to defend than between the kingdom of God and monarchy or aristocracy, let alone autocracy or tyranny, where any prevailing "rule of God" would be surely less obvious and probably completely overshadowed.

XXII. Are Church and State "Mutually Conducive"?

CRANSTON: Any discussion of the relation of democracy and the "kingdom of God" should logically start with Judaism. But because of problems connected with the international establishment of the state of Israel[1] and its special ethnic/religious requirements for citizenship,[2] the case is too anomalous to be used as a springboard for generalizations. So by default we are left with the somewhat more generalizable problem of the relationship of democracy to Christianity.

TURNER: To Christianity or to the "kingdom of God"?

CRANSTON: We will use "Christianity" as a generic term, with the full realization that there are differences of interpretation among Christians about whether the Church is a present Kingdom, or just the symbol or precursor of the future Kingdom, etc. So when we use the generic term, "Christianity," or refer to the Church, or "churches," we are simply referring to various communities grouped around various interpretations of the Kingdom.

TURNER: Various interpretations exist even within a single denomination. There's hardly any uniformity to get your teeth into. But as long as we realize this, I agree to the ground-rules for the use of these terms.

CRANSTON: I think we are ready, then, to work toward a conclusion: It seems to me quite obvious that democracy could exist and thrive in a non-Christian spiritual milieu, e.g. Hinduism; and that Christianity could likewise thrive under non-democratic political structures, e.g. a monarchy, even a non-constitutional monarchy

---

[1]See p. 165 above.
[2]See p. 164 above.

with a reasonably conscientious ruling family. So I can't agree with those who consider Christianity and democracy inseparable, mutually entailing each other. This would be like a revised version of the "Christian Republic" ideal of the middle ages.[3] But still, there is something special about the relationship between the two. They are mutually conducive to each other. Democracy sets up an optimum environment for Christianity, Christianity for democracy.

TURNER: It seems to me you are backing into those "utility of religion" approaches that, if I remember correctly, we both have abjured.[4] You're saying, in effect, "democracy is useful, even very useful, to religion (like many other things are useful to religion); and religion is useful, even very useful, *conducive*, to democracy (like many other things). Your "conduciveness" is just utility, warmed over.

CRANSTON: They are not the same thing. A pure utility-relationship would exist, for instance, when an incumbent administration in a democracy uses religious favoritism to swing the vote its way; or when a proselytizing and money-grabbing religion uses democracy to accomplish its nefarious goals more expeditiously. Immanuel Kant says that using persons just as a means to one's ends is immoral.[5] Democracy could use religion just as a means to an end, or vice versa. But that would be a worst-case scenario —certainly not what I mean by conduciveness.

TURNER: I'm not a Kantian, but I've never heard of applying Kant's principle beyond the relationship of individual persons.

CRANSTON: That would be problematic. But in referring to "democracy" and "Christianity" I am using metonymy for "democratic politicians" and "Christian leaders." In the final analysis, we're talking about persons using persons.

---

[3]See pp. 92, 93-92, 93 above.

[4]See above pp. 8ff.

[5]*Fundamental Principles of the Metaphysic of Morals*, Abbot trans. (Indianapolis & New York: Bobbs-Merrill, 1949).

TURNER: You're putting an awful bad face on "using" people. Even Kant would admit that most of the time we use people in a healthy and moral way. My children use my shoulders to sit on to get a better view of the parade; I use the services of my accountant to make out my income tax; I believe you are even using me now as a backboard to bounce your ideas off of.

CRANSTON: Yes, there are those good or at least innocuous ways of "using" people, too. And I admit that democrats can use Christians or vice versa in these good and innocuous ways. For example, democratic legislators may call on Christian constituents to back legislation that they consider to be morally imperative; Christian lobbyists could do the same thing in the other direction. But the relationship between democracy and Christianity is not *just* a relationship of utility—either the good kind or the bad.

TURNER: I take it that this is what you were trying to get at when you spoke of each "setting up an environment" for the other. But I'm afraid I fail to grasp how "setting up an environment" somehow surpasses relationships of "utility." Environments are, after all, useful.

CRANSTON: You're using the word, "useful," equivocally. One could say the world is useful or the sun is useful; but that is stretching the word beyond it's proper bounds. An environment is only properly "useful" when it is built up or provided by someone to be useful to someone. And that is not the case here.

TURNER: I think I understand what is "not the case." But I'm still not clear on what *is* the case. What is the positive content of this relationship that you refer to as "mutual conduciveness"?

CRANSTON: Democracy and Christianity are like two independent variables which show a positive correlationship with each other. For example, psychological tests may try to determine whether "respect for authority" correlates with political conservatism, or whether eroticism correlates with aggressiveness. They may come up with a negative correlation, an absence of correlation (statistical insignificance), or a positive correlation. If repeated tests show a positive correlation, one could say that the one factor is "conducive" to the other; that is, when you find one, there is a high probability you will find the other.

TURNER: Then you are asserting that when you find democracy, the probability that you will also find Christianity is significantly high; and vice versa? I'm sure you must realize how difficult any such "correlation" would be to verify empirically.

CRANSTON: The difficulty of verification emerges because of the differing definitions of democracy, and the differing interpretations of what is Christianity (e.g. visible church, faith in the Kingdom, etc.). But if a team of sociologists were to come to an agreement on the definition of democracy as "mixed government" in the sense we have been exploring,[6] and also agreed on, let's say, the "mediating" interpretation of the kingdom of God that we discussed,[7] I believe it would be in principle possible to determine one way or the other whether there is a positive correlationship between democracy and Christianity.

TURNER: In principle, but not in practice. For starters, how would you test democracy in a nation that had been overrun by a superpower or made a pawn in a "holy war"? And, as the exemplar of that "mediating" theological position, what church or denomination would you choose?

CRANSTON: I promise to steer clear of field work in sociology. But it does seem to me that the idea of a statistical "positive correlationship" in sociology (or, for that matter, in psychology or quantum mechanics) helps to illustrate how "conduciveness," as I have used that term, differs from mere "utility."

TURNER: I'm afraid that what you are referring to as a mutual conduciveness is just a historical convergence of two independent trends, one beginning in Canaan, the other in Athens, that happened to meet and interlock.

CRANSTON: I am not denying that. But now that they have met, there is a chemistry between the two. They're not going to just pull

---

[6]See p. 162 above.
[7]See p. 64 above.

apart from each other and go off in their own separate directions, like two trains passing each other in the night.

TURNER: What "chemistry" is there between a completely future-oriented Christianity and democracy? All the democracies I know of are present-oriented.

CRANSTON: Even such a version would keep democracy on its toes, challenging its immersion in the present and its control over the present. It functions as a symbol of a transcendent dimension, keeping the immanent from becoming an absolute. But a version with a more immanent interpretation of the kingdom of God would be conducive in a more positive way.

TURNER: But not completely immanent?

CRANSTON: I can't think of any species of Christianity that would exemplify complete immanence, except perhaps the "death-of-God" theological movement of the sixties, or (among Christian denominations) the humanist left-wing of Unitarianism. If there is a lack of belief in *any* transcendent dimension, including an afterlife, I would hesitate to use the designation, "Christian." The "death-of-God" movement was a metaphysical school of thought; and the humanist Unitarians seem to me to be best classified as an ethical fellowship.

TURNER: So by default you end up with the moderately-immanently-oriented version of Christianity as most conducive to democracy.

CRANSTON: Maybe also the most useful. For instance, Christians of this persuasion would be more likely than the strictly future-oriented transcendentalists to submit to a draft in times of war, and to pay taxes. But this version is not *just* useful. That's my point.

TURNER: But if you want to go beyond "mere" utility to designate some special kind of input that enhances democracy while also furthering the fulfillment of Christianity, you have to go beyond mere comparisons to "positive correlationships" in the sciences, or the metaphors you introduced about the "chemistry" that can exist between two independent movements. What sort of input or contribution do you have in mind?

CRANSTON: Moral leadership, for one thing.

TURNER: We don't need Christianity for moral leadership. Great moral leaders were there before Christianity. I know of no greater than Socrates. Certainly Confucius, who was more of a moral than a religious leader, was comparable to any of the great Christian moral leaders. Ethics is a philosophical discipline cultivated in the modern world independently of any religion. The separation from religious connections has been, as far as I'm concerned, a tremendous boon.

CRANSTON: A boon not only to ethics, but also to religion. I agree. But this is precisely what I'm getting at: We don't need religion to inform us about right and wrong, duties and rights. Religion worth its salt will go beyond that—beyond morality to values like love, compassion, generosity and benevolence—values that go above and beyond the call of duty.

TURNER: Then you're not talking about the moral leadership of religion, but of leadership beyond morality, or supra-moral leadership.

CRANSTON: That would be a technically more precise way of putting it.

TURNER: I would be supra-satisfied if religion would just strengthen morality. Why ask it to "go beyond" morality?

CRANSTON: Moral norms are not enough. Take, for example, utilitarianism, a moral viewpoint which prevails widely, explicitly or implicitly, in Western culture. The utilitarian goal—"the greatest happiness for the greatest number"—is a worthy goal, a tremendous step forward from the situation in pre-democratic cultures in which no one would have even conceived such a goal as possible. But "the greatest number" leaves out the minority. Utilitarianism has no agenda for bringing about maximum happiness for everybody.

TURNER: Marxism does. I have no doubt that this is precisely the reason for the attractiveness of Marxism in recent decades to the Third World, which considers itself to be the main disadvantaged "minority" left out of the "happiness"-calculations of Western capitalist utilitarians. Marxism proffered to them the high moral ideal of spreading out the happiness to everyone.

CRANSTON: A promise, of course, which it would be impossible to fulfill with even the most astute management of the liberated workers of the world.... And this is where Christianity comes in: going beyond utilitarianism with its doctrine of universal love, to show that the happiness of the minority is just as important as that of the majority; but without falling into the Marxist trap of trying to bring about a paradise on earth, and without short-circuiting individual rights or compromising the dignity of the individual person.

TURNER: It seems to me that these are ideals implemented largely by that "invisible church" that one hears about—*overly* invisible. In any case, you're putting the conduciveness of Christianity to democracy on a rather abstract level: Just "(supra-)moral leadership"?

CRANSTON: No. Practical, para-political leadership, too. This is one of the ways that the Church becomes visible. A great contribution of the visible Church to democracy is to provide constructive competition with the government.

TURNER: You obviously don't mean the old-fashioned competition, where the Church at various times was trying to get control of government, or manipulate it for its own purposes.

CRANSTON: Definitely not. I mean that other old-fashioned competition that you seem to have momentarily forgotten about: vying with the government, outdoing it if possible, in supplying first-class education and medical care to all, non-demeaning assistance to the homeless and unemployed, rehabilitation of miscreants.

TURNER: If I have forgotten about this competition, there is good reason for it: Church-related hospitals, schools, orphanages, etc. seem in recent decades to have become strapped with the same "bottom-line" problems as the government.

CRANSTON: This is where the contributions of *democracy* to *Christianity* come in. The genius of democracy is the decentralization which encourages creative volunteerism on the part of individuals and groups.

TURNER: I take it you have something else in mind than tolerance and freedom of religion.

CRANSTON: Yes. Tolerance is a start, but it's a negative kind of assistance—non-interference, non-imposition of beliefs. This has to be supplemented by positive assistance—financial, if necessary.

TURNER: Assistance to competitors? Human nature might balk at that.

CRANSTON: Christianity is not a competitor in the sense of an opposition party, but like a sparring partner in boxing, offering the sort of competition that will help keep the boxer in shape.

TURNER: I wasn't aware that anything like this was going on. If I knew about it, I probably would have become a Christian, just to belong to a class of people who would be assisted by the government to offer constructive competition to the government.

CRANSTON: That would be the wrong reason for converting.

TURNER: I hope you realize that some of the things you connect with "mutual conduciveness" are bordering on the grey area of unconstitutionality. Tuition rebates for parents sending their children to church-related schools, direct governmental support for religious hospitals, etc. would threaten traditions of the separation of church and state.

CRANSTON: Some of these traditions are *sui generis* to the United States, and may need to be challenged. They are reactions, of course, to the evil collusions of church and state in times past; but to go too far in the other direction is to "throw out the baby with the bathwater."

TURNER: The "baby" here being....?

CRANSTON:...being the tremendous benefits that a partnership, even a sparring partnership, between Christianity and a democratic state can bring.

TURNER: It seems to me that it was precisely the firm separation of church and state that made democracy possible in the first place—helped it to get off the ground, so to speak.

CRANSTON: That is in particular a profile of American democracy. But in many European democracies, there are more partnership-oriented constitutional provisions: clergy are paid in whole or in part by the state, church-related kindergartens, schools and hospitals are supported, Catholic and Protestant theological faculties are maintained at state universities.

TURNER: I think this emphasis on partnership rather than mere separation is probably a good idea. But I'm against paying the salary of clergy from public funds. I should think you would be against it, too, if you are anxious to preserve the "transcendent"-critical function of the church—sufficient independence from the state to criticize or censure acts of government, when this seems necessary. Clergy paid by the state would almost certainly be compromised when push came to shove. Weren't the clergy in Hitler's regime dependent on the state for their upkeep?

CRANSTON: I agree with you that putting clergy on the governmental payroll would be a mistake; and I am not advocating a reversion to past unification, but something more nuanced, which has to be worked out by trial-and-error in various democracies. What I advocate is something like a Hegelian unity-in-distinction of complementary and inseparable opposites—going beyond mere symbiotic or parasitic unity, but also avoiding the sort of alienation produced when the state is public but the church private, the state supported by the public treasury but the church left to its own devices, etc.

TURNER: I don't think any constitution could make a provision for a "unity-in-distinction." But "sparring partner"? That may turn out at least to be a productive metaphor.

XXIII. World Federalism and Ecumenical Christianity

Christian Universalism was reinforced by the universalism of the later Stoics, who created the ideal of an all-embracing city of reason—*cosmopolis*. Mediaeval Christians couched their universalist outlook in Hellenic terms. Thus two streams of thought, from Israel and Greece, flowed together. As a result the world today, although divided among nations often ferociously self-righteous and jealous, is haunted by the vision of a global community. —Glenn Tinder, "Can We Be Good Without God?"

History will not wait.... Communist Europe [is] exploding before our eyes.... Events are accelerating.... We must also accelerate ... and put in place institutions capable of assuming the exigencies linked to our external responsibilities.... A qualitative leap is necessary, both in our conception of the Community and in our modes of external action. —Jacques Delors, President, European Common Market, Speech delivered Oct. 17, 1989

[We support] an European Federal Union for the European Community's economic policies, [and also] a wider federation of democracies—at least the whole Atlantic Community, including Europe, the U.S., and Canada for common decisions in foreign policy and defense. —Rudolf Wagner, Planning Committee for the Security of the Atlantic Community, May, 1992

The unity to which we are called is a *koinonia* [community] given and expressed in the common confession of the apostolic faith; a common sacramental life entered by the one baptism and celebrated together in one eucharistic fellowship; a common life in which members and ministries are mutually recognized and reconciled; and a common mission witnessing to all people to the gospel of God's grace and serving the whole of creation. The goal of the search for full communion is realized when all the churches are able to recognize in one

another the One, Holy, Catholic and Apostolic Church in its
fullness. This full communion will be expressed on the local
and the universal levels through conciliar forms of life and
action. —Declaration of the Faith and Order Commission,
Seventh General Assembly of the World Council of Churches,
Canberra, Australia, Feb. 7-20, 1991

It is only in love that human freedom arrives at its truth. I
am free and feel myself to be truly free when I am respected
and recognized by others and when I for my part respect and
recognize them.... The alienation of person from person, the
division between human society and nature, the dichotomy
between soul and body, and finally, religious anxiety are
abolished; liberation is experienced when people are again one:
one with each other, one with nature, and one with God.
—Jürgen Moltmann, *The Trinity and the Kingdom*

Abstractions, in spite of the occasional vilification they receive,
can be a great help in intellectual analysis. They allow us to temporarily
put aside distracting and less important differences and concentrate on
essential features. But abstractions can also be the things that one
proverbially "gets lost in." We have been discussing both democracy and
the "kingdom of God" in the abstract. But of course there is no
democracy in the abstract, but only a variety of nation-states that call
themselves "democracies" with varying degrees of accuracy, and some
international organizations adhering to some extent to what are considered
to be democratic principles and/or procedures. And there is no "kingdom
of God" or Christianity in the abstract, but only a variety of churches,
denominations, and confessions that call themselves "Christian" and, as
we have seen, exemplify a wide variety of interpretations of, and
variations on, the Judaeo-Christian idea of a "kingdom of God". A
question naturally emerges: Should we be satisfied with this lush and
bewildering variety; or look forward, still dissatisfied, to an eventual
concrete, worldwide unity, such that democracy would reign not only
within individual nations but in a world federation, and Christianity
would exist as one Church rather than "the churches" or "the denominations"?

WORLD FEDERALISM

A worldwide democratic federation seems on initial consideration to be almost a contradiction in terms. This is because "world

government" in political ideologies and utopian schemes, not to mention science-fiction portrayals, conjures up images of world domination and oppression by some demagogic leader or group bent on whipping a world full of minions into conformity. In other words, it has become synonymous with political centralization taken to an absolute extreme. But neither theorists nor science fiction writers have succeeded in developing a credible scenario in which, say, five billion real people in a thousand democratic nations could be tabulated, computerized, directed and regimented (and for what? or to what?). There are probably no outer limits to the goals to which a true megalomaniac might aspire; but in any case the requirements of organization for a centralized *world* government would be clearly beyond the bounds of possibility (even more so than those fables of yesteryear about the takeover and transformation of America by loyal Soviet troops led by an urbane, English-speaking KGB with the help of overwhelming numbers of disenchanted American turncoats).

The main psychological obstacle to the serious pursuit of a world federation is the fear that its very size would make it unstable and unwieldy. But bigness does not of itself spell the immersion and absorption of smaller units. Thinkers as disparate as Madison[1] and Hegel[2] realized that the largeness of a political entity may actually rescue individuals from the provincial or ethnic or religious rivalries that are rampant on more local levels; and the same principle, if true, might also be extrapolated to the aspiration of individual nations to be rescued from endemic counterproductive national rivalries in which they are caught up. In actual fact, if democratization consists essentially in a process of measured and institutionalized decentralization, then a world federation would be the furthest conceivable extension of democratization—a way of avoiding the near-anarchy that has always prevailed among nations, without compromising the freedom and independence of any of them. If democracies were first established as an antidote to tyranny, a world democracy may be the only sure antidote to potential international tyrant-nations. If national democracies are the guarantee-of-choice of local autonomy from encroachment by powerful central authorities, a world federation will be the only hope of real and meaningful autonomy for the smaller and poorer nations of the world. It is a good question whether democracy in a world consisting almost exclusively of national democra-

---

[1]Alexander Hamilton, James Madison and John Jay, *The Federalist Papers*, #10.

[2]G. W. F. Hegel, *The Philosophy of Right*, §296.

cies could survive and even flourish without the creation of an international federation of democracies with mutual security arrangements.

Mikhail Gorbachev has observed that in planning future states of
the world, "we must proceed from the realities which exist."[3]   The
inchoate federative realities which exist in the world at present have been
established largely for security reasons and economic cooperation, and
have branched out into collaborative efforts in education, ecology, health
and other areas. The major pre-federative, more properly "confedera-
tive"[4] international effort in that direction is the United Nations Organization—the twentieth-century fulfillment of the dreams of Jean-Jacques
Rousseau, the Abbé de Saint Pierre, and Immanuel Kant in the eighteenth
century.[5] The United Nations is not quite conformable to the "strictly
democratic" criteria posed by President Wilson for his "League of
Nations" in the early 1900s, but is a formidable standing institution of
159 nations in the world working under parliamentary procedures
developed in democratic/constitutional traditions.   The U. N., which
possesses only minimal legislative and judicial powers, has recently
experienced, in the aftermath of a thawing of U.S.-U.S.S.R relations,
some strengthening of the Security Council's executive powers (which
depend on unanimity of the seated members), and some mitigation of the
ideological conflicts in the General Assembly which prevailed prior to the
disintegration of communist-block, pan-Arabist, and other allegiances.

Several years after the founding of the United Nations Organization, Justice Owen Roberts, John F. Schmidt and Clarence K. Streit,
under the pseudonym of "Publius II," published *The New Federalist*,
which they thought to be a natural and timely extension of the federative
idea originally defended by Madison, Hamilton and Jay in the *Federalist
Papers*. Their blueprint for a federation of the nations of the world was
probably overly influenced by specifically American constitutional
patterns; and until recently their ideal was perpetuated largely by
specialized organizations such as the American Association to Unite the
Democracies, the Union of European Federalists, and the International
Association for a Union of the Democracies, as well as some peace
movements sympathetic to the goals of international federation. But in
recent years steps have been taken by major international powers which
actually do seem to augur a gradual approximation to world federation.

---

[3]April 2, 1989, during the final round of state visits begun in 1988
but interrupted by the Armenian earthquake.

[4]See H. Kainz, *Democracy East and West*, pp. 116-117.

[5]See H. Kainz, *Philosophical Perspectives on Peace*, pp. 40-86.

The European Parliament proposed an European Treaty of Union in 1984; this proposal was endorsed by François Mitterand, Chair of the European Council, who in subsequent years has been joined by Helmut Kohl and other European leaders in laying plans for what could eventually amount to a United States of Europe. One instrument for the achievement of this goal has been the expansion of the existing European Economic Community (Common Market) into a political organization. In the United States, Francis Fukuyama, perhaps taking his cue from these European developments as well as from a loosening of Marxist ties in Eastern Europe, has suggested a "common marketization" of politics in which the U.S. and other nations would participate.[6]

It is clear in any case that, as Gorbachev indicated, any development in the direction of international democratic union will be based on the "realities" already in place. In addition to the U.N., these realities would almost certainly include the Conference on Security and Cooperation in Europe (CSCE), with 35 member states (including what used to be the Soviet "block" and neutral European countries, as well as the European allies); the Organization for Economic Cooperation and Development (OECD), with 24 members, including Australia, New Zealand, and Japan; the North Atlantic Treaty Organization (NATO), newly expanded to include 9 Eastern European nations and 10 former Soviet republics; and the European Common Market (including Ireland), with 12 members, as the area of most intense federative development at present. The problem of achieving an overall federative organization of what President Bush calls the "great and growing commonwealth of free nations"[7] is partly a problem of where to begin. U.S. Secretary of State James Baker has suggested that the logical starting place is the CSCE:

> The CSCE process could become the most important forum of East-West cooperation.... Free elections should now become the highest priority in the CSCE process.... We could involve parliamentarians directly in CSCE processes, not only as observers as at present, but perhaps through their own meetings.[8]

Representative Henry Reuss (Dem.-Wis., Ret.) has suggested that the 24 OECD countries, the industrialized democracies of the world, are

---

[6]See p. 120 above.
[7]State of the Union message to Congress, Jan. 31, 1990.
[8]Speech at the U.S.-U.S.S.R. Summit, Malta, Dec. 12, 1989.

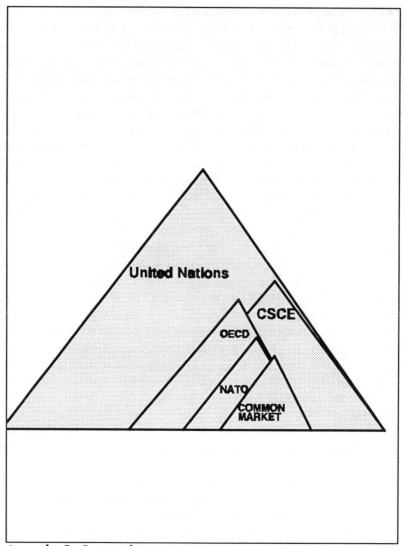

Quasi-federative movements

the "right" members to start with:

> The United States should take the initiative for the establish-
> ment of an Assembly of the OECD Democracies—the 24
> countries of free Europe, North America and the Pacific that
> the OECD has recognized as satisfying its requirements of
> political democracy and economic capability.... It would
> provide a "common democratic home" for additional countries,

in Eastern Europe and beyond, to join as they satisfy the requirements of political democracy and economic capability.[9]

Manfred Wörner, Secretary General of NATO, has suggested undertaking the transformation of NATO from a primarily military to a primarily political organization.[10] Others look to the European Common Market, which is already close to parliamentary organization, to spearhead confederation, probably in conjunction with the present European Parliament.   A major step in this direction has been taken by the Common Market's umbrella organization, the European Community. The EC at the Maastricht Conference in December 1991 signed treaties oriented towards the establishment by the year 2000 of a true European Parliament and European monetary and political union. The slim margin by which the French referendum on the Maastricht Treaty passed in September, 1992 is perhaps an augur that the process will take longer than expected.

It is obvious that many of these plans could be put into operation simultaneously; and the breakup of the Soviet Union may provide a suitable atmosphere for international coordination beyond original intentions.   Gorbachev emphasized the need for coordination in the planning, calling for a second Helsinki-type conference, to set up the mechanisms for establishing a "common European home."[11] Since the ascendancy of Boris Yeltsin to the Russian presidency, eleven nations of the former Soviet Union and the Balkan region have signed the Declaration of Black Sea Economic Cooperation, and Yeltsin has petitioned for the admission of Russia to the regular "Group of Seven" summits (along with the U. S., Great Britain, Japan, Germany, Italy, France, and Canada).

ECUMENICAL CHRISTIANITY

The qualifier, "ecumenical," is derived from the Greek, *oikoumenē*, "inhabited world".   In ecclesiology it was initially used to designate general councils such as the Council of Nicea in 325 and the Council of Chalcedon in 451, in which all parts of Christendom were represented. In the sixth century, the Patriarch of Constantinople was

---

[9]Henry S. Reuss, "Toward an Assembly of the OECD Democracies," *The Federator*, Dec. 1989.

[10]Speech to the North Atlantic Assembly, Rome, Oct. 9, 1989.

[11]Address at the Council of Europe, July 6, 1989.

entitled the "Ecumenical Patriarch," to indicate his primacy over all the other patriarchs in the Eastern Roman Empire (the Ecumenical Patriarch still holds the primacy of honor among the bishops of the 12 Orthodox churches in the world today); and this Patriarchate, acutely conscious of the damaging effects of divisiveness among Christians, showed itself open to exploring possibilities of union with Roman Catholics in the 13-15th centuries, with Protestants in the 16th century, and Anglicans in the 17th. In the 20th century, the term "ecumenical" has come to mean "world-wide," and, as Bell observes, it connotes in religious usage a "spiritual traffic between the Churches which draws them out of their isolation and into a fellowship of conversation, mutual enrichment, common witness and common action."[12] (In political science, however, Eric Voegelin uses "ecumenical" in a more specialized, and pejorative, sense—in contrast with what is beneficially "universal."[13])

If, as Niebuhr asserts, the kingdom of God is best described as neither an ideal nor an organization, but "a movement which ... appears in only a partial and mixed manner in the ideas and institutions in which men seek to fix it,"[14] the ecumenical movement gathering momentum in the latter half of the twentieth century seems to be an apt expression of the Kingdom. John's Gospel concludes that the only viable proof to the world of the divine origin of Christianity is the union of Christians among themselves.[15] If such unity of Christians is indeed so indispensable for the spiritual success of Christianity, the ecumenical movement looms on the horizon as the only reasonable hope for establishing the authenticity of Christianity. Although in the minds of some, ecumenism smacks of compromise and the dilution of the Christian faith, others see it as the vanguard of whatever presence the kingdom of God in a *visible* church can be expected to have.

An original impetus to modern organized ecumenical movements can perhaps be dated from the founding of the Franciscan Friars of the Atonement (Graymoor Friars) as an Anglican community by Rev. Paul Wattson in 1898. The Graymoor Friars, received into the Catholic Church in 1909, took ecumenism as their specific mission in the Church. From the side of Orthodoxy, the Ecumenical Patriarch of Constantinople, continuing in the long tradition of dialogue just alluded to, also initiated in 1902 a dialogue with Catholics, Oriental Orthodox, Anglicans and

---

[12]George K.A. Bell, *The Kingship of Christ*, p.18.
[13]See above, p. 153.
[14]H. Richard Niebuhr, *The Kingdom of God in America*, p. 164.
[15]John 17:20-23.

Lutherans. Since that time, the various attempts to bridge the splits caused by the Great Schism and the Protestant Reformation have generally taken the form of dialogues and conferences, sometimes but not always in conjunction with the organized movements within

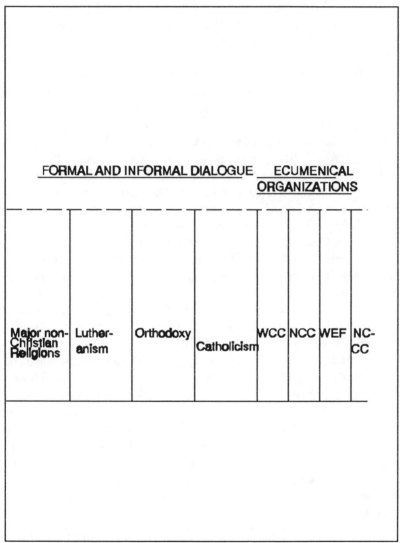

Ecumenical Developments

Catholicism, Orthodoxy and Protestantism that have gradually acquired official status.

The most organized of world ecumenical movements is the World Council of Churches (WCC), Protestant in its origins, founded in 1948 as an umbrella organization incorporating three early-twentieth-century Protestant movements concerned with various aspects of unification—namely, the International Missionary Conferences, the Faith and Order Conferences, and the Life and Work Conferences.   The American branch of the WCC, the National Council of Churches (NCC), which has just initiated dialogue with the "peace churches" (Quakers, Church of the Brethren, etc.) is outnumbered by the separate National Council of the Churches of Christ (NCCC), which includes African American churches.   The Reformed, Holiness and Pentecostal churches, differing from many mainstream Protestant churches in regard to issues of sacramentality, have formed their own separate ecumenical organization, the National Association of Evangelicals (NAE), which is affiliated with the World Evangelical Fellowship (WEF).   Pope John XXIII, belatedly following up on the initiatives of the Graymoor Friars, paved the way for the establishment of the Catholic Church's Secretariat for the Promotion of Christian Unity in 1961, and in the Second Vatican Council (1963-1965) offered a clear and unequivocal basis for an "Ortho-dox/Roman Catholic Consultation" (founded 1965), consisting of twelve Roman Catholic and twelve Orthodox theologians and pastors, and for numerous official bilateral theological dialogues on the international level between the Catholic church and the Anglican Community, the Lutheran World Federation, the World Methodist Council, some Evangelicals, the Baptist World Alliance, the World Alliance of Reformed Churches, the Disciples of Christ, and the Pentecostals.

Many areas of traditional doctrinal differences have been successfully bridged in the course of these dialogues.   Dialogues of Catholics with mainstream Protestants have demonstrated less disagreement than expected on the number and nature of the sacraments, and on various credal differences.   Lutheran/Roman Catholic dialogues have produced consensus on the formerly divisive issues of whether a person is justified by faith or by works, and whether Christ's presence in the sacrament of the Eucharist is something real and objective aside from the faith of the person who receives it.   The Lutheran/Roman Catholic dialogue concluded years of study of mariological problems with the issuance of a joint statement on *The One Mediator, The Saints, And Mary* at the conclusion of their meeting in Florida on Feb. 17, 1990 (the only differences still remaining are with regard to papal definition of the dogmas of the Immaculate Conception and the Assumption of Mary).   In the Orthodox/Roman Catholic Consultation, where the main differences had to do with ecclesiastical authority rather than doctrinal points, consensus has been reached concerning the importance of seven ecumenical councils in the early church, and regarding the necessity for collegiality and synodal leadership, although there is still disagreement concerning the authority of the Pope operating independently of episcopal colleagues. Anglican/Roman Catholic dialogue has produced agreement regarding the doctrine of the eucharist and the ministry, and surprisingly a considerable amount of consensus on issues of ecclesiastical authority; but new problems have emerged recently with regard to the issue of the ordination of women.

It would seem that the main differences remaining among Christians are largely reducible to the one difference regarding official Catholic papal interpretations of "Petrine" authority and the "keys of the Kingdom".[16] Perhaps enough ground has been broken in the dialogues which have already taken place, for that crucial topic to be put at the top of the agenda. Evangelicals, however, have additional differences with mainstream Protestantism, as well as with Catholicism and Orthodoxy regarding the relative importance of creed over ethical commitments (which are emphasized in evangelical Protestantism).

THE RELATIONSHIP BETWEEN WORLD FEDERATION AND CHRISTIAN ECUMENISM

If, as Everett asserts, the legal/constitutional apparatus of federalism is best complemented by, and perhaps even requires, cultural consolidation and cementing with the biblical spirit of covenant[17]; and if Christianity, with its emphasis on love of all men and salvation of the whole world, is the most universalistic expression of the biblical idea of covenant; then a truly ecumenical Christianity as the most visible manifestation of the kingdom of God and a truly international federal union of the world's democracies as the highest expression of communality in history would seem to be maximally complementary. In lieu of such a conjunction, one would have to visualize a harmonious international federation somehow operating amid centuries-long sectarian and denominational rivalries; and/or an ecumenically united Christianity somehow having a compound moral effect on, and getting its message across to, a world still plagued by innumerable conflicts between democratic and non-democratic sovereign nation-states. Either of these

---

[16]Matt. 16:19.

[17]William Johnson Everett, *God's Federal Republic*, pp. 101-2.

two conjunctions defies imagining. This is not to say that ecumenism and federalism necessarily entail each other. But, prima facie, complementarity is certainly indicated.

A major obstacle to both religious and political unification in the world is the widespread confusion of unity with homogeneity and/or conformity. Modern communications and streamlined transportation are increasing homogeneity of a superficial and often detrimental sort at such a rapid pace in the world, that a thoughtful person might begin to view socio-political unification itself as a homogeneity, and thus as a major deadening and levelling force in the world. This seems to be the "unity" that Tillich has in mind when he writes:

> [A united mankind] certainly did not exist in the past; nor can
> it exist in the future because a politically united mankind,
> though imaginable, would be a diagonal between convergent
> and divergent vectors. Its political unity would be the frame-
> work for a disunity that is the consequence of human freedom
> with its dynamic that surpasses everything given.[18]

This counterproductive type of unity seems to be on the mind of the "convergence theorists" who see in the recent dismantling of communist power in the Soviet bloc a vindication of their predictions, beginning in the 60s, that communism would inevitably veer towards capitalism and be overtaken by capitalism.[19] That capitalism should gain a permanent victory not only over Marxism but over the socialist and welfare-state ideals is probably not desirable (at least from the vantage point of the handicapped and disadvantaged in the world), even if it were possible.

A similar misconstrual of unity in terms of homogeneity is also found at times among Christian ecumenists. Paul Crow, for example, in his treatment of ecumenism discusses various models of unity—covenanted, organic, and cooperative unity, and finds all of them wanting if they do not lead to absolute unity. This leads him to reject overhastily a Roman Catholic proposal in the early 70s for a "communion of communions," a variety of typologies within the same ecclesial allegiance. This proposal was approved by some Episcopalians, but Crow seems to over-interpret it in terms of his ideal absolute unity.[20]

---

[18]Paul Tillich, *Systematic Theology III*, p. 311.

[19]See Jutta Kneisel, "The Convergence Theory."

[20]See Paul Crow, *Christian Unity*, Ch. 7.

True unity is not only compatible with diversity, but requires maximal diversity. Teilhard de Chardin's principle, "unity diversifies," applies with full force to the human level. Human personalities bring the greatest diversity of organs and faculties into unity; and human societies are distinguished not by a sameness of aptitudes and interests and ends and means, but by bringing the great diversity of all these things into unity. Thus in the second century Irenaeus, when questioned about the differences existing among Christians regarding observance of fasts, replied that, not only should such differences be tolerated, but "the divergency in the fast emphasizes the unanimity of our faith."[21] If ecumenists are looking for an eventual unification of Christians such that there would no longer be a distinction between the present Catholic and Protestant and Orthodox confessions and rites, then they are making the same sort of mistake that a world-order theorist would make whose plan for unity required obliteration of differences between conservatives and liberals, or capitalist and democratic socialist camps.

There exist, of course, some types of diversity which are obstacles to unity. The tremendous disparity of languages in Europe would be a major obstacle (perhaps *the* major obstacle at present) to the formation of any European federation. Doctrinal differences have traditionally been a leading cause for the major splits and schisms among Christians. But is it really intolerable that those sharing the Christian faith should have sharp differences of opinion regarding, e.g. whether the Holy Spirit proceeds just from the Father or from the Son as well as the Father, whether Mary the mother of Jesus was conceived without original sin and assumed into heaven without dying, whether a person is justified by faith alone without consideration of his/her works, etc.? If Christians are already in agreement, in spite of a diversity of interpretations and emphases, on the pivotal importance of the idea or symbol of the "kingdom of God" in their religion, the other differences that still remain seem to be relatively anticlimactic.

The path to unification has to be, and should be, through diversity. For sovereign democracies considering the possibilities of international federation, this may mean that the tentative but precarious alliance between democracy and capitalism should not be extrapolated into a standard for democratization. The failures of Marxism should not lead us to sound the death knell for socialism too early. In the wake of Marxism, the voices for egalitarianism and social democracy in a world sharply divided between haves and have-nots still must be heard. If they

---

[21]Cited by Eusebius, in his *History of the Church*, p. 232.

are not heard, some "-ism" worse than Marxism is sure to appear on the horizon.

For religious confessions considering the possibilities of ecumenical union, a major consideration might be ... leaving most of the differences that distinguish the confessions where they now are: Catholics defending tradition, the special prerogatives of Mary the Mother of Jesus, and (along with Episcopalians and Swedish Lutherans) apostolic succession; Protestants defending guidance by Scripture and the priesthood of the laity and, in some confessions, the ordination of women; Orthodox defending diverse interpretations concerning the procession of the Holy Spirit or concerning the existence of a true human nature in Christ or concerning the right of priests other than bishops to marry. Differences regarding ethical matters may be greater obstacles to unity than differences over doctrine, although some areas of agreement have been found -- e.g. agreement between Catholic and Presbyterians that we should try to build the sort of society in which abortion will rarely be resorted to, and agreement between Catholics and United Methodists that "extraordinary" technological means need not be used for prolonging life.[22]

This is not to derogate from the importance of formulating doctrines correctly, so far as this is possible in theology; but to raise a question about the nature of that "faith" that all Christians agree is of the utmost importance. Faith itself seems to be in need of redefinition. Catholics, and some Protestants and Orthodox, seem to read "faith" as a belief in certain dogmas or doctrines; for others it is belief in Scripture; and for still others it is a simple trusting belief in Christ, or in being saved by Christ.

In the New Testament "faith" is scarcely ever used in a doctrinal sense—e.g. believing in the Trinity or in Transubstantiation or the Immaculate Conception. "Faith" in the New Testament is always used in the sense of a belief in Christ, in God's power, in the fact that Christ was sent by God, and/or in the coming of the Kingdom. Oversimplification of obstacles is always a danger; but it seems that if Christians could interpret, or reinterpret, faith just in these New Testament terms, the major "faith"-related obstacle to union would be dissipated.

The most formidable obstacle to the reunion of Catholics with other Christians is, as already indicated, the insistence that papal primacy is not just a primacy of honor (the sort of primacy that exists also in

---

[22]See Eugene J. Fisher, "Moral Issues in Interfaith Dialogue," *Ecumenical Trends*, 20:6, June, 1991, pp. 89-90.

Orthodoxy) but a primacy of jurisdiction over the entire Church. Faith in the jurisdictional primacy of the "successor of Peter" is, again, another one of the extensions of faith beyond the normal New-Testament parameters of faith. But even this obstacle could be dealt with in a way satisfactory to many Christians if Roman Catholicism would accept the principle of Orthodoxy that primacy has to be exercised in conjunction with episcopal and/or patriarchal consultation—so that, e.g. the Pope could not make a pronouncement contrary to the opinions of the majority of his episcopal advisors (thus rendering the influence of the Holy Spirit on the episcopate rather questionable!).

For some Christians, of course, the key to unification of Christians is not any settlement of doctrinal disputes or even of jurisdictional conflicts, but a collaboration in the practical and personal sphere. Thus Emmidio Campi, with this in mind, proposes a "Post-Constantinian Christian Community" no longer constituted according to traditional patterns (e.g. diocese, parish, etc.), but based on individual choice and mutual recognition of individual and corporate responsibility.[23] (This would seem to involve "churches" mobilized for various individual goals—e.g. combatting drugs? fighting homelessness? studying the Bible? family literacy?) Even if one wants to maintain the traditional structures—parish, hierarchical jurisdiction, etc.—it is not completely clear why Christians with opposite viewpoints regarding e.g. the Immaculate Conception or original sin could not join together to run ecumenical schools or universities or hospitals, or provide ecumenical welfare services.

LIMITED UNIVERSALISM

The really intractable problems are the ones omitted even by the most serious and dedicated ecumenists or federalists. These have to do with the outer peripheries of the worlds which they are trying to visualize. For those committed to international federalism, these outer peripheries are the "third" and "fourth"[24] worlds, so poor or illiterate or disorganized that "democratization" is not even a meaningful aspiration. For Christian ecumenists, the outer peripheries are the great oriental

---

[23]Emmidio Campi, "Renewal as Liberation and as Spiritual Development in the Future of Ecumenism -- a Perspective," p. 341.

[24]The "fourth" world is conventionally defined as areas of the world lacking natural resources, as well as falling far short in standard of living.

religions—especially Hinduism, Buddhism and Taoism, which, unlike Islam, have no common roots in the Judaeo-Christian tradition. It is of course to be expected that ecumenists should try to "close ranks" in their own domains before branching out into the unknown. But to an observer from another planet it might seem strange that Christians and religious non-Christians cannot find sources of unity either in their theism or in their moral views. Possibly the obstacle to this sort of unity is the traditional Christian conception of "preaching the Gospel" which is thought to involve the turning away of "pagans" from their religion in their "conversion" to Christianity (as if there were nothing spiritually worthwhile that had to be preserved from their former religions and the culture with which the religion is associated). Matteo Ricci in China in the 16th century, as already mentioned,[25] was prevented from continuance in his mission because of such a traditional "one-way" conception of conversion. But in most and perhaps all human intercourse, conversion seems to be a rather complex bidirectional process.

---

[25]See p. 76.

Conclusion

BEYOND UTOPIANISM

As has often been observed above, the major thrusts in the theological interpretation of the "kingdom of God" seem to be in the direction of a future Kingdom. One great benefit from this development may be the weaning-away of Christians from utopian thinking, and the realization that *only* God could establish perfect justice and peace in either church or state. As Lord Acton once observed, "the surest way of bringing about hell on earth is to try to make it a heaven." H. Richard Niebuhr emphasizes "Christian Realism" as an antidote to the utopian expectations often connected with the kingdom of God, and as an antidote to the optimism of "Social Gospel" leaders about realizing the kingdom of God on Earth in spite of human sinfulness and deeply rooted social evils.[26]   And Eric Voegelin's warning against repeating the mistakes of the overoptimistic ancient Israelites is timely:

> The derailment [of the Israelite goals]...found its expression in the symbol of Canaan, the land of promise.... The promised land can be reached only by moving through history, but it cannot be conquered within history. The Kingdom of God lives in men who live in the world, but it is not of this world. The ambiguity of Canaan has ever since affected the structure not of Israelite history only but of the course of history in general.[27]

We, like the ancient Israelites, says Voegelin, are in danger of trying in frustration "to bring the obstreperous reality of the world, through metastatic imagination and action, to conformity with the demands of the

---

[26]See *Moral Man and Immoral Society*, passim.

[27]*Order and History*, I, p. 114.

Kingdom."[28] The "metastatic" attempt to bring present earthly reality once and for all into conformity with the Kingdom, or a particular interpretation of the Kingdom, is no doubt the main cause for all the great "abuses" that have been chronicled by the critics of Christianity and religion—the Inquisitions, the Holy Wars, the witch-burnings, the pogroms, etc., etc. These have resulted from attempts to make the Kingdom a "sure thing," rather than a matter of hope and faith. The truth is, of course, that mankind will never get to some "metastatic" point putting it beyond the need for faith—not just faith in God and in a self-reforming, self-critical church, but also a very basic human faith in the powers of human organization, in the potentialities of the earth, and (with appropriate reservations) in human nature itself.

BEYOND THE "BEYOND"

We have seen that there have been concerted attempts by contemporary theologians to establish, or reestablish, the "transcendent" significance of the kingdom of God in Christianity. Such attempts emphasize that the Kingdom can never be finalized in the here and now, and by human efforts—an emphasis that may indeed help mankind to avoid future holy wars and Inquisitions and repetitions of the attempts to establish dictatorial New Zions in Florence or Muenster or Geneva or elsewhere. But might not one reasonably expect something other than an unknown and invisible kingdom of God, to be expected in the "beyond," from Christianity? Isn't it Christianity which traditionally distinguishes itself from other religions in being a "revealed" religion—well beyond the pale of the "unknown God" syndromes? The commonly alleged "symbolic" presence of the future Kingdom in the present Church is probably *not* enough to constitute a bona fide revelation. In this respect, the objections of the liberation theologians seem to be on target, although their expectations of perfection in social justice and brotherhood edge into utopianism, or at least a disregard of the proven realities of human nature. Also relevant are the criticisms of the ecumenists, who insist on Christians "getting their own act together" as a prerequisite for the authentic revelation of Christianity to the world. Those objections and these criticisms can be bypassed only if one is willing to maintain that somehow God can be revealed without his Kingdom; or, alternatively, that the Kingdom can be revealed purely in an inner faith-experience that

---

[28]Ibid., p. 453.

somehow stands clear of any essential connections with real-worldly operations. But such intellectual compartmentalizations may turn out, like the dismantling of Humpty-Dumpty, to be embarrassingly irreversible as well as counterproductive.

If it be granted that the kingdom of God is revealed in some partial manner in time and in the world (perhaps even in the Church!), it is also to be hoped that the Kingdom would *not* be actualized and present in such a way that it becomes identified with any present regime or political institutions. Looking back over history, even non-Christians might perceive the Christian ideal of a present but non-political (or para-political) Kingdom—like the idea of "natural law"—as a valuable corrective upon, or counterforce to, the power of prevailing governments. In other words, just as the concept of a natural law (even if no natural law exists) has provided at times a defense against the unjust and inhumane "positive laws" which have been enacted not infrequently by governments, so too the idea of a kingdom of God standing directly over against, and competing for allegiance with, the various political pursuits of more earthly "kingdoms," may be an indispensable corrective on the excesses connected with the latter. But paradoxically even such functions of judging and correcting the political realm will always have to be carried out from a position of dependence on the political, since a church which lays claim to the Kingdom is just one organization or corporation among others ordered and controlled by the state which actually governs. In this respect, the church is something like the "loyal opposition" in parliamentary governments—although not competing for accession to power through election, and even less predictably "loyal" than the loyal opposition—*especially* if the church conceives itself and is perceived by the state as having in some sense a mandate to implement in the here and now the kingdom of God, to which even governmental expediencies must be subordinated.

Although it is not to be identified with any particular political institution, the kingdom of God may have a special relationship with democracy. Everything in the Judaeo-Christian tradition leads us to believe that if the Kingdom is in any way present, it is a special type of kingdom, far removed from the images of glory and pomp and power that we tend to associate with kings and kingship. Why not entertain the hopeful vision of the struggles of many generations finally being crowned with success in worldwide democratization—a vision in which high-profile leadership is so conspicuously absent that it finally becomes clear to mankind that the *demos* are indeed, after all, ruling themselves? This of course does not seem to fit in well with apocalyptic visions of a miraculous imposition of the Kingdom from on high. But the greatest and most challenging, God-class miracle might just be ... making it possible for humans to accomplish the impossible themselves.

BIBLIOGRAPHY

Albrecht, Reinhardt, *Hegel und die Demokratie*. Bonn: Bouvier Verlag Herbert Grundmann, 1978.

Appleton, Nicholas, "Democracy and Cultural Pluralism: Ideas in Conflict," *Proceedings of the Philosophy of Education Society*, Vol 38, 1982, pp. 151-158.

Arendt, Hannah, *On Revolution*. NY: Viking, 1965; Middlesex: Penguin, 1973.

Aristotle, *Politics*

Augustine, Aurelius, *De Corpore Christi, quod est ecclesia*, Ch. IX, "De Ecclesia et Statu."

Augustine, Aurelius, *The City of God*, Marcus Dods trans. Edinburgh: T&T. Clark, 1934, Books XI-XIX.

Aveshai, Bernard, *The Tragedy of Zionism: Revolution and Democracy in the Land of Israel*. N.Y.: Farrar Straus Giroux, 1985.

Baillie, John, *What Is a Christian Civilization?*. Chas. Scribners Sons, 1945.

Bars, Henry, *La Politique selon Jacques Maritain*. Paris: Les Editions Ouvrieres, 1961.

Barzun, Jacques, "Is Democratic Theory for Export?" *Society* 26:3, Mar/Apr. 1989, pp. 16-23.

Bekker, Simon, "Pluralism and Conflict Regulation," *Philosophical Papers*, South Africa, vol. 6, Oct. 1977, pp. 33-50.

Bell, George K.A., *The Kingship of Christ: The Story of the World Council of Churches*. Baltimore: Penguin Books, 1954.

Bell, Daniel, "The Return of the Sacred: The Argument about the Future of Religion," *Zygon*, 13:3, Sept. 1978, pp. 187-208.

Bellah, Robert N., *The Broken Covenant: American Civil Religion in Time of Trial*. N.Y.: Seabury-Crossroad, 1975.

Ben-Asher, Naomi, *Democracy's Hebrew Roots*. Hadassah, 1951.

Ben-Ezer, ed., *Unease in Zion*. NY: Quadrangle, 1974.

Bercovitch, Sacvan, *The Puritan Origins of the American Self*. New Haven: Yale University Press, 1975.

Bergson, Henri, *The Two Sources of Morality and Religion*, R. A. Audra and C. Brereton trs. NY: H. Holt and Co., 1935.

Berkhof, Louis, *The Kingdom of God: The Development of the Idea of the Kingdom Especially in the Eighteenth Century*. Grand Rapids, Mich.: Eerdmans, 1951.

Bobbio, Norberto, *Which Socialism?: Marxism, Socialism, and Democracy*. Minneapolis, Minn.: University of Minnesota Press, 1987.

Boff, Leonardo, *Church, Charism and Power: Liberation Theology and the Institutional Church*, John W. Diercksmeier trans. N.Y.: Crossroad, 1985.

Boff, Leonardo, *Ecclesiogenesis: The Base Communities Reinvent the Church*. Maryknoll, N.Y.: Orbis, 1977.

Bonsirven, Joseph, *Le regne de Dieu*. Paris: Aubier, Editions Montaigne, 1957.

Bowden, John, *Edward Schillebeeckx: In Search of the Kingdom of God*. N.Y.: Crossroad, 1983.

Brandt, Richard B., ed., *Social Justice*. Englewood Cliffs, N.J.: Prentice-Hall, 1962.

Bright, John, *The   Kingdom of God: The Biblical Concept and Its Meaning for the Church*. N.Y. and Nashville: Abingdon Press, 1953.

Bryce, James, *The Holy Roman Empire*. London: Macmillan, 1922.

Brzezinski, Zbigniew, "Post-Communist Nationalism," *Foreign Affairs*, 68:5, Winter, 1990, pp. 1-25.

Buber, Martin, *On Zion: The History of an Idea*, Stanley Godman, trans. London: East and West Library, 1973.

Burnham, James, *The Managerial Revolution: What is Happening in the World*. N.Y.: John Day, Inc., 1941.

Campi, Emidio, "Renewal as Liberation and as Spiritual Development in the Future of Ecumenism—A Perspective," *The Greek Orthodox Theological Review* XXVI, 4, Winter, 1981, pp. 332-42.

Chesterton, G. K., *Orthodoxy*.   Garden City, NY: Doubleday-Image, 1959.

Clarke, Desmond M., *Church and State: Essays in Political Philosophy*. Cork, Ireland: Cork University Press, 1984.

Cohen, Mitchell,   *Zion and State: Nation, Class and the Shaping of Modern Israel*. Oxford: Basil Blackwell, 1987.

Cohen, Carl, *Democracy*. Athens: University of Georgia Press, 1971.

Cohn, Norman, *The Pursuit of the Millenium*. London: Secker & Warburg, 1957.

Comte, Auguste, *The Positive Philosophy*, Vol. II, Harriet Martineau, tr. London: Kegan Paul, Trench, Trübner, & Co., 1893.

Cone, James, *Speaking the Truth: Ecumenism, Liberation, and Black Theology*. Grand Rapids, Mich.: Eerdmans Publ. Co., 1986, II.5, "Black Ecumenism and the Liberation Struggle."

Cooper, Barry, *The Political Theory of Eric Voegelin.* Lewiston/Queenston: Edwin Mellen Press, 1986, in *The Political Religions.* 1938.

Cox, Harvey, *Religion in the Secular City.* N.Y.: Simon & Schuster, 1984.

Cox, Harvey, *The Secular City: Secularization and Urbanization in Theological Perspective.* NY: Macmillan, 1965.

Crites, Stephen, *In the Twilight of Christendom: Hegel vs. Kierkegaard on Faith and History*, Chambersburg, Pa.: American Academy of Religion, 1972.

Crow, Paul, *Christian Unity: Matrix for Mission.* NY: Friendship Press, 1982, Ch. 5, "The Unity of the Church and the Reconciliation of the Human Family", pp. 95-110.

Dahl, N. A., "The Parables of Growth," in *Studia Theologica*, 5:2. 1952.

Dawson, Christopher, "The Kingdom of God in History," in H. G. Wood et al., *The Kingdom of God and History.* Chicago and N.Y.: Willet Clark and Co., 1938.

Denton, Robert C., "The Kingdom of God in the Old Testament," *The Interpreter's One Volume Commentary*, C. Laymon, ed. Nashville: Abingdon, 1982.

Dimant, Max, *Jews, God, and History.* N.Y.: Signet, 1964.

Dorrien, Gary J., *The Democratic Socialist Vision.* Totowa, N.J.: Rowman and Littlefield, 1986.

Duchrow, Ulrich, *Global Economy: A Confessional Issue for the Churches*, David Lewis trans., W.C.C. Publications, 1987.

Dussel, Enrique, *History and the Theology of Liberation*, John Drury trans. N.Y.: Orbis-Maryknoll, 1976.

Eddy, Sherwood, *The Kingdom of God and the American Dream: The Religious and Secular Ideals of American History.* N.Y. and London: Harper and Bros. Publishers, 1941.

Edhud Ben-Ezer, ed. *Unease in Zion.* NY: Quadrangle Books, 1974

Elan, Amos, "Jerusalem: The Future of the Past," *New York Review*, Aug.17, 1989, pp. 37-39.

Ellis, Marc, *Toward a Jewish Theology of Liberation.* Maryknoll, N.Y.: Orbis Books, 1987.

Elmessiri, Abdelwahab M., *The Land of Promise: A Critique of Political Zionism.* New Brunswick, N.J.: North American, Inc., 1977.

Epp, Eldon Jay, "Mediating Approaches to the Kingdom: Werner Georg Kuemmel and George Eldon Ladd," in Willis, *The Kingdom of God...*

Eusebius, *The History of the Church from Christ to Constantine*, G. A. Williamson trans. NY: Dorset Press, 1965.

Everett, William Johnson, *God's Federal Republic.* N.Y.: Paulist Press, 1988.

Ferguson, Everett, "The Kingdom of God in Early Patristic Literature," in Willis, *The Kingdom of God....*

Ferm, Deane William, *Third World Liberation Theologies.* NY: Orbis-Maryknoll, 1986.

Friedman, Robert, "The Settlers,". Letters, *New York Review of Books*, June 15, 1989.

Friedrichs, Carl, *Transcendent Justice: The Religious Dimensions of Constitutionalism.* North Carolina: Duke University Press, 1964

Fuller, Reginald Horace, *The Mission and Achievement of Jesus: an Examination of the Presuppositions of New Testament Theology.* Chicago: A.R. Allenson, 1954

Gascoigne, Robert, *Religion, Rationality and Community: Sacred and Secular in the Thought of Hegel and his Critics*. Dordrecht and Boston: Nijhoff, 1985.

Germino, Dante, *Political Philosophy and the Open Society*. Baton Rouge and London: Louisiana State University Press, 1982.

Gilson, Etienne, *Les Metamorphoses de la Cité de Dieu*. Paris: J. Urin, 1952.

Goldmann, Nahum, "Zionist Ideology and the Reality of Israel," *Foreign Affairs* 57:1, Fall, 1978, pp. 70-82.

Gould, Carol, *Rethinking Democracy*. Cambridge: Cambridge University Press, 1988.

Graham, Keith, *The Battle of Democracy: Conflict, Consensus and the Individual*. Totowa, NJ: Barnes & Noble, 1986.

Green, Philip, *Retrieving Democracy: In Search of Civic Equality*. Totawa, N.J.: Rowman & Allanheld, 1985.

Gutierrez, Juan, *The New Libertarian Gospel: Pitfalls of the Theology of Liberation*, Paul Burns trans. Chicago: Franciscan Herald Press, 1977.

Gutierrez, Gustavo, *Teologia de la Liberacion*, Novena Edicion. Salamanca: Ediciones Sigueme, 1980.

Hall, Cline; and Combee, Jerry, "The Moral Majority: Is It a New Ecumenicalism?", *Foundations* 25, April/June 1982, 204-211.

Harkabi, Yehoshafat, "Israel's Fateful Hour," *World Policy Journal*, Spring 1989, 6:2.

Harkniss, Georgia, *Understanding the Kingdom of God*. N.Y.: Abingdon, 1974.

Harris, Errol E., *Annihilation and Utopia: The Principles of International Politics*. London: Allen & Unwin, 1966.

Harris, Errol E., "Hegel's Theory of Sovereignty, International Relations, and War," *Hegel's Social and Political Thought*, Donald Verene, ed. N.J.: Humanities Press, 1980.

Hegel, G.W.F., *The Christian Religion: lectures on the Philosophy of Religion*, Peter Hodgson trans. Missoula, Mt: Scholars Press, 1979.

Hegel, G. W. F., *Werke*. Frankfurt am Main: Surkamp Verlag, 1969.

Hegel, G. W. F., *The Philosophy of History*, Sibree trans. NY: Dover, 1956.

Heine, Heinrich, "Zur Geschichte der Religion und der Philosophie in Deutschland," Book III, *Heines Werke*, Bong & C., Vol. IX, pp. 274-277.

Heller, Agnes, *Beyond Justice*. N.Y.: Oxford University Press, 1988.

Hendrikx, E., "Die Bedeutung von Augustinus 'De Civitate Dei' für Kirche und Staat," *Augustinianum*, 1:1, pp. 79-93.

Herrick, Henry Martyn, *The Kingdom of God in the Writings of the Fathers*, in *Historical and Linguistic Studies in Literature Related to the New Testament*. Chicago: University of Chicago Press, 1903, vol. I, Part III.

Hiers, Richard H., *The Kingdom of God in the Synoptic Tradition*. Gainesville: University of Florida Press, 1970.

Hirsch, Emanuel, *Staat und Kirche im 19. und 20. Jahrhundert*. Goettingen: Vandenhoeck & Ruprecht, 1929.

Hirsch, Emanuel, *Die Reich-Gottes-Begriffe des neueren europaischen Denkens: ein Versuch zur Geschichte der Staats- und Gesellschaftsphilosophie*. Goettingen: Vandenhoeck & Ruprecht, 1921.

Holl, Adolf, *Jesus in Bad Company*, Simon King trans. N.Y.: Avon, 1971.

Honderich, Ted *Violence for Equality: Inquiries in Political Philosophy*. London and New York: Routledge, 1976

Hoover, Kenneth R., *Ideology and Political Life.* Monterey, Calif.: Brooks/Cole, 1987.

Huxley, Aldous, *The Perennial Philosophy.* N.Y. and London: Harper, 1970

Hyams, Edward, *The Millennium Postponed: Socialism from Sir Thomas More to Mao Tse-tung.* N.Y.: New American Library, 1973.

James, William, *The Varieties of Religious Experience.* N.Y.: New American Library, 1958

Jamme, Christoph, "Hegel and Hölderlin's Tübingen View," CLIO 15:4, 1986, 359-77.

Johnston, David, *The Rhetoric of Leviathan: Thomas Hobbes and the Politics of Cultural Transformation.* Princeton, N.J.: Princeton University Press, 1986.

Kainz, Howard, *Democracy East and West: a Philosophical Overview.* London and NY: Macmillan and St. Martin's Press, 1984.

Kantorowicz, Ernst, *The King's Two Bodies: a Study in Mediaeval Political Theology.* Princeton, N.J.: Princeton University Press, 1957.

Khouri, Fred J., *The Arab-Israeli Dilemma.* Syracuse, NY: Syracuse University Press, 1985.

Klein, Charlotte, "The Theological Dimensions of the State of Israel," *Journal of Ecumenical Studies*, vol.22, Fall, 1973, 700-715.

Kneissl, Jutta, "The Convergence Theory," *New German Critique* 1:2, 1974, pp. 16-27.

Knoll, Erwin: "O Promised Land!", *The Progressive*, April, 1979, pp. 14-19.

Kuenning, Paul P., "Two Kingdoms: Weighed and Found Wanting," *Lutheran Forum*, 20:21, Lent, 1986, pp. 22-27.

Küng, Hans, *Theology for the Third Millenium.* N.Y.: Doubleday, 1988.

Küng, Hans, *The Church*, Ray and Rosaleen Ockenden trs. N.Y.: Sheed & Ward, 1967.

Küng, Hans, *The Church*, R. Ockenden trans. NY: Sheed and Ward, 1957

Küng, Hans, *On Being a Christian*, Edward Quinn trans. NY: Pocket Books - Wallaby, 1978.

Lakeland, Paul, *The Politics of Salvation: The Hegelian Idea of the State*. Albany: N.Y.: State University of New York Press, 1984.

Lampe, B. W. H., "The Kingdom of God in the New Testament," *The Interpreter's One-Volume Commentary*. Nashville: Abingdon, 1971, pp. 1176-1186.

Lange, Ernst, *And Yet it Moves: Dream and Reality of the Ecumenical Movement*, Edwin Robertson trans. Grand Rapids, Mich.: Eerdmans, 1979, Ch. 2, "The Significance of the Ecumenical Movement for the Survival of Mankind".

Langemeyer, Georg, *Menschsein in Wendekreis des Nichts*. Muenster: Aschendorff, 1988.

Lischer, Richard, *Marx and Teilhard: Two Ways to the New Humanity*. Maryknoll, N.Y.: Orbis, 1979.

Lochman, Ian, *Encountering Marx: Bonds and Barriers between Christians and Marxists*, E. Robertson trans. Philadelphia: Fortress Press, 1971

Lowenthal, Richard, "Development *vs.* Utopia in Communist Policy," in *Change in Communist Systems*, Chalmers Johnson, ed. Stanford: Stanford University Press, 1970.

Löwith, Karl, *Meaning in History*. Chicago & London: University of Chicago Press, 1949.

Löwith, Karl, *From Hegel to Nietzsche*. Garden City, NY: Anchor, 1967.

Lundström, Gösta, *The Kingdom of God in the Teaching of Jesus: A History of Interpretation From the Last Decades of the 19th*

Century to the Present Day. Edinburgh and London: Oliver and Boyd, 1963.

Luther, Martin, *On Secular Authority*, 1523.

MacIntyre, A. C., "Recent Political Thought," in *Political Ideas*, David Thomson, ed. N.Y. and Hammondsworth, Middlesex: Penguin, 1969.

Maritain, Jacques, "Christianity and Democracy," *Pour la justice.* NY: Éditions de la maison Française, 1945.

Maritain, Jacques, *La Philosophe dans la cité.* Paris: Alsatia, 1960

Maritain, Jacques, *Challenges and Renewals.* Notre Dame: Notre Dame University Press, 1966.

Marty, Martin E., *Religion and Republic: The American Circumstance.* Boston: Beacon Press, 1987.

Maspetiol, Roland, *Ésprit objectif et sociologie Hégelienne.* Paris: J. Vrin, 1983.

Mazlish, Bruce, *The Meaning of Karl Marx.* London and NY: Oxford University Press, 1984.

McGovern, Arthur, *Marxism: An American Christian Perspectives.* N.Y.: Orbus, 1980.

Miller, Irving, *Israel: The Eternal Ideal.* N.Y.: Farrar, Straus & Cudahy, 1955.

Moltmann, Jürgen, *The Trinity and the Kingdom: the Doctrine of God*, Margaret Kohl trans. San Francisco: Harper & Row, 1981.

Moorhead, James H., "Between Progress and Apocalypse: A reassessment of Millennialism in American Thought, 1800-1880", *Journal of American History*, Dec. 1984, 524-542.

Mulford, Elisha, *The Republic of God.* Boston, 1981.

Murray, John Courtney, S.J., *We Hold these Truths: Catholic Reflections on the American Proposition.* Kansas City, Mo.: Sheed & Ward, 1960.

Niebuhr, H. Richard, *The Kingdom of God in America.* N.Y.: Harper, 1959.

Niebuhr, H. Richard, *Moral Man and Immoral Society.* NY: Charles Scribners Sons, 1932.

Norman, Richard, *Free and Equal: A Philosophical Examination of Values.* Oxford: Oxford University Press, 1987

Novak, Michael, *Will It Liberate? Questions About Liberation Theology.* N.Y.: Paulist Press, 1986.

Novak, Michael, "The Case Against Liberation Theology," *New York Times Magazine*, Oct. 21, 1984, pp. 50-1, 82-7, 93-5.

O'Brien, Conor Cruise, : "God and Man in Nicaragua," *The Atlantic Monthly*, Aug. 1986, pp. 50-72.

O'Malley, Joseph, "Hegel on Political Sentiment," *Zeitschrift für Philosophische Forschung*, 41:1, Jan.-Mar., 1987, pp. 75-88.

Offe, Claus; and Keane, John, *Contradictions of the Welfare State.* London: Hutchinson, 1984.

Otto, Rudolph, *The Idea of the Holy*, John Harvey trans. N.Y. and London: Oxford University Press, 1977

Pagels, Elaine, *Adam, Eve, and the Serpent.* N.Y.: Random House, 1988.

Pannenberg, Wolfhart, *Theology and the Kingdom of God.* Philadelphia: Westminster Press, 1969.

Pangle, Thomas, *The Spirit of Modern Republicanism: The Moral Visions of the American Founders and the Philosophy of Locke.* Chicago: University of Chicago Press, 1988.

Parsons, Howard L., *Christianity Today in the USSR*. N.Y.: International Publishers, 1987.

Patrick, Dale, "The Kingdom of God in the Old Testament", in Willis, *The Kingdom of God*.

Paz, Octavio, *One Earth, Four or Five Worlds*. N.Y.: Harcourt Brace Jovanovich, 1985.

Perrin, Norman, *Jesus and the Language of the Kingdom: Symbol and Metaphor in New Testament Interpretation*. Philadelphia: Fortress Press, 1976.

Plant, Raymond, *Hegel*. Oxford: Blackwell, 1983, Ch. 10, "The Absolute in Politics and History."

Popper, Karl, *The Open Society and Its Enemies*. London: Routledge & Sons, 1945.

Rahner, Hugo, *Kirche und Staat im frühen Christentum*. München: Kosel-Verlag, 1961.

Rauschenbusch, Walter, *The Righteousness of the Kingdom*, Max Stackhouse, ed. Nashville: Abingdon Press, 1968.

Reich, Robert B., *Tales of a New America*. N.Y.: Random House-Times, 1987.

Revel, Jean-François, *The Totalitarian Temptation*, David Hopgood trans. N.Y.: Penguin Books, 1977.

Rhodes, James, "The Kingdom, Morality and Prudence—The American Bishops and Nuclear Weapons," *Center Journal*, Winter, 1983, pp. 31-79.

Rhodes, James, *The Hitler Movement*. Stanford, Ca: Hoover Institution Press, 1980.

Rhodes, James M., "Voegelin and Christian Faith," *Center Journal*, Summer, 1983, pp. 55-105.

Riemer, Neal, *Karl Marx and Prophetic Politics*. NY: Praeger, 1987

Riemer, Neal, *The Future of the Democratic Revolution.* NY: Praeger, 1984.

Roberts, J. M., *The Triumph of the West.* Boston: Little, Brown, and Co., 1985.

Rorty, Richard, "The Priority of Democracy to Philosophy," in *The Virginia Statute for Religious Freedom: Its Evolution and Consequences in American History*, Merrill D. Peterson and Robert C. Vaughn, eds., Cambridge University Press, 1988.

Rose, Gillian, *Hegel Contra Sociology.* London and New Jersey: Athlone and Humanities Press, 1981.

Rouner, Leroy S., ed., *Civil Religion and Political Theology.* South Bend: Notre Dame University Press, 1986.

Rubinstein, Amnon, *The Zionist Dream Revisited: From Herzl to Gush Emumim and Back.* N.Y.: Shocken, 1984.

Runkle, Gerald, *A History of Western Political Theory.* NY: The Ronald Press Co., 1968.

Rusch, William, *Ecumenism.* Philadelphia: Fortress, 1985, Ch. 7, "Ecumenism—Its Promise for the Future."

Sanders, E.P., *Jesus and Judaism.* Philadelphia: Fortress Press, 1985.

Sanford, John, *The Kingdom Within: A Study of the Inner Meaning of Jesus' Sayings.* Philadelphia: J. B. Lippincott Co., 1970.

Sayers, Sean and Norman, Richard, *Hegel, Marx and Dialectic.* Brighton, Sussex, and Atlantic Highlands, N.J.: Harvester Press and Humanities Press, 1980.

Schlink, Edmund, *Oekumenische Dogmatik: Grundzüge.* Goettingen: Vandenhoeck and Ruprecht, 1983, Kapitel 22, "Die Einheit der Kirche und die uneinige Christenheit."

Schlitt, Dale M., "Hegel on the Kingdom of God," *Église et théologie* 19. 1988, p. 33-68.

Schlosser, Jacques, *Le regne de Dieu dans les dits de Jesus.* Paris: J. Gabalda, 1980.

Schmitt, Carl, *Political Theology: From Chapters on the Concept of Sovereignty*, George Schwab trans. Cambridge, Mass. and London: M.I.T. Press, 1985.

Schnall, Rabbi David J., "Strategic Theology," *America*, Sept. 13, 1980, pp. 117-119.

Schneider, Herbert W., *A History of American Democracy.* N.Y.: Columbia University Press, 1946, Ch. 15, "Idealistic Democracy."

Segundo, Juan Luis, *Liberation of Theology*, John Drury trans. N.Y.: Orbis, 1986.

Eddy, George Sherwood, *The Kingdom of God and the American Dream: the Religious and Secular Ideals of American History.* NY and London: Harper & Brothers, 1941.

Simon, Yves, *The Community of the Free*, W. Trask trans. Lanham, Md.: University Press of America, 1984.

Sinclair, R.K., *Democracy and Participation in Athens.* Cambridge: Cambridge University Press, 1988.

Sowell, Thomas, *A Conflict of Visions.* N.Y.: William Morrow, 1988.

Spetnak, Charlene, "Postmodern Directions," in David Ray Griffin, ed., *Spirituality and Society: Postmodern Visions.* N.Y.: State University of New York Press, 1981.

Spinoza, Baruch, *Tractatus Theologico-Politicus*, Samuel Shirley trans. NY, Leiden, København, Köln: E.J. Brill, 1989.

Stace, W. T., *The Teachings of the Mystics.* N.Y.: New American Library, 1960.

Suchocki, Marjorie, *God, Christ, Church: a Practical Guide to Process Theology.* NY: Crossroad, 1982.

Sullivan, Clayton *Rethinking Realized Eschatology*. Mercer University Press, 1988, Part VIII.

Susser, Bernard, *Existence and Utopia: The Social and Political Thought of Martin Buber*. Rutherford and London: Fairleigh Dickinson University Press and Associated University Presses, 1981.

Talmon, J.L., *The Origins of Totalitarian Democracy*. London: Secker and Warburg, 1955.

Tertullian, *Apologeticus*, T. R. Glover trans. (Loeb Classical Library, 1931).

Theunissen, Michael, *Hegel's Lehre vom absoluten Geist als theologisch-politischen Traktat*. Berlin: de Gruyter, 1970.

Thiel, Andreas, ed., *Epistolae Romanorum pontificum genuinae*. Hildesheim and New York: Georg Olms Verlag, 1974.

Thompson, W. D. J. Cargell, "Martin Luther and the 'Two Kingdoms,'" *Political Ideas*, David Thomson, ed. N.Y. and Hammondsworth, Middlesex: Penguin, 1969.

Thompson, Kenneth W., *Toynbee's Philosophy of World History and Politics*. Baton Rouge and London: Louisiana State University Press.

Tillich, Paul, "The Kingdom of God and History," in H.G. Wood et al., *The Kingdom of God and History*. Chicago and New York: Willet, Clark, and Co., 1938.

Tillich, Paul, *Systematic Theology*, Vol. III. Chicago: University of Chicago Press, 1963.

Tinder, Glenn, "Can We Be Good Without God?" *Atlantic Monthly*, Dec. 1989, pp. 69-85.

Tocqueville, Alexis de, *Democracy in America*. NY: Mentor, 1956; London: New English Library, 1956.

Toynbee, Arnold J., *A Study of History*, Sommervell Abridgement. N.Y. and London: Oxford University Press, 1957.

Turner, Denys, *Marxism and Christianity*. N.Y.: Barnes and Noble, 1983.

Ungar, Roberto Mangabeira, *Knowledge and Politics*. NY: Free Press, 1975.

Viereck, Peter, *Metapolitics: The Roots of the Nazi Mind*. NY: Capricorn, 1941.

Vital, David, *The Origins of Zionism*. Oxford: Clarendon Press, 1975.

Viviano, O.P.; Benedict, *The Kingdom of God in History*. Wilminton, Delaware: Michael Glazier, 1988.

Voegelin, Eric, *From Enlightenment to Revolution*. Durham, N. C.: Duke University Press, 1975.

Voegelin, Eric, *Order and History I*, Israel and Revelation. Louisiana State University Press, 1956.

Voegelin, Eric, *The Ecumenic Age*. Baton Rouge: Louisiana State University Press, 1974.

Voegelin, Eric, *The New Science of Politics: an Introduction*. Chicago: University of Chiciago Press, 1952.

Weigel, George, "Catholicism and Democracy: The Other Twentieth-Century Revolution", in *The Washington Quarterly*. Autumn, 1989, pp. 5-25.

Weiss, Paul, *Toward a Perfected State*. Albany, N.Y.: State University of New York Press, 1986.

Weittman, Paul, "Sex and Sin". Letters, *New York Review of Books*, June 15, 1989.

Willis, Wendell, ed., *The Kingdom of God in 20th-Century Interpretation*. Peabody, Mass.: Hendrickson, 1987.

CONCORDANCE OF NAMES AND SUBJECTS

STUDIES IN PHILOSOPHY AND RELIGION

1. E.-R. FREUND: *Franz Rosenzweig's Philosophy of Existence.* An Analysis of 'The Star of Redemption'. (Translation from the German revised edition) 1979
ISBN 90-247-2091-5

2. A. M. OLSON: *Transcendence and Hermeneutics.* An Interpretation of the Philosophy of Karl Jaspers. 1979　　　　ISBN 90-247-2092-3

3. A. VERDU: *The Philosophy of Buddhism.* A 'Totalistic' Synthesis. 1981
ISBN 90-247-2224-1

4. H. H. OLIVER: *A Relational Metaphysic.* 1981　　　　ISBN 90-247-2457-0

5. J. G. ARAPURA: *Gnosis and the Question of Thought in Vedānta.* Dialogue with the Foundations. 1986　　　　ISBN 90-247-3061-9

6. W. HOROSZ and T. CLEMENTS (eds.): *Religion and Human Purpose.* A Cross Disciplinary Approach. 1987　　　　ISBN 90-247-3000-7

7. S. SIA: *God in Process Thought.* A Study in Charles Hartshorne's Concept of God. 1985　　　　ISBN 90-247-3103-8

8. J. F. KOBLER: *Vatican II and Phenomenology.* Reflections on the Life-World of the Church. 1985　　　　ISBN 90-247-3193-3

9. J. J. GODFREY: *A Philosophy of Human Hope.* 1987
ISBN Hb 90-247-3353-7; Pb 90-247-3354-5

10. R. W. PERRETT: *Death and Immortality.* 1987　　　　ISBN 90-247-3440-1

11. R. S. GALL: *Beyond Theism and Atheism.* Heidegger's Significance for Religious Thinking. 1987　　　　ISBN 90-247-3623-4

12. S. SIA (ed.): *Charles Hartshorne's Concept of God.* Philosophical and Theological Responses. 1990　　　　ISBN 0-7923-0290-7

13. R. W. PERRETT (ed.): *Indian Philosophy of Religion.* 1989　ISBN 0-7923-0437-3

14. H. E. M. HOFMEISTER: *Truth and Belief.* Interpretation and Critique of the Analytical Theory of Religion. 1990　　　　ISBN 0-7923-0976-6

15. J. F. HARRIS (ed.): *Logic, God and Metaphysics.* 1992　　ISBN 0-7923-1454-9

16. K. J. CLARK (ed.): *Our Knowledge of God.* Essays on Natural and Philosophical Theology. 1992.　　　　ISBN 0-7923-1485-9

17. H. P. KAINZ: *Democracy and the "Kingdom of God".* 1993
ISBN 0-7923-2106-5

KLUWER ACADEMIC PUBLISHERS – DORDRECHT / BOSTON / LONDON